The Queen

The Queen

KENNETH HARRIS

St. Martin's Press
New York

Library of Congress Cataloging-in-Publication Data

Harris, Kenneth
The queen : royalty and reality / Kenneth Harris.
p.   cm.
ISBN 0-312-11878-3
1. Elizabeth II, Queen of Great Britain, 1926-   .   2. Monarchy—
Great Britain—History—20th century.   3. Great Britain—History—
Elizabeth II, 1952-   4. Queens—Great Britain—Biography.
I. Title.
DA590.H376   1995
941.085'092—dc20
[B]   94-37943   CIP

First published in Great Britain by Orion

First U.S. Edition: February 1995
10 9 8 7 6 5 4 3 2 1

Contents

Illustrations

The Queen

Prologue

NOT SINCE THE Abdication crisis of 1936, possibly not since the scandal surrounding the accession to the throne of the profligate Prince Regent in 1820, has there been so much speculation about whether or not the British monarchy has a future. There is argument about who and what has done most to put the monarchy in danger, but it seems that there is one proposition about which few people disagree: by far the greatest asset the monarchy has today is the high reputation of and affection for the Queen.

The great majority of public opinion respects her both as a human being and as a professional person who carries out her role with dedication, dignity and charisma. She is generally thought of as an attractive, engaging and dutiful woman. Above all she is thought of as virtuous. The monarchy may have made her much of what she is, but that is not nearly so much as she has made of the monarchy.

The international reputation which she holds has been achieved in spite of, some may say as a result of, forty strenuous years. Some of what has happened, and which she helped to make happen, has been agreeable. Much of what happened to her has been hard to bear. Seen as existing entirely in the present her personal image is much to be admired, but to be objectively appreciated it should be seen as the end-product of forty difficult years, in which every problem inevitably was liable to exposure by the press. This book gives an account of those years. It is not a biography, but it has a biographical character since it gives a selection of episodes, influences, problems and successes, which have combined to produce the redoubtable character who occupies and preserves the monarchy today.

The strength of the monarchy at all times is the respect of the people, and the people will not respect the monarchy if they do not respect the man or woman on the throne. There may come a day when though the people respect the monarch they may prefer to do without the monarchy, but history makes it clear that they have not been so minded in the past, and there is no consensus that they are so minded in the present. History also makes it clear that when the people perceive, or believe, that the monarch is "good", the monarchy is secure, and that when they do not take that view the monarchy is in danger. The monarchy has not been in so much danger in two hundred years as it was in 1820 when the Prince Regent succeeded to the throne as George IV. His private life, only too public, that of his estranged wife Caroline, who behaved scandalously but was regarded by the London crowds as a wronged woman, pulled down the reputation of the monarchy to such depths and so encouraged republicanism that had not Caroline suddenly died the British monarchy might have come to an end.

The reign of his niece, Victoria, provides two lessons: the first was that even when the reputation of the monarchy is still so low that its existence is endangered the succession to the throne of a respectable person revives its fortunes remarkably quickly, particularly when the new monarch has a consort, as Victoria had in Albert, with his or her own ability to inspire popular regard. The second lesson taught by the reign of Victoria was that even the virtuous and respected monarch can soon lose the affection and regard of the people. When in 1861 the good Prince Albert died the Queen was so stricken with grief that she retreated into what the people saw as seclusion. She continued to be as hardworking, conscientious and influential as ever, but it seemed to the people that she had turned her back on them, and they resented it. Again the standing of the monarchy dipped rapidly, and republicanism prospered. In the latter years of her life, coaxed out of seclusion by Disraeli, Queen Victoria, whose virtue had never been doubted, lifted the image of the monarchy, and when she died in 1901 the reputation and significance of the monarchy had never been so great.

Her son, and successor, Edward VII, was a libertine, and the nation knew it, but he had the benefit of the reputation of the monarchy which his mother had created, of his own attractive and outgoing personality, of his *bonhomie* and *joie de vivre*, and of undoubted skills and achievements as an international diplomat. His son, George V, did nothing but good to the monarchy: he was a wise man; his private life was without criticism, he was married to a much admired and much respected wife. His son, Edward VIII, popular, but with no reputation for wisdom or virtue, abdicated so that he was free to marry the last of his many mistresses, Mrs Wallis Simpson, a twice divorced American of dubious reputation. He precipitated a crisis for the monarchy and an opportunity for republicanism the like of which had not been known for nearly two hundred years. With the accession to the throne of his brother George VI, whose gradually revealed shining virtues, with those of his universally beloved wife, were given a unique challenge and success by the Second World War, the monarchy more than recovered the ground which had been lost by the Abdication, and restored it to the level at which Elizabeth II, with her supportive and protective consort, has vigorously and courageously maintained and enhanced it.

The burden of the book is to convey how the Queen has coped with her vicissitudes and successes to place the monarchy on the level which it occupies today. It deals also with the happenings to her family, and their behaviour, which have created ongoing controversy about the future of the monarchy not only while she is alive but more importantly after she has gone. At the time of writing, January 1994, it is impossible to forecast what the effects of these are going to be. But what is certain is that whoever may come into serious consideration as the heir to the Queen, that person, if he or she is to last sufficiently long in that capacity, will have to convince the people of his or her regard for the practice of the basic virtues without which the monarchy ceases to be acceptable or viable.

I

Parents and Grandparents

QUEEN ELIZABETH II grew up in an exceptionally closely knit self-sufficient and affectionate family, which, since it was also royal, gave her a childhood unusually remote from the outside world. She was far more influenced by her parents than most children are, by the example they set, by what they taught her, by their attitude to one another, by what she observed in them and by what she saw happening to them. For somebody who was destined to become the country's most public figure hers was an extraordinarily private upbringing. To know *her*, and understand her, it is important to know about the personalities of her parents and their relationship with one another. To understand *them* it is necessary to understand *their* parents.

Elizabeth's grandfather, George V, was a kind man, but one whose behaviour and manner more often than not created a quite different impression. The life he understood best and which had taught him most were his years in the Navy. The sensitivity in his nature was belied by a bluff, rough, sometimes brutal manner which alarmed many of those who served him and made his children afraid of him. Harold Nicolson, his official biographer, said that Lord Derby, a close friend of the King, once told him that the King had said: "My father was frightened of his mother; I was frightened of my father, and I am damned well going to see to it that my children are frightened of me." Whether the King had said this or not, the frequency with which it has been quoted suggests that the remark is not without some basis near the truth.

As well as being a martinet the King sometimes exhibited a fierce temper and a sadistic tongue. His eldest son, later to be Edward VIII, and, later still, to become Duke of Windsor, told his mother's biographer: "My father had a most horrible temper. He was foully rude to my mother ... I've seen her leave the table because he was so rude to her, and we children would follow her out ..." His father, the Duke said, believed that children were to be seen and not heard. When they were heard he could become very angry. His outbursts were exacerbated by frequent bouts of dyspepsia. One of his grandsons, the Earl of Harewood, recalls that "visits to Windsor for Easter usually provided their quota of uneasy moments". At the age of eight he made one such visit just after he had got over a serious illness but was still suffering from hay fever. On the morning of their departure, the Harewoods went to their grandfather's sitting-room to say goodbye. Lord Harewood began to sneeze "either from the pollinating grass or from sheer nerves". The King was extremely annoyed, and "no amount of assurance that I had hay fever could stop the shouts of 'Get that damn child away from me.'"

His more recent biographer, Kenneth Rose, gives us a more sympathetic portrait of him, pointing out that both Edward VIII and George VI left some very happy recollections of their childhood. "Yet," says Mr Rose, "even by the stern standards of the age he was a watchful and exacting father who let nothing go by default. His early years in the navy had trained him to instant submission and he saw no reason why his own sons should not benefit from the same discipline." He enjoyed the company of children, and got on well with them, was relaxed and indulgent with them. He treated them differently from the way he treated his own. "But then his own children", observes Mr Rose, "were destined for a royal role which, he believed, could be learned only under a quarterdeck discipline tempered by the equally alarming badinage of the gun-room."

George V had some fine qualities, but they were of character not of intellect. He was uneducated, ignorant and uninterested in things of the mind. He was a magnificent shot, an expert yachtsman, and a considerable philatelist. His many hours with his twelve-bore guns and his stamp collection were the centre of his life, and he spent little time with his children, or indeed by choice with adults, an exception being his wife, to whom, in spite of frequent appearances to the contrary, he was deeply attached.

Having read no books worth speaking of – he is recorded as having said, "People who write books should be locked up" – being no student of people or society, and indifferent to the arts, he had, though he read *The Times* every day, no substantial conversation. In any case he was by nature uncommunicative and did not encourage the expression of views by others. Nevertheless it would be a mistake and an injustice to underestimate his concern about public affairs, his interest in politics and politicians and his grasp of his duties as a constitutional monarch. Little was expected of him when he came to the throne, but, says Mr Rose:

> King George V confounded every doubt. Under the tutelage of two experienced private secretaries, Knollys and Stamfordham, he set about learning the trade of a constitutional monarch. To each of the problems which relentlessly crowded in on him, day after day, for a quarter of a century, he brought an inspired common sense and kindliness. His welcome to the first Labour Government in 1924 was considerate, uncondescending, almost paternal. He was without prejudices of class, colour or race. If he did have a preference, it was for his poorer subjects, on whose behalf he would plead with his ministers to show generosity and compassion.

He was neither the first nor the last monarch, or political leader, of whom it has been said that they did well by their people but not so well by their children.

In his case, even if he had wanted to he did not have the resources creatively to guide and form the minds of his children. What they got from him was a guilt-inducing sense of duty and an unimaginative discipline, albeit with an affection which it took them years to recognise and understand. This, more than the anxiety he bred in them, may have done them damage. Scolding and punishment taught them only too well and early what they were supposed not to do; to know what they were supposed to do took them a long time, and by then they had to some degree lost the will to do it.

Some idea of the effect of their father's influence on his sons is

7

conveyed by an anecdote of the Duke of Windsor about his father's reaction to a speech he had made at a public dinner:

> I asked his old secretary, Lord Stamfordham, to help me with (this) speech, and he put in quite an amusing little paragraph which had a great success with the audience ... my father read the report (of the speech) sent for me and said: "I'm very surprised that you made those flippant remarks in your speech ... I've *never* made a joke in a speech." Sometimes when my father admonished me for something I had done with "My dear boy, you must always remember who you are" I used to think: Now, who am I? No answer.

However well-intentioned, the King was not an easy or a helpful parent, and the effect his shortcomings had on his sons was compounded by the gloomy quasi-religious sense of duty he urged them to acquire. Whenever he wished to direct or correct his sons' behaviour he instructed a servant to go and tell them to report to the Library. This was the room – there were hardly any books there – where the King kept his guns and his stamps and to which he retired in the evenings to read *The Times*. The boys, recorded the Duke of Windsor, came to regard the so-called Library as "the seat of paternal authority, the place of admonition and reproof". The room was not large but it was dark and forbidding. On the desk was displayed that motto so favoured by heavily dutiful Victorian parents: "I shall pass through this world but once. Any good thing, therefore, that I can do or any kindness that I can show any human being, let me do it now. Let me not deter or neglect it, for I shall not pass this way again." The ambience of the room evoked feelings of failure, fear and guilt.

Though her personality was quite different from that of their father their mother too fell short of what is required in a good parent. Queen Mary was a very regal figure, tall and elegantly upright, with fine carriage and a most dignified manner and bearing. Her German background had given her a profound conception of what royalty was, and of how royals should behave: predictably, ritualistically, theatrically. This she exemplified devotedly at some cost to her other obligations, including the welfare of her sons. She idolised the King, whom she revered not so much as husband but as monarch. Her children did not interest her as children so much as little people who one day would grow up to be royals and take their place in the élite above all élites. She was incapable of hugging or caressing them, or of otherwise showing them normal human affection. Looking after them as human beings she found difficult and unrewarding. Childbirth, postnatal care, and the mothering of infants she regarded as necessary interruptions in regal existence which should be as brief as possible. She was so dominated by her husband that she would not have displayed much affection to her children even if she had had it to give. Notwithstanding the offensive manner in which he sometimes treated her she admired and respected her husband, and, since she did not conceal this, in the children's eyes she became identified with him, which made her even more remote. Consequently, she did little to ease the repressive regime under which they were brought up. She was never stern nor harsh with them, but she was never warm. She spent some time in their company. When the King was away on his own, perhaps shooting, which the Queen did not care for, she would read to them, play cards and sing songs with them. They saw and felt this softer, though not much more intimate, side of parenthood, but, sadly, saw too that it came to an abrupt end when the King returned. These brief moments with their mother made them conscious of what they were missing when their father was at home.

The story of the upbringing of the five children is in some respects a sad one, and quotations from accounts of it often make the King and Queen sound far harder parents than they were. The most imaginative comment on it, perhaps, is to be found in the memoirs of Mabell, Countess of Airlie, close friend and lady-in-waiting to the Queen for many years. In her *Thatched with Gold*, published in 1962, Lady Airlie wrote:

> [they] were more conscientious and more truly devoted to their children than the majority of parents in that era. The tragedy was that neither had any understanding of a child's mind ... they did not succeed in making their children happy.

They could feel, but they were unable to show their feelings. Just before they got married in 1893 Princess May of Teck, as she was then, wrote to her husband to be:

> I am very sorry that I am still so shy with you ... It is so stupid

to be so stiff together & really there is nothing I would not tell you except that I love you more than anybody in the world, and this I cannot tell you myself so I write it to relieve my feelings.

George wrote back the same day:

Thank God we both understand each other, & I think it really unnecessary for me to tell you how deep my love for you my darling is & I feel it growing stronger & stronger every time I see you; although I may appear shy and cold ...

There was much comment on how little affection "the happy pair" showed to each other in public, how shy and reserved they both were. That being so, it is easy to understand how little affection they were able to show to their children. For most of the day the children, especially Edward and Albert, were in the hands of their governesses and nannies. In his memoirs the Duke of Windsor describes the misery he was subjected to at the hands of one of them – the (as it turned out) psychopathic Miss Green. Part of her daily duties was to take the little prince to spend tea-time with his parents. On arrival outside the door of the drawing-room Miss Green would pinch and twist the prince's arm until he began to cry. "The sobbing and bawling this treatment invariably invoked", the Duke recorded, "puzzled, worried and finally annoyed [my parents]" and he would be taken back to the nursery in disgrace. Miss Green did harm to the younger brother in a different way – she totally neglected him. Various explanations have been put forward of Miss Green's behaviour to the little princes. The most important aspect of it is that it went on for three years before Queen Mary became aware of it, and then only because Miss Green, having become obviously mentally ill, had to be removed.

All five children suffered to one degree or another from the imperfections of the King and Queen as parents but there seems little doubt that it was the second son, Albert, who suffered most. The first born, Mary, being a girl, was treated the most favourably by her father, who forgave her more than he would ever have tolerated in the boys. Though his father was strict with him, Edward got away with many transgressions because he was articulate, charming, a natural little showman, and very attractive. His father was proud of him. Albert, on the other hand, was shy, slow, unengaging, and at the age of six had developed a pronounced stammer. This affliction irritated his father – "Get it out!" he would growl at the boy sometimes – and amused the other children – they teased Albert about it. The stammer became worse. Albert was left-handed, but was forced to write with his right hand. He was knock-kneed. At the age of eight, to correct this, he was made to wear splints for several hours of the day and in bed at night. He developed a tendency to lose his temper. Whether this was a trait inherited from his father, whose quick temper was notorious, or brought about by his frustrations, he would sometimes get into a fit of rage, usually brought on by such setbacks as failure to do a simple sum of arithmetic.

In fact, by the time he was ten years old Albert had become something of a "problem child", the main feature of the syndrome being a sense of inferiority. Physically, apart from the knock-knees, which affected his posture but not his performance, there seemed nothing wrong with him. He was well built, and, knock-knees notwithstanding, he walked well. He learned to ride early – "If you can't ride, you know, I am afraid people will call you a duffer" his father had said in a milder moment – took to it with enthusiasm, and became an outstanding horseman. He learned to skate, play golf, and shoot. In later life he was rated one of the best shots in the country.

The only education a man needs, said their father, "is a spell in the Navy". So until Edward and Albert entered the Royal Naval College, Osborne, at the age of thirteen, they were tutored at home. They showed little aptitude for studies. When Albert entered Osborne his tutor, Mr Hansell, did not hold out high hopes for success at examinations: "We must remember that he is at present a scatter-brain [but] I have always found him a very straight and honourable boy, very kind-hearted and generous; he is sure to be popular with the other boys.'

Apart from dancing classes, occasional football matches with sons of workers on the royal estates, and meetings with the children of the courtiers, the royal children had made little contact with others of their age. When Albert went to Osborne he did not have much idea of what other boys were like. He had a rude awakening. There was not much bullying, but the life was tough, the boys were rough, and young Albert, shy, and undersized for his age, nicknamed "Sardine", had some uncomfortable times. The main problem for him was adjusting to living in a group. As the months went by he became popular, but he did not improve academically. He was a poor student. His father wrote to him regularly, and not unsympathetically, but frequently telling him that his teachers complained that he did not take his work seriously, and urging him to concentrate. To no avail; in Albert's final exam at Osborne he was placed bottom of a class of sixty-eight.

This was not a promising beginning to the next stage of his career – Royal Naval College, Dartmouth. Here his early days were marred by an attack of mumps. Three months later Edward VII died, his father became King and his elder brother became Prince of Wales, and heir to the throne. This widened the gap which had already appeared between the two brothers, and Albert was very conscious of it. His feeling that he was being outshone by David* added to the sense of inadequacy already growing as a result of his stammer and his poor results at school. He and his elder brother were frequently spoken of at this time as the ugly duckling and the cock pheasant.

On 15 September 1913, Prince Albert, Midshipman, aged seventeen, was commissioned to his first ship, the battleship *Collingwood*. He was treated like the others of his rank, slept in a hammock, and enjoyed no privacy. Even after the rough time he had had at Dartmouth he found life in the Navy was hard. When war was declared he was at Scapa Flow. In May 1916 *Collingwood* took part in the Battle of Jutland, the only major naval engagement of the war, and the last between full-scale fleets. He was immensely proud of this, and of being mentioned in dispatches, but alas for his hopes of a naval career, he spent the great part of his war at home or in hospital. The gastric trouble which had afflicted him at Dartmouth recurred, and a few weeks after war broke out he was taken ashore to have his appendix removed. Other troubles followed. Before the end of the war he had become a semi-invalid for the time being, able to go on wearing uniform only because he was given a staff job at the Admiralty. It irked him to be on the sidelines while almost every other man of his age was in the fight, and became more and more conscious that while he was almost out of action his elder brother was in the thick of it. He was being completely

---

* Although he took the name as monarch of Edward, to his family he was always known as David.

eclipsed by his elder brother: Edward visited the front lines in France, lived a life in which glamour and danger were excitingly combined, and won the Military Cross.

It was not long before the already unhappy Albert heard from his doctors that he must abandon all hope of a career in the Navy. It was a crushing rejection, harder to bear knowing what a disappointment this would be to his father. The King's behaviour in these troubled years had shown him at his best, understanding and supportive, but clearly father and son did not have the same view of the attractions of life at sea. George V believed passionately that life in the Navy was the happiest a man could have. His son thought differently: "I had a miserable time in the Navy." He was aware that it was his rather than the Navy's fault, and it mortified him to think that this was probably his father's opinion.

The setback did not sap his determination to stay in the war as long as he could. Refusing to go back into civilian life he was commissioned into the newly created Royal Air Force. Just before the war ended he was flown over to France, where he served as a staff officer at Air Force Headquarters in Autigny. Compared with what his elder brother had done this was not very much, but it was better than nothing. Looking back on it, the war for him had been a frustrating and depressing experience which had lowered his morale and diminished his self-confidence.

The King now decided that Albert should spend a year at Cambridge. As a young man in 1894, the King had been tutored in constitutional history by J. R. Tanner, a Fellow of St John's College, his instruction consisting almost entirely of the study of Walter Bagehot's classic, *The English Constitution*, of which Tanner made him write a condensed version. The contents of this book were to be practically the whole of his formal education. His notes on it are preserved in the archives at Windsor. Kingship in Britain, he concluded, was "still a great political force and offers a splendid career to an able monarch". Albert, he thought, should be given a similar grounding in constitutional history, so the young man went up to Trinity College, Cambridge, his syllabus being wider than that of his father, including, as well as constitutional history, economics and civics. According to his official biographer, Sir John Wheeler-Bennett, Albert became very interested in the development of the Constitution – much more interested than his father had been: "This he learned from Dicey's solid and uncompromising

Law of the Constitution, relieved by the brilliant and scintillating pages of Walter Bagehot." Though Wheeler-Bennett regrets that the Duke did not leave on record, as his father had done, "the fruit of his reading in Bagehot's fascinating work … many of the author's apophthegms must have remained in Prince Albert's mind and recurred to him in later years." According to Sir John, of all Bagehot's precepts the one which impressed the Prince most was the one which emphasised the *moral* role of the monarch. Sir John wrote:

Mr Bagehot was also admonitory. "We have come to regard the Crown as the head of our *morality*," he wrote. "We have come to believe that it is natural to have a virtuous sovereign, and that domestic virtues are as likely to be found on thrones as they are eminent when there." To all Bagehot's principles of Monarchy – its necessary dignity, its social value and its essential morality – Prince Albert dedicated himself with a solemn rectitude and an upright probity. He believed that the Crown must of necessity represent all that was most straightforward in the national character …

Albert passed nothing on to his daughter with more conviction than Bagehot's conception of the monarch as the head of the nation's morality, and she seems to have been as imbued with it as her father had been. In due course Prince Charles was to be versed in this and Bagehot's other precepts. According to Lady Longford, regarded as an expert on the lives of the royal family, it would be impossible to "catch out Prince Charles on the meditations of St Bagehot, who has become patron saint of all royal historians, biographers and journalists". More of Bagehot later.

Apart from this indoctrination in the philosophy of monarchy, riding around the pretty countryside on motor-cycles, punting on the Cam, drinking an occasional beer at the Hawks Club, and on one occasion being fined by the proctors for smoking in academic dress, Albert does not seem to have done very much at Cambridge or to have derived a great deal of benefit from having been there. He met few of his fellow students; most of his contacts were with dons. Instead of residing in college, as his elder brother had done when he was an undergraduate at Magdalen College, Oxford, Albert, with his younger brother Henry, lived on the outskirts of the city in a rented house. This was at his father's wish – a well-intentioned one: his father thought this would give him more freedom than residence within the confines of a college. The only friend of his own generation he seems to have had at the University was Lord Louis Mountbatten, five years his junior, already as full of life and redolent of success as Albert was lacking in these qualities. However, Albert seemed to have enjoyed his time at Cambridge. While he was there his father created him Duke of York, writing him one of those friendly letters which were so difficult to reconcile with the harsh and discouraging criticisms which he so often inflicted on his sons:

> I know that you have behaved very well, in a difficult situation for a young man & that you have done what I asked you to do ... I hope you will always look upon me as yr. best friend & always tell me everything & you will always find me ever ready to help you and give you good advice.
> Looking forward to seeing you tomorrow
> Ever my dear boy
>
> > Yr. very devoted Papa

Cambridge was at least a change for Albert, and meant that for several weeks in the year he did not have to live incarcerated with his parents in the palace. But his time at the University came to an end, and it looked as though he would then have to re-enter the rut: more boredom, more frustration. Then came the first stroke of luck in a life that hitherto had sadly lacked it.

Just before Albert went up to Cambridge it had been mooted that he might be asked to become President of the Boys' Welfare Association, an organisation which had been founded to mobilise the support of employers to provide better working conditions for boys working in industry. The invitation had been steered in his direction by Lord Stamfordham, Private Secretary to the King. Stamfordham was looking around for means of protecting the monarchy from the potential consequences of the widespread disillusionment with the political and constitutional system which had immediately followed the war. Recently demobilised ex-servicemen were now demanding the "houses fit for heroes to live in", which they had been promised during the war by the wartime prime minister, Lloyd George. These houses were not forthcoming.

Unemployment, swollen by men coming out of the forces who could not get jobs, was rising. Now that war contracts had come to an end industry was in recession. The prospect was of fewer not more jobs. While popular frustration and resentment was largely directed against the government the monarchy also came within the line of fire. Some of the Labour Party leaders praised the Bolshevik revolution of 1917 for demolishing the class system, liberation of the workers from the tyranny of the aristocracy, and for abolition of the monarchy, the main barrier, they claimed, to social progress. They attacked the political role of the British royal family, complained about the financial cost of maintaining it, and hailed the day when the Red Flag would fly over Buckingham Palace. Nobody was more aware of this hostility than wise courtiers such as Stamfordham. The best way of dealing with it, he believed, was to make the monarchy look more useful, less associated with class and conservative attitudes, more involved in the life of the nation, nearer to the people, and in particular to the working man. The idea of the newly created Duke of York becoming President of the Boys' Welfare Association fitted into his policy very well.

The idea of having a prominent member of the royal family as President had become very attractive also to the organisers of the Association. Awareness of the problems arising from the political situation had converged with other considerations to inspire a crucial change in their objectives. That same year they announced that in future the Association would promote the interests not only of boys but of all workers in industry, and would henceforth be known as the Industrial Welfare Society (IWS). Its aims remained the same – to improve relations between employers and employees by bringing about better working conditions and amenities, instituting education programmes, and making provision for medical care. The activities of the new and expanded Society were to be financed by the employers: support from these would be more likely to be forthcoming if the new President were a member of the royal family.

By now the King had reluctantly accepted the view that the monarchy was, if only temporarily, on the defensive. One incident towards the end of 1919 made a particularly unpleasant impression on him. Accompanied by the Prince of Wales the King rode from the palace to Hyde Park to a review of 35,000 ex-servicemen. He was given an enthusiastic reception, many of them breaking ranks, milling around his horse, and cheering him. Suddenly banners were unfurled carrying protests about lack of houses and of work. Though he was in no danger, the police decided that the King must be extricated from the throng, which was accomplished without trouble and with no mishap. According to Wheeler-Bennett the King and the Prince of Wales rode back to the palace in silence: "Dismounting, the King said, more to himself than to the Prince, 'Those men were in a funny temper' – and shaking his head, as if to rid himself of an unpleasant memory, he strode indoors."

The monarchy, the King decided, must take measures to make itself more acceptable to public opinion. This he made clear to his sons. If it were not done, he said, the future of the monarchy would be at risk. Albert, who to some degree faced a similar situation at the end of the war in 1945 – listening to his father in 1919 may have been a very useful experience – saw this at once, as is clear from observations he made much later. He saw that "the family firm", as he came to call it, must work hard to project an image of the monarchy agreeable to the people who had to pay for it. It would be unfair to both father and son to suggest that their views were determined only by a sense of dynastic self-preservation. George V always showed strong feeling about the conditions of his poorer subjects, and sometimes complained behind closed doors that politicians did not do enough to improve it. Albert had inherited that disposition. He regarded the Presidency of the Industrial Welfare Society as an opportunity to try and help the working man, and stipulated that he would take the job only "provided that there's no damned red carpet about it".

Having decided to embrace this opportunity he worked on it wholeheartedly. It was the more to his credit that he did not at the time realise how valuable the opportunity would turn out to be. He began a round of visits to industrial plants, met employers and employees, inspected machinery, asked questions and learned a great deal about production and industrial relations. Newspapers applauded him. He was extolled as a royal who exemplified enlightened concern for social welfare, and earned his keep. The grateful family firm nicknamed him "the foreman". The best known of his activities in this field came later, the annual Duke of York's Camp, to which he invited 200 boys from public schools and 200 from firms contributing to the IWS, the tents being pitched for the first few years at a site near the sea on Romney Marshes. The boys, with the Duke of York in attendance, played games, swam and sang songs. Today it might sound a somewhat corny operation, but in the early 1920s it was regarded as radical. There were mixed feelings about the association of a royal Duke with the Society. Many political leaders, trade union leaders and industrialists, for different reasons, had misgivings about the forging of this unprecedented link between industry and the monarchy. Stamfordham, while supporting the venture, was careful to avoid the impression being created that the royal family was favouring the interests of the workers against the employers. But consensus was soon established that the image of the Duke of York as President of the Industrial Welfare Society was good for the country and good for the monarchy. It was certainly good for Albert. It was his first success. Important for him at the time, it was to pay much greater dividends in years to come.

In spite of the uplift the Industrial Welfare Society brought him, Albert's life on the whole continued to be depressing. He still spent most of his time at Buckingham Palace, and found life there duller than ever. Except when they went out to perform a monarchical duty, which in itself was performed in a rarefied atmosphere, the King and Queen lived nearly always not only in a world of their own, but a world largely constructed for the satisfaction of only two people. They rarely went out for what even by their standards could be called fun, and they rarely had people in for the purpose. Except for their official engagements there was little variation in their daily routine. To his shooting, sailing, and stamps, the King added no other interests. What he knew about social life after the war he did not find very much to his taste, and so far as he could he lived in the previous century. His wife, though she took an interest in works of art, and in the contents of museums – the interest of a collector rather than of an *aficionado* – was equally content, or seemed to be, with their way of life. Most nights they dined together in solitary state, and went to bed at ten or ten-thirty. When the princes came for dinner the King interrogated them perfunctorily on what they had been doing since he had seen them last, and then with altogether more vigour told them what they should have been doing, and aired his opinions and prejudices on whatever took his fancy. Notwithstanding his work as "the foreman" Albert had the least to say for himself, partly because of his stammer, and therefore suffered the most from this depressing routine. It became worse for him when David was allowed to leave his parents' home and set up his own establishment in St James's Palace, shortly afterwards embarking on a series of world tours. Henry went into the Army and George went into the Navy. Albert wrote to David deploring their parents' habits, and complained to Lady Airlie of "no originality in the talk – nothing but a dreary acquiescence in the order of the day ..."

The King did nothing to encourage or stimulate Albert. On the contrary, he continued, unwittingly, to undermine his son's confidence. Sir John Wheeler-Bennett gives an example in the official biography. In October 1922 Albert was sent out to represent his father at the coronation of Queen Marie of Romania. He made a good job of it, and the British Minister in Bucharest reported as much to Lord Curzon, the Foreign Secretary. "The Duke's soldier-like appearance, his bearing, his good looks, and horsemanship ... were all the subject of many flattering observations." Curzon was impressed, and, thinking that the King would like to see this tribute to his son, passed on a copy of the report to Lord Stamfordham, who showed it to the King. The King read it, and mentioned it to Queen Mary, at a time when Stamfordham happened to be within hearing. The King spoke of the contents of the report in such perfunctory terms that Stamfordham felt that the Queen could have had no idea of how well her son had done, and that Albert had been most unfairly treated. His sense of an injustice being done was so acute that he took the unusual, and somewhat questionable, step of writing privately to the Queen and saying so:

I venture to trouble Your Majesty with this letter in case you may not quite realise what an unqualified success the Duke of York was in Rumania.

I happened to be in the King's room when His Majesty was talking on this subject to Your Majesty. *I* had been talking to Colonel Waterhouse [the Duke's very able Private Secretary, who had been with him in Romania] and I felt His Majesty's praise was quite inadequate. For Colonel Waterhouse said he could not exaggerate how admirably in every way His Royal Highness had done – and that when once he got away "on his own" he was a different being and never failing to "rise to the occasion", and proved himself to be far away from the most important of the foreign visitors at the Coronation.

19

Wheeler-Bennett comments: "it was not always easy for the sons of King George V to please their father."

The King's unfortunate influence on his sons was due partly to being indifferent or critical when he should have been sympathetic and involved, and partly to interfering when he should have given them their heads. He continued to do what he could to control and direct their lives as he had when they were children. He was to some extent motivated by his fear that his sons might get mixed up with "bad company", especially women, and embark upon the kind of life his father had led, a fear compounded by his belief that the morals and manners of young people of their generation were in danger of corruption by what he thought were the new and reprehensible "goings-on" of the early twenties. Of the four sons, Albert suffered the most from his father's criticisms because he had to spend more time at home listening to them. Life was indeed difficult for Albert: a domineering father; a distant mother; a dominant elder brother; and a daunting stammer.

This last had become a most worrying problem. Though more often than not described as a stammer, his problem was not what is usually understood by that term. His affliction manifested itself mainly in the form of sudden long silences occurring without warning and illogically at, for instance, the beginning of a sentence; sometimes, which was even more disturbing for his listeners, in the very middle of a phrase. His audience heard the long silence and saw the working of his jaw muscles as he tried to control his fear so that he could begin to speak again. In these silences his mouth writhed as he tried to shape words which he could not utter. It was an embarrassing experience for those present, made worse by seeing and hearing how the Prince was suffering from his ordeal. His delivery of a speech made at the closing of the British Empire Exhibition at Wembley Stadium, an occasion extremely important internationally for British trade and industry, so embarrassed his listeners that many people thought he should never be asked to speak in public again.

Following this débâcle Albert became a patient of Lionel Logue, an Australian therapist practising in Harley Street. In Logue's view the cause of the Prince's affliction was his relationship with his father. The problem was a lack of self-confidence; if he applied himself there was no reason why the Prince could not acquire it. Logue also prescribed physical treatment, mainly to teach the Prince how to control his breathing. Under Logue's direction Albert's speech began to improve. Though over the years Logue's methods did not remove all traces of the impediment the results were beneficial, a by-product being an easier relationship between Albert and his father. Logue later insisted that the greatest improvement came after Albert's marriage to the Duchess, and that it was due to her support, and to Albert's determination, that the problem had become manageable.

The improvement in Albert's speech enabled him to make considerable progress in coping with another of his problems: his temper. Irascibility, with prolonged gloom suddenly ending in an explosion of undue wrath, were a family syndrome inherited from the Hanoverians. Some of Albert's occasional outbursts, always triggered by failure or frustration, had taken place in public, and had caused comment. One of them had occurred in a tennis match at Wimbledon. Albert was a very good tennis player – in 1920 he won the RAF doubles championship. Later he was persuaded to enter the Wimbledon men's doubles. He and his partner were drawn against a very experienced pair. Defeat at their hands would have been no disgrace, but in the course of the game Albert gave many signs of taking his own mistakes very badly. That was the last time he played tennis in public.

Albert's marriage to Elizabeth Bowes-Lyon transformed his life. Accounts differ about how and where they first met. The most favoured version is that they did so as small children at a party, and that Elizabeth, sitting next to him at tea, with typical generosity, gave him the cherries off her sugar cake. It seems that he first became attracted to her in June 1920 when he saw her at a private dinner talking to his equerry, James Stuart, younger son of the Earl of Moray, and a direct descendant of the Stuart kings of Scotland. Stuart, later Conservative chief whip in Churchill's wartime coalition government, was a handsome and attractive man, who had had a brave career in the First World War. It was said then and later that Elizabeth Bowes-Lyon had at one time been in love with him. Certainly many other beautiful and desirable women had been, and were to be.

In his short autobiography, more memorable for what it did not say than for what it did, Lord Findhorn, as Stuart later became, records with characteristic economy that immediately after Elizabeth moved away from him that evening Albert went over to him and asked: "Who was that lovely girl you were talking to? Introduce me to her." Which Stuart did.

Elizabeth had just "come out". She was judged one of the most beautiful and likeable débutantes of the "season". Nineteen years old, petite, five foot four inches tall, with cornflower-blue eyes and the famous pink and white complexion which her daughters were to inherit, she had, as they were to have, that equally famous suddenly beaming smile. Her spontaneity and sense of fun charmed everybody. She was completely natural and unspoiled. The night Albert met her, even the simple unfashionable dress she wore distinguished her from the smart, sophisticated and very 1920s young ladies who were present.

Albert soon made up his mind that he wanted to marry Elizabeth. To succeed in that, he knew, would not be easy: she was out-standingly attractive, self-confident and sought-after. She was not easily impressed. The world was at her feet. By comparison he was a failure; lonely within his family, unhappy with himself, ill at ease with the world. But he lived up to the Captain of Osborne's report on him when he left the Royal Naval College – "He shows the grit and 'never say I'm beaten' spirit which is strong in him." He resolved to try his luck. It was one of the best decisions a member of the British royal family has ever made.

Elizabeth Bowes-Lyon was not royal, though she came from one of the oldest families in the kingdom, tracing their ancestry back to Robert Bruce, King of Scotland, in the thirteenth century. She was the ninth child of ten, and fourth daughter, of the fourteenth Earl of Strathmore, her mother being a daughter of a son of the Duke of Portland. This son had become a clergyman. Elizabeth's mother was a strong character, in whose life being the daughter of a clergyman played an important part. But as well as inheriting and embracing positive religious values she took a keen interest in the arts, had a gift for gardening, and played the piano well. She had the sense of fun which Elizabeth inherited.

Elizabeth's father was a man of admirable character, much respected by all who knew him, though of a cast of mind which some of his contemporaries thought grave if not sombre. Though he carried out all his civic duties conscientiously he much preferred private to public life, and left contacts outside the family to his wife and children. In some respects his personality resembled Albert's, which may ultimately have helped Albert's cause. The fourteenth

Earl of Strathmore was a wealthy man, his income coming mainly from ownership of coalmines in County Durham. He was not a recluse. He loved shooting and fishing, and playing cricket, a game at which he was outstanding. He was a thoughtful man with a keen sense of his social responsibilities. His concern for his tenants and employees was widely cited as an example of how a rich aristocratic landlord should behave, this reputation being enhanced by widespread appreciation of his courtesy, modesty and unostentatious devotion to his Christian faith. He was no admirer of that part of society which centred on the Court, possibly because of what he knew about the private life of Edward VII. His wife shared his views. She did not venerate royalty, and was critical of people who did.

Elizabeth had been brought up in a large and loving family to whose happiness she made a great contribution. An attractive brood, they had plenty of friends, but enjoyed being with each other more than socialising. The ambition of the boys was to grow up like their father as countrymen, understanding the land and caring for it, and doing good by all who lived on it. They fished and shot and looked after their workers. The girls were taught to look after the house, to cook, to sew – they made their own clothes – to sing and play the piano, and to create their own entertainment. They grew up in a moral atmosphere based on Christian belief and example.

The Strathmores owned an eighteenth-century mansion at Walden Bury in Hertfordshire, a town house in London's exclusive St James's Square, a castle in Durham and a more famous one at Glamis in Scotland. "I have nothing but wonderfully happy memories of childhood days at home," wrote Elizabeth in later life to Osbert Sitwell: "fun, kindness, & a marvellous sense of security." They were not all halcyon days. The First World War broke out when she was fourteen; four of her brothers went off to fight in it, one was killed when she was fifteen and for a long time another was believed dead. Her mother converted Glamis into a military hospital and ran it. When she became ill Elizabeth stood in for her.

Albert's family and friends were soon aware of his attachment. For such a shy young man he seems to have been remarkably forthcoming about it. Elizabeth did not immediately reciprocate. She liked him very much – they had many interests in common – and did not conceal the fact, but in the early days of her friendship with him that was as far as the relationship went. Many handsome and eligible young men besieged her with their attentions, some of them quite dashing figures. Elizabeth appreciated spirited young men. She always would. And Albert, whatever his virtues, was not dashing or even spirited.

Albert's parents wanted him to marry as soon as possible, particularly since his elder brother showed no signs of doing so, and there was no sign therefore of the family firm being provided with an heir. David too wanted him to marry, in spite of the fact that he was in love with a married woman, Freda Dudley-Ward, and had no intention of getting married himself: he was fond of Albert, empathised with his problems, and wanted him to escape from the parental dungeon and breathe a different air.

Albert's family and friends all shared his opinion of Elizabeth. His father told him: "You'll be a lucky fellow if she accepts you," not the most tactful remark, however well meant, to make when it was quite on the cards that Elizabeth would, however considerately, turn young Albert down. Everybody seemed in favour of the match except Elizabeth. In the course of the next two years Albert proposed twice and was refused twice. He became desperately unhappy – he still took reverses badly – and there are some interesting records of the despondency with which he talked so candidly about his predicament to his friends. He decided to propose to Elizabeth for a third and last time. The occasion he chose for it was a walk with her in the woods of the Strathmores' Hertfordshire home at Walden Bury, the house where she had been born. This time she accepted. He could hardly believe it. Up until now he had experienced almost nothing but failure in his personal life; now he had achieved his ideal. His jubilation was the greater because he knew how impressed his father and mother would be.

Why did Elizabeth refuse Albert twice? When she first met him she was only nineteen. She had not been brought up to think highly of life as a royal, and what she knew of it so contrasted with the life she knew and loved that it did not appeal to her. There were several young suitors who would have vied with each other to provide her with a more congenial life style. Albert, unlike David, did not impress on first acquaintance. A number of people who were his friends at the time, or became friends with him later, have recorded that on early acquaintance his personality put them off. He was shy, unsure, tense, his conversation often at first heavy to the point of being boring. It took some time for newcomers to get used to the impediment in his speech, which they found more embarrassing than a simple stammer because it obviously caused so much embarrassment to him. When they got to know him better, and he them, they found a different person. When he was relaxed he displayed a sense of humour, kindness, sensitivity and considerateness for other people, qualities not evident in the early stages of acquaintanceship. He was without his father's roughness and his brother's selfishness. He had character.

As she came to perceive these virtues, and his efforts to overcome his shortcomings, Elizabeth's attitude to Albert changed. She saw him not as a member of the royal family so much as a loving and lovable individual who displayed some of her father's qualities. She saw him as a serious fellow, but with a sense of humour and a desire for fun, a Christian and a gentleman, who understood and loved the way of life in which she and her family had been brought up. She saw he had the moral qualities and the sense of social responsibility which she had been brought up to respect. His superficial defects, his shyness and his stammer, appealed to that mother instinct in her that was strong then and would become stronger. And it had by now become clear to her that he adored her.

Lady Airlie may have played a crucial role in bringing about the marriage. She had known Albert and Elizabeth since their childhood. He had confided in her, even to the point of criticising his parents to her. He knew that Mabell Airlie, respected by everybody, with her own Scottish connections a friend of the Strathmores, might have influence with Elizabeth. He made frequent visits to her to get her advice. Elizabeth also visited Lady Airlie frequently. Lady Airlie talked to her about Albert. She spoke up for him.

Albert's feelings at discovering he had been third time lucky are enshrined in a letter he wrote to his benefactor:

> How can I thank you enough for your charming letter to me about the wonderful happening in my life which has come to pass, and my dream which has at last been realized ... It seems so marvellous to me to know that my darling Elizabeth will one day be my wife.

As soon as Elizabeth had accepted him he sent a telegram to his parents: "All right. Bertie". Two days later the King wrote in his diary: "Bertie ... arrived after tea and informed us that he was engaged to Elizabeth Bowes-Lyon, to which we gladly gave our consent ... She is a pretty and charming girl & Bertie is a very lucky fellow." The Queen wrote in her diary: "We are delighted ... Elizabeth is so charming, so pretty and engaging and natural. Bertie is supremely happy ..."

The wedding took place on 26 April 1923 at Westminster Abbey. It was the beginning of a marriage which must be outstanding for the record which it has left behind it of the fulfilment and mutual devotion of the partners. The husband idolised his wife; she dedicated herself to cherishing and helping him. He was a good man for whom the most important thing in life was to do his duty. For her, equally good, the most important thing in life was to help him to do it. Outside their inner world of love and duty everything was secondary and some of it remote, even Albert's stammer, his shyness, his occasional outbursts of ill temper, and his frequent loss of confidence. They shared a love for the simple things in life, and just being together. He would have liked more than anything to live the life of a country squire; she had been brought up as the daughter of one.

It was a good match, a happy marriage. It was into this self-sufficient world that their first child, Elizabeth, was born, and in which she grew up, the child of a dutiful and loving man and a brave, unselfish, devoted woman. The life of the Queen to be was to reflect that breeding from the start.

2

Birth and childhood. Her uncle abdicates 1926–36

THE FUTURE QUEEN ELIZABETH the Second was born on 21 April 1926 at 17 Bruton Street, a house in central London, midway between Bond Street and Berkeley Square, the recently acquired London residence of her mother's parents. Albert had been advised in advance that the birth might have complications and that a Caesarian section might be necessary, so instead of the child being born at the Yorks' home, White Lodge, Richmond Park, several miles away from the centre of London, the delivery was to take place near whatever medical facilities might be required. All went well. The baby was called Elizabeth, not after Queen Elizabeth the First, but after her mother. When the child began to talk she had difficulty in pronouncing her name, and called herself "Lilibet". And to her family "Lilibet" she remained.

In his biography of King George V Kenneth Rose includes some anecdotes about Elizabeth when she was about two years old. One came from Winston Churchill. He was invited to stay with the King and Queen at Balmoral. "There is no one here at all," he wrote to his wife, "except the family, the household and Princess Elizabeth – aged 2. The latter is a character. She has an air of authority and reflectiveness astonishing in an infant."

Much of what is known about Elizabeth's childhood comes from

The Little Princesses, a book written by her governess, Marion Crawford. Many students of the royal family have drawn extensively on this book, and while some of them have not cared for the vein in which it is written, they have made generous use of its contents. Whether her account is accurate from beginning to end is hard to say, but the bulk of it seems consistent with what over the years has become known from other sources. Elizabeth Longford, an expert on the royal family, has been critical of some of the things said in the book but has quoted far more than she has questioned. The royal family dissociated themselves from the book when it appeared in 1950 not because of what Miss Crawford had written but because she had, in their view, betrayed a trust in writing it at all.

At the age of twenty-two, having taken a course at the Moray House Training College in Edinburgh, and intending to become a child psychologist, Marion Crawford was filling in time teaching small children in families living near her home at Dunfermline. One of her employers was a sister of the Duchess of York, Lady Rose Leweson-Gower, then living at Rosyth. One day Lady Rose told Miss Crawford that the Yorks were coming to stay, and that she would like Miss Crawford to meet them. She did not say why.

The Yorks arrived. On the appointed morning Miss Crawford went to the Leweson-Gowers' house, still not knowing why she had been invited.

> As I crossed the lawn I remember there came over me an eerie feeling that someone was watching me. It made me look up towards the house. Then it was I saw there a face at the window, and for the first time I met that long cool stare I was later to come to know so well.

Two weeks later Lady Rose told Miss Crawford that the Yorks wanted to know if she would go to London as governess of the Yorks' two daughters, then aged six and two. Miss Crawford thought the matter over for two weeks, and then wrote to the Duchess suggesting that she came down for a short trial period. "The Duchess wrote me a charming, friendly little letter: 'Why not come for a month and see how you like us and how we like you?'" Miss Crawford went.

The Yorks' town house was 145 Piccadilly. Demolished many

years ago, it was a tall narrow building, with a glass dome, in the corner of Hyde Park made by Park Lane and Piccadilly, just west of where Apsley House stands today. Their country residence was now Royal Lodge, Windsor, situated in the middle of Windsor Great Park, and it was here that Miss Crawford reported for duty. When she arrived she was told that the Duke and Duchess were in London but would return later. Meanwhile, they would like her to meet the Princess before she went to bed: Mrs Knight, Elizabeth's nanny, would take her up to the night nursery and introduce her. Mrs Knight's Christian name was Clara, but from the days when she had been nanny to the Princess's mother she was known to all as "Alah", the little children finding it difficult to say "Clara".

A small figure with a mop of curls sat up in bed. She wore a nightie with a design of small pink roses on it. She had tied the cords of her dressing-gown to the knobs of the old-fashioned bed, and was busy driving her team.

"This is Miss Crawford," said Alah.

The little girl said, "How do you do." She then gave me a long, comprehensive look I had seen once before, and went on, "Why have you no hair?" I pulled off my hat to show her. "I have enough to go on with," I said. "It's an Eton crop."

She picked up her reins again.

"Do you usually drive in bed?" I asked.

"I mostly go once or twice round the park before I go to sleep, you know," she said. "It exercises my horses ... Are you going to stay with us?"

"For a little while, anyway," I replied.

"Will you play with us tomorrow?"

Alah had by now unhitched the team, and laid her flat. She allowed herself to be tucked away like a small doll.

"Good night. See you tomorrow," she said to me.

Miss Crawford had her supper, and thought about the "long comprehensive look" Elizabeth had given her. In the sixty years since then many other people have thought about that look. A little later the Duchess came to see her.

Her way of speaking was the easy, friendly one of any girl in her own home speaking to another girl who was far from home and

might be a little homesick and needed to be put at her ease …
When she said, "I do hope you will be happy here, and like us,"
I replied, "I am sure I shall." And I meant every word of it.

Miss Crawford proved her point. Having agreed to come to the
Yorks on a month's trial she stayed for seventeen years.

"Crawfie", as Elizabeth soon began to call her, had charge of the
two Princesses from nine o'clock until six. Alah, the nanny, who
had charge of them for the rest of the time, had the help of an
under-nanny and a nursemaid, the MacDonald sisters, Margaret
(Bobo) and Ruby. In Crawfie's view, Alah was "what every good
nurse ought to be – calm and kind, exuding that comfortable air of
infallibility and security so necessary to the welfare of the young".

Crawfie soon learned that the Yorks had decided to employ her
against the advice of many people, including the King and Queen,
who thought a much older governess would be more appropriate.
But the Yorks knew what they wanted, and were adamant about it.
"The Duke, I gathered, had throughout his own childhood been
hampered by somewhat immobile pastors and masters. He wanted
someone energetic with his children, and had been impressed by
the amount of walking I did." Above all the parents wanted a happy
childhood for their two little girls, the mother because she had had
one, and had never ceased to be grateful for it, and the father
because he had not, and knew what he had missed. Neither cared
about formal education; the mother because she had never had one,
and he because his had made him miserable. The Duke, says
Wheeler-Bennett, "was determined that, come what might, Princess
Elizabeth and Princess Margaret should look back upon their early
years as a golden age".

Soon after Crawfie's appointment the King and Queen invited
themselves to tea – so that they could have a look at her, she learned
later. Before being formally presented to them she chanced to meet
them as they strolled across the lawn. They stopped. Queen Mary
smiled, and said: "You are Miss Crawford." Crawfie curtsied.

King George grunted and prodded the ground with his stick. At
first acquaintance he was rather disconcerting. He had a loud
booming voice, rather terrifying to children and young ladies
who did not know him. After a moment he said: "For Goodness's
sake, teach Margaret and Lilibet to write a decent hand, that's

all I ask of you. None of my children can write properly. They all do it exactly the same way. I like a hand with some character in it."

He walked on. Queen Mary smiled again, and followed him.

Crawfie soon found that the planning of the Princesses' education was to be left to her. Later she wrote:

As far as education was concerned, the Duke and Duchess reposed great confidence in me, leaving much to my judgement. No one ever had employers who interfered so little ... Perhaps it was generally conceded in those days that the education of two not very important little girls did not matter a great deal. Nothing then seemed less likely than that they would ever have to play any important role in life ...

I had often the feeling that the Duke and Duchess, most happy in their own married life, were not over concerned with the higher education of their daughters. They wanted most for them a really happy childhood, with lots of pleasant memories stored up against the days that might come, and, later, happy marriages.

As a result Princess Elizabeth was given as unacademic an education as any British sovereign has had or is likely to have. This is not surprising. Nobody thought she would one day become Queen. Apart from Crawfie, the only other person who took a real interest in Elizabeth's studies was her grandmother. Queen Mary asked to see Crawfie's curriculum, and made a number of suggestions. She recommended plenty of history and geography – she had little use for arithmetic – and study of the genealogical trees of their families. She suggested more time for Bible reading.

School for Elizabeth started at the age of six. She was awakened at 7.30, and given her breakfast. At 9 she went downstairs to her parents. Lessons took place in a boudoir off the drawing-room. The week began with thirty minutes of religious instruction. For the rest of the week the first thirty-minute period of the day was given to arithmetic. There were four periods on History, two on Grammar, one each on Literature, Writing and Composition, Poetry and Geography. At eleven o'clock there was an hour's break for orange juice and play in the garden. From twelve to one there was reading, thirty minutes' silent reading, thirty minutes of Crawfie reading aloud. Elizabeth could read long before Crawfie arrived; she had been taught by her mother, who had been taught by her mother, mainly by reading Bible stories to her. After lunch came drawing and painting, out of doors if possible, the parents' love for horses, dogs, trees, flowers and country life showing in the choice of subjects; next, dancing and music. The Princesses had good voices. Lessons ended at 4.45. Then came tea. Occasionally some other children might be invited, such as their cousins the Harewood boys. The Prince of Wales often dropped in, and stayed for a game of Snap or Happy Families. He enjoyed himself tremendously; playing cards with his nieces brought out the little boy in him. When he lost he pretended to fume, and the little girls shouted and jumped with glee. Whenever possible the parents would spend the hour between 5.30 and 6.30 with Elizabeth, and when she was old enough Margaret too. The girls had their supper at 7.15. Then, bathtime. Their parents always came to see them in their bath. There would be splashing, squealing, screams and laughs. According to Crawfie:

> Then, arm in arm, the young parents would go downstairs, heated and dishevelled and frequently rather damp ... The children called to them as they went, until the final door closed, "Good night, Mummie. Good night, Papa."

Whatever we are to make of this daily routine, it was certainly very different from life in the palace a few decades previously, when a forbidding father intended his sons to grow up frightened of him, and a mentally unstable nanny pinched the heir to the throne to make him cry.

Most weekends were spent at Royal Lodge. The family drove down on Friday afternoon, accompanied by Governess and Nanny. There was school again on Saturday morning: revision of the week's work. On Sunday morning everybody went to Church. A very family weekend. Their father loved working in the garden; he chopped logs, hacked dead wood away, and burned rubbish on bonfires. Their mother planted and pruned. A relaxed weekend; as their father said sometimes, savouring his remark: "a very *ordinary* weekend".

Their home, in the middle of Windsor Great Park, was a splendid place for riding. Elizabeth was given her first pony when she was three, and was being seriously taught to ride before she was six.

Her mentor was the famous Mr Owen, of whom the Duke once said, not entirely in jest, that he had more influence over his daughter than her father. It was Mr Owen who asked Elizabeth what she would like to do when she grew up and received the reply: "Live the life of a country lady, with lots of horses and dogs." Crawfie recorded that Elizabeth "went through a phase of being very farm-minded". She built up a large "farm", buying most of the pieces in Woolworth's, and at that time used to say that when she grew up she would marry a farmer. "I shall have lots of cows, horses, and children."

Elizabeth loved horses. As a child she leaned out of the window at 145 Piccadilly not only to see the horses canter in Hyde Park but to watch the carthorses pull their drays around Hyde Park Corner. She kept a "stable" of thirty to forty horses on the landing outside her bedroom, each with its own saddle and bridle, which she personally polished, and which she took off at night when they were fed and watered. The treat of the year for her was the Olympia horse show; as soon as she got back home the horses outside her bedroom "would be put through several weeks of intensive training".

Crawfie was struck by the warmth the parents showed towards the children. She knew the little girls' experience was very different from their father's, and different from that of the children of most upper-class British families. Visits abroad separated the Yorks from their children for long periods, but when they were home "No matter how busy the day, how early the start that had to be made, each morning began with high jinks in their parents' bedroom."

Elizabeth was a very lovable little girl, according to Crawfie, good natured, easy to deal with, affectionate and devoted to her parents, and to her grandparents, especially to her grandfather. She and the King were great friends. She seems to have been the only person in that large family who brought out all of the very considerable affection which was latent in that off-putting personality. To the astonishment of the rest of the family, who would have thought him incapable of it, when little Elizabeth told him it was time for play he would get down on all fours and let her lead him along by his beard. He had never behaved like this with his own children. When he was convalescing from an illness at Bognor she used to walk along beside his Bath chair, telling him what she had been doing, he commenting with as much gravity as though this was an audience with his Prime Minister. The top floor of 145 Piccadilly could be seen from Buckingham Palace. After breakfast the King used to train his binoculars on Elizabeth's nursery and she would wave to him. She thought he was marvellous. The old man adored her. His death, in January 1936, was her first grief. According to Crawfie:

> Lilibet in her sensitive fashion felt it all deeply. It was very touching to see how hard she tried to do what she felt was expected of her. I remember her pausing doubtfully as she groomed one of the toy horses and looking up at me for a moment. "Oh, Crawfie ... ought we to play?" she asked.

A few months before he died George V talked to his Prime Minister, Stanley Baldwin, about his son and heir the Prince of Wales. He was worried. "After I am dead," he told Baldwin, "the boy will ruin himself in twelve months." By then the King and the Prime Minister and some others, including the Press Lords, knew that the Prince's latest mistress was a divorced American woman now in her second marriage, Mrs Ernest Simpson. There was gossip that he wanted to marry her.

In his first ten months as King, Edward's record had not been good. Those close to him knew that some of it had been disgraceful. Soon after his father's death he had declined an invitation to open new hospital premises at Aberdeen the following September, when he would be at Balmoral. He gave as his excuse that he would still be in mourning for his father. He asked the Duke of York to deputise for him, and the Duke agreed. On the day the new hospital premises were opened the King was seen at Aberdeen station meeting Mrs Simpson off the London train.

That week the King, when he was supposed to be in mourning, gave a grand party at Balmoral. The Yorks, having represented him at Aberdeen, were staying at nearby Birkhall. The King invited them to his party. When they arrived at the castle they found that the guests were being received by Mrs Simpson, who was behaving as the King's hostess. They learned later that she was sleeping in Queen Mary's bedroom. From that moment the Yorks feared the worst. For a long time they had been conscious of the change in Edward since he had become enthralled by Mrs Simpson. He had always tended to be irresponsible, inconsiderate and selfish, but it seemed to them now that these traits were in the ascendancy, that his personality was dominated by his mistress and that her evil influence was corrupting the goodness and niceness in his character.

Since he came to the throne in January the King had embarrassed the Prime Minister by making comments on international affairs inconsistent with government policy. This was unconstitutional. He had also made questionable statements about domestic politics. In many other ways he made it clear that he was not going to be a representational king. He was going to rule as he thought fit. Thirty-five years later when he was asked in a BBC television interview if he would have liked to have gone on being King he replied: "Yes, if they had let me do it in my own way." The fact was that he could not have been allowed to do it in his own way.

In November it was becoming impossible to keep news of the King's relationship with Mrs Simpson from the British public – American and continental newspapers were full of it – and in the middle of the month the King and Baldwin met to discuss the situation. It was not much of a discussion: the King delivered to his Prime Minister, though amicably, what was in effect an ultimatum: he was going to marry Mrs Simpson, and if necessary he would give up the throne to do so. The King then told his mother and arranged to meet each of his brothers separately to break the news to them.

Albert was stunned, and because of the shock and his shyness was so unable to express himself that he asked for another meeting a few days later. This time his way was paved by a letter to the King from the Duchess of York, which, in the words of Edward's biographer, Philip Ziegler, "illustrates, perhaps better than any other document, the turmoil of emotions in which the royal family were floundering at the time."

The Duchess wrote in a letter whose existence she concealed from her husband:

Darling David,
   Please read this. Please be kind to Bertie when you see him, because he loves you, and minds terribly what happens to you. I wish that you could realize how loyal and true he is to you, and you have no idea how hard it has been for him lately. I *know* that he is fonder of you than anybody else, and as his wife I must write to tell you this. I am terrified for him – so DO help him, and *for God's sake* don't tell him that I have written. We both

uphold you always. We want you to be happy more than anything else, but it's awfully difficult for Bertie to say what he thinks, you know how shy he is – so do help him.

As well as illustrating "the turmoil of emotions in which the royal family was floundering at the time" the letter tells us much about the character of the Duchess, as does a letter she wrote to Queen Mary: "every day I pray to God that he will see reason, and not abandon his people."

The idea of his brother ceasing to be King, and the prospect of having to replace him brought Albert close to the point of breakdown. The Duchess was almost as consternated as he was. Nobody knew better than she did how unfitted her husband was for the responsibility. As well as by his personal shortcomings, Albert would be handicapped by his lack of training for the throne. According to Wheeler-Bennett he told Mountbatten, in great distress, "I'm quite unprepared for it," and, when Mountbatten demurred, added: "David has been trained for this all his life. I've never seen a state paper. I'm only a Naval Officer. It's the only thing I know about." Not only did he not have the knowledge; he feared the responsibility; he felt that he could not shoulder it. Conscious of his disabilities, he saw himself being caught up again in those frustrations and miseries of his childhood and his early youth which he thought he had put behind him. He knew too that he would take over a monarchy with a reputation smirched and dented by his brother's recent behaviour. The family firm's honour had been compromised. Its reputation for unselfish devotion to the public good had been sullied if not lost.

The nightmare of the burden to be thrust upon him was made worse by what he now began to learn about the previous conduct of his elder brother. It was now clear that Edward, while Prince of Wales, had lied to their father about his relationship with Mrs Simpson, had deceived members of the family about his intentions, and in order to try and get both throne and marriage had involved himself in politics in a manner inconsistent with the constitutional duty of the monarch.

It was one thing for Albert to tell himself that he was not qualified to succeed his brother; another to hear that other people thought so too. He had to suffer the indignity of hearing that there was talk of his younger brother, George, becoming King. Everybody knew about his stammer; but there were rumours also that he suffered from "falling fits" – epilepsy – and that his health would not stand up to the demands of state occasions and tours abroad. The Abdication crisis raised all the old questions of what the monarchy was for and whether it was worth while, and the new question, whether after this trauma it could recover its position. Albert did not look the man for that task. His youngest brother, George, Duke of Kent, on the other hand, looked as if he might be. He was tall, handsome, elegant and gregarious. He was married to the beautiful and popular Princess Marina, and already had a male heir. His reputation was not beyond criticism. Among his friends were several homosexuals, and at one time he had taken drugs, an episode from which he had been rescued by Edward. But at the time these things were known to only a few: generally the Duke of Kent was well thought of. It is still not known how far the Prime Minister and royal family went in considering whether Albert had better be passed over in favour of his brother; or whether they considered the matter at all. Two books written by the historian Dermot Morrah, widely regarded as an expert on the monarchy, both written with the approval and assistance of the royal family, one published in 1947, the other in 1958, indicate that the matter *was* seriously discussed. Baldwin's official biographers, Middlemas and Barnes, could find no evidence of this when they examined the Abdication papers.

These were agonising weeks for Albert. The worst were the week before and the week after the public announcement of the Abdication, his misery being the worse because his wife was confined to bed with influenza. His diary recorded "a terrible lawyer interview", demanding discussions of constitutional technicalities and other unpleasant sessions. At one of these Edward, complaining about his "poverty", tried to get King George V's will altered in his favour, bringing back painful memories of the bereavement ten months previously. Albert's grief was heightened by his rapidly growing suspicion that his brother was not to be trusted. He began to doubt whether Edward would honour the legal and financial arrangements being negotiated. He was angry and hurt when he found out how much information Edward was keeping back about the size of his private fortune. Tortuous legal conferences with the lawyers, emotional outbursts from Edward, his own grief and fear, combined to weigh Albert down. After these exhausting meetings

37

he found it impossible to relax. Elizabeth spent these two critical weeks in her sickroom – "I could not rest alone." Elizabeth grieved the more at being unable to give him her best support. She wrote later: "The agony of it all has been beyond words."

It says much for the progress Albert had made with his own psychological problems that at this moment he did not collapse. As it was, on one occasion he lost control of himself, as he described in the account of the crisis written in his own hand at the time, now in the royal archives at Windsor. Returning from the last harrowing session with his brother as King, Albert recorded, "I went to see Queen Mary & when I told her what had happened I broke down and sobbed like a child." Many years later Queen Mary confirmed this to Harold Nicolson. "He sobbed on my shoulder for a whole hour – there, upon that sofa."

During these days, Crawfie recorded, the Duke and Duchess never spoke of what was happening, "but it was plain to everyone there was a sudden shadow over the house." She and the little girls used to look down into the well of the dome at the important people coming and going. "The Prime Minister, Mr Baldwin, bishops and archbishops passed below, all looking anxious and harried." One afternoon she was asked to go and see the Duchess. When she got to her bedroom she was asked to wait – the Duchess had a visitor. Crawfie looked out of the window at the crowds below, like her wondering what was to be.

And then something happened that told me the Abdication had taken place. The bedroom door opened. Queen Mary came out of the Duchess's room. She who was always so upright, so alert, looked suddenly old and tired. The Duchess was lying in bed, propped up among pillows. She held her hand out to me. "I'm afraid there are going to be great changes in our lives, Crawfie," she said. We talked for a little while as to how we were going to break this news to the children, and what differences it would make. The break was bound to be a painful one. We had all been so happy in our life at 145.

"We must take what is coming to us, and make the best of it," the Duchess said ...

When I broke the news to Margaret and Lilibet that they were going to live in Buckingham Palace they looked at me in horror.

"What!" Lilibet said. "You mean for ever?"

The new King was proclaimed on 12 December. He decided to be called "George", since "Albert", he thought, sounded too Germanic.

The new Queen was still confined to bed. The two girls spent the day at home with Crawfie, talking about the changes in their lives which lay ahead. Elizabeth was old enough and perceptive enough to be aware of the stress her father had been under even if she did not understand all the reasons for it. She could see the effort he was making to behave as though all was normal. She may not have sensed with how much anxiety her mother viewed the future but she sensed that both parents preferred the life they had been leading to the one that was now beginning. She understood too, according to Crawfie, that they were changing their lives only at the call of duty. She was aware that her own life had become different in the last few days. Preparations for the move from the house in Piccadilly to Buckingham Palace brought this home. Her "horses" had to be packed up and taken away, and new stabling had to be found for them. Her new home was only a few hundred yards away, and she was no stranger to it, but whereas 145 Piccadilly was familiar, warm, comfortable and intimate the Palace, by comparison, was vast, dim, cheerless and cold. Overall, one was a home, the other a museum.

The unfamiliar ambience in which the family had lived in the past few weeks had not cleared up overnight. Her parents continued to be preoccupied. Her father still looked strained. Though she could not have known it, as well as being apprehensive about his future, the King was immediately involved in most painful exchanges with his brother. The personal tensions within the family created by Edward in his last few days in Britain did not end when he left the country. On the contrary they took on a new and more unpleasant lease of life. The newly created Duke of Windsor had barely arrived on the Continent before he sent off a series of complaints and demands which the King found deeply hurtful and disturbing. The tone and content of the Duke's letters confused him. Much of it was quite irrational. It depressed the King to find the Duke insisting on being given privileges which he must have known he could not have. It depressed him even more – it shocked him – that his beloved and admired elder brother now displayed such insensitivity, acquisitiveness and aggression.

The Duke's main complaint, which he reiterated frequently until he died, was initially made not to the King but to Queen Mary. He had been bitterly hurt, he wrote, by his brother's "humiliation" of him in denying the title of Her Royal Highness to his wife, and by Albert's claim that he had done so on the advice of his government. This explanation, said the Duke, was "a sorry enough show of weakness" but, worse, it was not the true one: the real reason for his humiliation was "Bertie's personal attitude towards myself ..." He went on to say: "I regret to say, your attitude and that of the whole of my family can have had but one important result; my complete estrangement from you all."

Queen Mary showed this letter to the King, who at once wrote a personal letter to the Duke saying that far from wishing to humiliate his brother what he had done was "absolutely necessary for the sake of the country". He was as hurt as he was indignant. "How do you think I liked taking on a rocking throne, and trying to make it steady again?" He urged the Duke not to go on writing letters of this kind, at any rate to his mother; "... If you do want to let yourself go, do write to me and not Mama, as it makes her absolutely miserable."

The Duke replied with a letter which repeated some of the complaints he had made previously – mainly relating to money – and rejected his brother's assessment of the situation when he came to the throne. "I do not agree with your description of the throne as 'tottering' ... I have done a great deal to preserve the system, over which you now preside ... What other motive had I in abdicating except a patriotic one, and to avoid a conflict between Crown and Government?" Far from moderating his criticisms of the way his family had treated him the Duke extended them. He wrote later to his youngest brother, the Duke of Kent: "I tell you, here and now, that I will never forgive or forget the lead Bertie has given you all in your behaviour to me ever since I left England."

Whenever the Duke decided to launch an attack on his family, the Duchess almost invariably backed him up, and sometimes instigated these assaults. But this case was an exception. When she saw his original letter to the Queen she told him he should not have written it. Thereafter she always referred to it as "the offending letter". The wound it inflicted lasted throughout the King's life. The knowledge of it darkened the memories of his daughter. To what extent at the age of ten Elizabeth was aware of these tensions within the royal family is difficult to assess. Some aspects of the situation could not have escaped her. In earlier days Edward's visits to 145 Piccadilly and to Royal Lodge at weekends had been a happy part of her life. As he became involved with Mrs Simpson he visited his nieces far less frequently. When he became King, he became even more remote. Then, suddenly, he ceased to be spoken of at all, seemed no longer to exist. Then came the news that beloved Uncle David was no longer King. He was going away, and nobody was happy about this, certainly he was not, and her father was going to take his place, and nobody seemed happy about that either, and everybody seemed sad and disturbed about everything, and a cloud seemed to hang over 145 Piccadilly.

Elizabeth would certainly have not been told much about the Abdication by her parents. They wanted life for their daughters so far as possible to go on as before. The King said as little to them as he felt he could. This was not hard for him; except to his wife he had never wanted to unburden himself to anybody. His shyness and reserve, and his impediment, had discouraged him from doing that, and reticence about personal matters and private situations had long since become a habit with him. He and his elder brother had grown up sharing the same view of the necessity of circumspection. Edward wrote of his and Albert's feelings as young men:

> People were watching us. Our lives were under the surveillance of some who might not be understanding of ordinary human frailties ... One learned to be withdrawn, wary, non-committal, and, above all else, to keep one's emotions under a tight leash.

Though Elizabeth was now the heir presumptive to the throne, her parents wanted no change in the balance of her education, or in her upbringing. Education was still not going to be a burden, and school would continue to be a happy place. When the girls moved into the Palace somebody earmarked a schoolroom for them. The King and Crawfie went to inspect it, standing at the door and looking in. It was, said Crawfie, "the cheerless room in which he had spent many unhappy hours as a child". They moved on. A pleasant airy room was soon selected. The Princess's syllabus continued on much the same lines as before. There were exceptions. A crash course in monarchy was added – Queen Mary's idea – as a preparation for the Coronation, now arranged to take place the following May. Miss Crawford produced the reading for it, and Queen Mary produced pictures and drawings to illustrate it. The other change in Elizabeth's syllabus was an extension of the history course. Later, like her grandfather, uncle and father before her, she would be given special instruction in constitutional history, and in the works of Bagehot.

Notwithstanding the feeling of many people that the wrong king was being crowned the Coronation was hailed as a great success. Huge crowds lined the streets to see the royal procession go by, and there was general enthusiasm. As the coaches went from Buckingham Palace to the Abbey and back there was tremendous cheering for the Princesses, more, some people said, than for the King and Queen. Elizabeth thoroughly enjoyed herself. She regarded herself as being in charge of her sister, particularly in the Abbey. When she got back to the Palace she told Crawfie that Margaret had behaved very well: "I only had to nudge her once or twice ... when she played with the prayer books too loudly." Drawing on the course of instruction which Queen Mary and Crawfie had devised for her Elizabeth wrote an account of the Coronation for her parents in red pencil in an exercise book, preserved in the royal archives at Windsor:

> The Coronation, 12 May, 1937.
> To Mummy and Daddy. In Memory
> of Their Coronation,
> From Lilibet By Herself.
>
> At 5 o'clock in the morning I was woken up by the band of the Royal Marines striking up just outside my window. I leapt out of bed and so did Bobo. We put on dressing-gowns and shoes and Bobo made me put on an eiderdown as it was so cold and we crouched in the window looking on to a cold, misty morning. There were already some people in the stands ...

Once the new Queen had got over her influenza and the shock of the Abdication she became herself again. And more. She not only began to behave like a queen; she evidently enjoyed it, and nobody begrudged her evident pleasure, with the exception of the Duchess of Windsor, who could not see a picture of her in a newspaper without making disparaging remarks about her. The new Queen turned her back on the convention, honoured notably by Queen Mary, that no member of the royal family should be seen to smile in public. Some people claimed that she smiled all the time. She was aware of the criticism. She said to an old friend: "Some people say I do it for effect. It's much worse than that: half the time I don't know that I'm doing it." There were no signs of her having changed or having been changed by the trauma of the Abdication and her husband's precipitate elevation to the throne. She was as admired and loved as ever, good will towards her deepened by sympathy on account of her husband's limitations, which, always there, and always evident, would now be in the light of day as never before. Few people knew at this time how tough her character was, that though she was understanding, tolerant and forgiving she had an uncompromising almost Calvinist conviction of what was right and wrong, especially in relation to the conduct of the monarch, and that her very visible velvet glove was lined with steel.

The King's performances in public soon began to reassure the doubters. He delivered his speeches better than his friends had expected. His family saw the steady increase in his self-confidence. They watched him as he toured the city among cheering crowds, and heard him say, "I did not know I was so popular." This was all to the good, but the new pressures caused some of his imbalances to re-surface. Occasionally, his nervousness, his barking ill temper, his fretfulness, even the occasional explosion of rage – his "gnashes" – returned to plague him.

The greatest problem for him in the short term was still his brother. As well as the personal problems the Duke was creating within the family, he was behaving publicly in a way which was embarrassing to the new King and the government, mainly by making statements about world affairs which conflicted with the policies of the British government. In October 1937 the Duke announced that he proposed to visit Germany and the United States to study how they handled housing and working conditions. The new King and his Queen interpreted his announcement as the beginning of a campaign to create publicity for himself preparatory to re-establishing himself on the British political scene. There were also reports that the Duke was considering heading a World Peace Movement financed by a Swedish millionaire, Wenner-Gren, the founder of Electrolux, the main objective of this movement being to reconcile Labour to the capitalist system by improving the standard of living and working conditions. The Duke's visit to Germany took place, but reports of his praise for the Nazis so angered American opinion, that he decided, reluctantly, to call the

American visit off. He told Lord Beaverbrook, who, in order "to bugger Baldwin", had tried to keep him on the throne throughout the Abdication crisis:

> Of course, you know as well as I do, that it is for no other reasons than for fear lest the attitude my mother and sister-in-law seem likely to adopt to my wife may provoke some controversy in England and adverse criticism of them in America, that I have been advised to postpone our projected visit this Spring.

In the meantime reports reached the British Foreign Office that the *Daily Herald* would publish an interview with the Duke in which he had said that if the Labour Party came to power, established a Republican form of government, and invited him to become its first President he would accept. If such an interview took place it was never published.

It is unlikely that the King and Queen believed that the Duke seriously intended to come back to Britain and head a campaign to oust them. But they knew he might cause trouble. He was beginning to miss the popularity and publicity that for so long he had been accustomed to. They knew too that he was irresponsible, insensitive, feckless. He never paused to consider the implications of what he said or did. They put nothing past the mesmeric influence on him of "that woman". So, though the new King continued to make ground, impressed more and more people at home and abroad with his personality, and built up the confidence of the Establishment in his capacity to rule, he and his wife began their reign looking over their shoulders at the Windsors. This the King tried hard to conceal from everybody except his wife. But he was not sufficient of an actor to conceal it from those near him. He was frequently tense and strained. Elizabeth, whose cool gaze, according to Crawfie, missed nothing, observed her father's behaviour and her mother's reactions. When the Duke made a brief visit to London to talk to the King at the Palace, Elizabeth noted that the Queen went out for the day.

Early in 1938 the full scale of the threat from Hitler and Mussolini began to reveal itself. In March Hitler invaded Austria, and in September would have absorbed Czechoslovakia but for the last-minute agreement with Chamberlain at Munich – "peace in our time" the British Prime Minister claimed. For the time being Hitler was content to annex only the Czechoslovakian Sudetenland, but the following March he sent in his troops, and the whole of Czechoslovakia became part of Germany. The Prime Minister's appeasement policy had long been denounced by many members of his own party, outstandingly by Winston Churchill, on the grounds that far from appeasing Hitler it would lead to further aggression. The invasion of Czechoslovakia forced Chamberlain to abandon appeasement. Poland seemed to be Hitler's next target. Chamberlain announced that in the event of the Poles being attacked Britain would go to their defence.

In May of that year, the prospect of war with Germany staring Britain in the face, the King and Queen were to set out on the first state visit of their reign – to Canada and the United States. The Duke of Windsor chose this moment to renew his campaign for international peace. While the King and Queen were in mid-Atlantic the Duke, at the invitation of the National Broadcasting Company of America, made a broadcast to the United States which was virtually a call to the Americans to save the world from war. He claimed in his memoirs that he did this because "I became convinced that Europe was headed down the slippery slope to war. Only the Americans had the influence to arrest the slide."

Many people believed at the time that the Duke's real aim was to upstage the King and Queen in the United States. He had many friends in America. Many of them had read recently published newspaper and magazine articles which alleged that the Duke had not given up the throne of his own free will but had been manoeuvred into exile on account of his radical reforming views. When he was King, the Duke had certainly made public statements which lent some colour to this contention, the most memorable of them only three weeks before the Abdication, when he visited an area of high unemployment in South Wales and, visibly moved by what he saw and heard, said, "Something must be done to find them work."

The Duke may have made his broadcast for entirely personal reasons. By now he knew that there was no possibility of his being able to return to Britain and play a significant public role, and he believed that he had been denied this at the insistence of the King. In that belief he was mistaken: according to Walter Monckton, the Duke's lawyer and contact with the royal family, the King did not at this time rule out such a possibility, and the Prime Minister was not opposed to it. Lord Birkenhead's authorised biography of Monckton records:

> The King himself ... was not fundamentally against the Prime Minister's view. But [noted Monckton] I think the Queen felt quite plainly that it was undesirable to give the Duke of Windsor any effective sphere of work. I felt then, as always, that she naturally thought that she should be on her guard because the Duke of Windsor, to whom the other brothers had always looked up, was an attractive, vital creature who might be the rallying point for any who might be critical of the new King, who was less superficially endowed with the arts and graces that please.

Before the King left London for the United States several articles appeared in the American press which questioned his capacity for discharging his new responsibilities. One of these, written by Josef Israels, included the following passage:

> The important fact about the United States is that a large part of the country still believes that Edward, Duke of Windsor, is the rightful owner of the British throne, and that King George VI is a colourless weak personality largely on probation in the public mind of Great Britain, as well as of the United States.

According to Israels the attitude of well-informed British and American citizens to the new King and Queen had been influenced by accounts of:

> George's alleged epileptic seizures, his speech impediment and an impression that he is of poorer royal timber than has occupied England's throne in many decades.
>
> As for Queen Elizabeth, by Park Avenue standards, she appears to be far too plump a figure, far too dowdy in dress, to meet American specifications of a reigning Queen. The living contrasts of Queen Mary (as regal as a woman can be) and the Duchess of Windsor (chic and charmingly American) certainly does not help Elizabeth.

The King and Queen set foot on American soil with apprehension. They need not have feared. The visit was a triumph. The King came back to London to find glowing reports from the Foreign Office, enthusiastic cuttings from the press, and congratulatory messages from relations and friends all over the world. Plaudits had poured in from the countries of the Commonwealth. Even without these accolades he felt a different man. The tour had immensely boosted his confidence. He had held his own in talk about world affairs with the President of the United States and the Prime Minister of Canada.

President Roosevelt had told the world how much he admired the King, who, now completely at ease with him after a weekend at his private home, described him to Mackenzie King, the Prime Minister of Canada, as his "new found friend". Washington and New York rang with praise of the new King. "The British Sovereigns have conquered Washington," proclaimed the *New York Times*. Great crowds had turned out to cheer them. The King had got through his speeches without mishap. Eighteen months later, Harry Hopkins, President Roosevelt's confidential emissary to Churchill, told the Prime Minister, according to Colville: "It was the astounding success of the King and Queen's visit to the U.S. which had made America give up its partisanship of the Windsors." The King's homecoming speech, made at the Guildhall, the day after he arrived back, was hailed as by far the best he had ever made. There was widespread comment on his new self-confidence.

By now, Elizabeth had reached her thirteenth birthday. In many respects she was mature beyond her years, in some respects younger than her age. She had inherited traits from both sides of the family: from her father's their shyness and inwardness, and some awkwardness in human relationships; from her mother's, resilience and outgoing affection. Now and again she might seem "a little down", moody, sulky, a dark, heavy expression on her face. But not for long. The warmth she had inherited from her mother would return; the smile would suddenly beam out like the sun appearing from behind a cloud. Unlike Margaret, she was serious, earnest, self-sufficient and dutiful. She was rather a cool child, already bringing to mind that comment about her frequently to be heard in later life: "matter-of-fact". At the top of the page in her diary on the day her uncle had given up the throne she had written the words "Abdication Day" and had immediately proceeded to record her progress at swimming that day. Seeing a letter on the hall table addressed to her mother as "H.M. The Queen" she said to Lady

Cynthia Asquith, standing nearby, "That's *Mummy* now, isn't it?"

Crawfie says that in these early days Lilibet never seemed to feel the need for friends; parents, sister, horses and dogs gave her all she needed. Somebody who remembers her at this stage in her life, and continued to see a good deal of her, said: "You knew where you were with her, even when she was a child. As children go she was very matter-of-fact. She still is matter-of-fact. If you don't know what matter-of-fact means, you don't know the Queen."

Even as a very young child she had been neat, methodical and orderly. Nothing was left lying around. Everything must be tidy. Her toys, books and clothes were taken out and put away carefully. The "horses", thirty of them, all about a foot high, mounted on wheeled platforms, "stabled" outside her bedroom, had always to be ranged in their right order and strictly in line. At one time Crawfie "got quite anxious about Lilibet and her fads" and felt something should be done:

> She became almost too methodical and tidy. She would hop out of bed several times a night to get her shoes quite straight, her clothes arranged just so. We soon laughed her out of this. I remember one hilarious session we had with Margaret imitating her sister going to bed. It was not the first occasion, or the last, when Margaret's gift of caricature came in very handy.

Crawfie began to worry that Elizabeth's life was becoming remote from what was normal. It was not good that a planned and protected visit to the local YWCA should be regarded as a great adventure, or to take a ticket on the tube and pay for it out of her own purse seem like an expedition into the unknown. When she walked in Hyde Park she gazed on other children as though they had arrived from another planet; she wanted to talk to them but did not know quite how. The essence of the problem, as she saw it, was that Elizabeth had grown up in a world of adults, and of adults of a special kind. Even when she was a little girl her father had talked to her as though she were much older than her age, and she had responded in kind. Walking with him to feed the horses at Royal Lodge of a weekend, her hand in his, she would solemnly describe a visit to an art exhibition with her grandmother as though she were making a report, her father equally solemnly listening and making comments.

Crawfie raised this with the King and Queen and they agreed with her. Some experiments were made. One was to create the 1st Buckingham Palace Company of Girl Guides, with vacancies for a few Brownies so that Princess Margaret could be included. After some modifications the experiments were successful. The original recruits arrived at the Palace escorted by their nannies and dressed as though for a dancing party. On their way through the corridors to meet their royal highnesses the doors were opened for them by footmen wearing scarlet coats. Nobody saw the need for change sooner than Elizabeth, said Crawfie:

> There was one Guide game we played where all the shoes are heaped together in the middle of the room, and their owners have to find their own, put them on, and see who can get back to the starting-line first. This never went very well, as quite half the children did not know their own shoes! Lilibet and Margaret told me this with scorn. There was never any nonsense of that kind in *their* nursery.

The 1st Buckingham Palace Company of Guides had considerable success. When at the beginning of the war the two girls went to live at Windsor the company was restructured to include recruits from the village school and evacuees from the East End of London.

Crawfie worried not only about Elizabeth's remoteness but about her seriousness. She smiled, felt for people and situations, got excited, laughed; but the main impression she made was of being dutiful. She was "a very good little girl". If she felt ill she never wanted to rest in bed – "I must not take the easy way out." Parts of Crawfie's narrative made the Queen sound a little priggish, a trifle prim, and some of her elders began to liken her to the young Queen Victoria. The examples not only of her great-grandmother but of her grandfather, grandmother and above all her father, conditioned her at a preternaturally early age to believe that above all the most important thing in life for a member of the royal family was *duty*. This was what "the family firm" was *for*.

Lilibet's sense of duty extended to her feelings about Margaret. She felt she had to look after her sister, a feeling not reciprocated, and not always appreciated. Elizabeth felt this more as a result of the change in status relative to each other when she became the heir presumptive. Crawfie overheard her say to Margaret as they

49

followed their parents downstairs to a Buckingham Palace garden party: "AND if you do see someone with a funny hat, Margaret, you must *not* point at it and laugh, and you must *not* be in too much of a hurry to get through the crowds to the tea table. That's not polite either."

She looked on Margaret as not only much younger but as different. Margaret was playful, wilful, sometimes naughty, a performer, a mimic, an actress, a comedienne, volatile, and very often the spoiled child. Elizabeth was reserved, controlled and, by comparison with her sister, sedate; mature beyond her years. The long absences of her parents away from home, she thought, meant that she must supervise Margaret. She must set her an example. She was extremely fond of her. Margaret was part of her life. A close, more affectionate and more mutually dependent relationship between little sisters would be difficult to imagine. And it never changed.

According to Crawfie:

Lilibet was very motherly with her younger sister. I used to think at one time she gave in to her rather more than was good for Margaret. Sometimes she would say to me, in her funny responsible manner, "I really don't know what we are going to do with Margaret, Crawfie," and go on to tell me of something she had been up to.

There were frictions, occasional fights. Now and again Elizabeth got a dig in the arm, and now and again Margaret had her arm pinched. But the age gap between them made more for compatibility than conflict, and their happy relationship with their parents was another bond. As they grew older, they saw in each other traits they would like to have had in themselves. Elizabeth enjoyed her sister's sense of fun, her jokes, her cracks, her sometimes outrageous mimicry, her originality. Up to a point she would have liked to have been like Margaret. On the other hand, Margaret, though sometimes she became impatient with it, admired her sister's unshakeable solidity.

According to Crawfie Elizabeth never lost her feeling that she must protect Margaret:

All her feeling for her pretty sister was motherly and protective. She hated Margaret to be left out; she hated her antics to be misunderstood. In her own intuitive fashion I think she saw ahead how later Margaret was bound to be misrepresented and misunderstood. How often in earlier days have I heard her cry in real anguish, "Stop her, Mummy. Oh, please stop her," when Margaret was being more than usually preposterous and amusing and outrageous. On more than one occasion the official camera has caught her giving Margaret a nudge and a sisterly look that has said plainer than any words, "Margaret. Please behave!" or "You must *not* laugh here."

Elizabeth had very early on developed a sense of how a royal should behave at all times. She felt that Margaret had not. Elizabeth had a precocious sense of being royal, and that being royal was different from being any other kind of human being. She was highly aware that the masses of the people outside the Palace were interested in her, and that she must behave towards them, and in front of them, in a special kind of way. And that it was her duty to do so.

In this she may have been much influenced by her grandmother. After her father became King, and had to be away from home much more, she saw more and more of Queen Mary, who, now a widow, was glad to see more of her grandchildren. Queen Mary, with Crawfie's enthusiastic encouragement, became a second governess. Shy, uncommunicative, of regal mien, she was undemonstrative to her granddaughter but very attentive. Especially when the Yorks were away she would take Elizabeth out for the afternoon, usually to exhibitions and galleries. Queen Mary was very knowledgeable about paintings and sculpture, and talked about them interestingly. She also talked about being royal, with that devout Germanic feeling for the dignity and mystery of royalty which was mentioned earlier. She had precise ideas of how royals should behave and how they should be treated. Just as she had looked upon George V as monarch first and husband second she expected to be treated as Queen first and grandmother second. Even when there was nobody else with them she behaved to her little granddaughter like a Queen to a subject, and expected this behaviour to be reciprocated. When Elizabeth entered her presence she must curtsy.

It was even more important, in Queen Mary's view, that royals should behave royally in public. They should never allow themselves to be photographed while smiling. They should show themselves aware of the crowds with dignity and grace but not in any way play to the gallery. Observing that Elizabeth was becoming increasingly aware of the interest that the public showed in her Queen Mary discouraged her from responding to it. Royals must not behave like film stars.

Whatever Elizabeth learned from Queen Mary, according to Crawfie she modelled herself more on her mother. Even before the Abdication, when she was only ten years old, Elizabeth loved to look down from the dome of 145 Piccadilly at the prominent people who came and went, passing "some astonishingly acute judgements, too, on this one or that". She seemed to think about her image.

Already Lilibet was developing a charming little manner of her own in company, and she made the most brave efforts to model herself on her mummie and always say the right thing at the right time. This was charming, but not always entirely successful. One day Ramsay MacDonald (then Prime Minister) bent low over her small hand, and she said in that clear ringing voice of hers:

"I saw you in *Punch* this morning, Mr MacDonald, leading a flock of geese."

Mr MacDonald gave her a wan smile.

In Elizabeth's upbringing, however, the most important influence was her father. Above all she was impressed by his sense of duty, his industry and conscientiousness. He did things the hard way. Whereas after an important meeting his father would dictate notes to his Private Secretary the new King wrote a full report in his own hand. He opened his own mail. Consequently he came across many facts and figures he might not otherwise have come by, and developed his memory. He was methodical, and liked routine. For him, routine went hand in hand with duty. His devotion to routine, like his father's before him, may have been a shelter from royalty, but next to duty it was the most important thing in life for him. Wherever they were, at Buckingham Palace, Windsor or Sandringham, the day would be predictable, built up around what had to be done, not around what people might want to do, all about duty, rather than self-expression.

The King influenced his daughter by example rather than precept, and she came to regard the example as a moral one. She saw her father working extremely hard at a job he had never wanted, and had thought himself ill-fitted for. She saw the struggle he had had with his speech impediment, and how he had succeeded. Physically and emotionally she was developing slowly, but her values and her perceptions were in many respects beyond her age. She looked at life with "that long cool stare".

This, 1939, was the year in which Elizabeth, aged thirteen, first became aware of the man she was later to marry. With her father and mother and Margaret, and accompanied by Crawfie, she made a visit to the Royal Naval College at Dartmouth. They went there on board the royal yacht, *Victoria and Albert*, and with them was Lord Louis Mountbatten. In the course of the visit – accounts of what happened differ in detail – the party was joined from time to time by Prince Philip of Greece, Mountbatten's nephew, who at the age of eighteen had become a cadet at Dartmouth that year, according to Crawfie "a fair-haired boy, rather like a Viking, with a sharp face and piercing blue eyes". Elizabeth "never took her eyes off him". Prince Philip on the other hand, "was quite polite to her, but did not pay her any special attention ... At the tennis courts I thought he showed off a good deal, but the little girls were much impressed."

In the next few days Elizabeth and Philip were together frequently. According to Prince Philip's biographer, Tim Heald, there was an outbreak of an infectious disease at the Naval College, possibly mumps or chicken-pox, and the Queen did not want Margaret and Elizabeth to run the risk of contracting it by going to morning chapel. Philip was exempted from the service and invited up to the Captain's House to help entertain the two little girls. Mr Heald recorded that Prince Philip, "an eighteen-year-old man-of-the-world, was resentful at having to squire a thirteen-year-old girl and her nine-year-old sister, no matter how regal. Nevertheless he carried off the chore or privilege to general satisfaction."

When the royal party left, the cadets, in a great variety of small craft ranging from rowing boats to launches, escorted the royal yacht down the river to the sea. Some of these boats got so close to the royal yacht that the King feared there might be an accident so he gave instructions for them to be told to turn back. The order was given through the loud-hailer. All obeyed, except one. On his own in a rowing boat the young Viking continued to ply his oars. Eventually a stentorian voice came from the royal yacht, probably Lord Mountbatten's: "Uncle Dickie" was already thinking about a marriage between his nephew and the heir presumptive. The young Viking, albeit reluctantly, turned and rowed back towards the shore.

According to Crawfie, the King commented: "The young fool." Whether Elizabeth heard the remark Crawfie does not say, but she did record that as Philip rowed away Elizabeth "watched him fondly through an enormous pair of binoculars".

Prince Philip told Mr Heald that the Crawfie version of what happened is not altogether correct. "The boats followed the Royal Yacht for only two hundred yards, turned round and went home. And that was that." Mr Heald quotes an earlier biographer of the Prince, Basil Boothroyd: " 'There's a fair consensus' writes Boothroyd, in his breezy, matter-of-fact way, 'that this was the day that romance first struck.' "

In Elizabeth's early and late teens her emotional life was to be dominated by two men, her father and her husband-to-be. For better or for worse this was to be, however formative an experience, a limited one.

As recorded more fully later in this book her father was not happy about her marrying after so little experience of meeting other men. And he had misgivings about her marrying a man who seemed at that time so much a dependent of the ambitious and politically active Labour Party supporter, Lord Mountbatten. But the die had been cast. The King's daughter had fallen in love with Prince Philip. The seeds of great prospects for the monarchy, and for the country, were then planted. And, also, the seeds of some problems.

3

Growing up in the war 1939–45

THE WAR WAS the making of George VI, and gave a new lease of
life to the monarchy. As a man he had the opportunity to display
to the full his sense of duty; as the monarch he rose to it. It
displayed the institution as was not possible in times of peace as
the symbol of embattled patriotism and national identity. In the
terrible context of a war in which the British people might be
defeated and subjugated the person of the King and the institution
of the monarchy were fused incandescently by the eloquence of
Winston Churchill.

The way the King conducted himself in the war showed that he
welcomed its challenge. People saw this and applauded it. His
shortcomings now seemed of no consequence; they were more
reason for admiring him. He was no warlike king, but he was a
worthy king to have in war. Elizabeth observed this. With her
familial piety grew an admiration of her father as a king. She saw
that it was his devotion to his duty which most endeared him to
the people. Her father, a hero for her already, was now a hero to
the nation.

In the war she learned to admire her father not only for what he
was but for what he had achieved. He had conquered his speech
impediment; he had wrestled with kingship, and had won; he had

refurbished the image of the monarchy; now he was the nation's acclaimed symbol, leading Britain's single-handed struggle against the dictators.

Her father put much of what he said and did into a religious context. For him the war was not only a fight for democracy but for Christianity. His first wartime Christmas broadcast spoke of war in "the cause of Christian civilisation". He concluded his broadcast with the quotation from M. Louise Haskins:

"I said to the man who stood at the Gate of the Year, 'Give me a light that I may tread safely into the unknown.' And he replied, 'Go out into the darkness, and put your hand into the hand of God. That shall be better than light, and safer than a known way.'"

May that Almighty Hand guide and uphold us all.

Hitler had invaded Poland on the first day of September 1939. In accordance with their pledge to preserve Poland's independence the British and French governments immediately issued an ultimatum to the German government. This was ignored. Two days later Chamberlain announced that Britain and France were at war with Germany. For several months all was quiet on the Western front. The feeling grew in Britain and France that Hitler did not wish to involve Germany in a full-scale European war, and that seeing that the Allies were prepared to fight he might offer to negotiate. Even at this late stage many people in Britain and France could not believe that after the slaughter of the First World War the governments of Europe would engage in a second one. Even some of the experts on foreign affairs predicted "Peace by Christmas". The "phoney war" continued until May 1940. Then the Panzers swept like a suddenly undammed flood across the Low Countries and northern France. By now Chamberlain, ill and broken in spirit – a British invasion of Norway in April had proved a disaster – had lost the confidence of the House of Commons. There was pressure for the formation of a national government. The Labour Party was willing to join, but not under Chamberlain. He hung on to the last minute, and had virtually to be pushed out, resigning ungracefully on 10 May. The King asked Winston Churchill to form a national government.

The King was deeply unhappy that Chamberlain had been forced to resign. As he saw it, a world war had been averted the previous year by the last-minute agreement Chamberlain had negotiated at Munich. He believed that Chamberlain's downfall had been brought about by malcontents within his own party, that he had been maligned and betrayed by people who should have been grateful and loyal to him, and that he had been unjustly treated. Queen Mary shared her son's feelings. So did the Queen and Princess Elizabeth. After Chamberlain made a broadcast to the nation announcing his resignation, almost immediately to become one of the most ill-regarded of British prime ministers, the Queen told him: "My eldest daughter told me that she and Margaret Rose had listened to it [the broadcast] with real emotion. In fact she said, 'I cried, Mummy.'" When Chamberlain, now dying of cancer, left the government the following October, the King wrote him a particularly warm and personal letter: "You were my Prime Minister in the earliest years of my reign, & I shall ever be grateful for your help & guidance during what was in many ways a very difficult period. For me too it will always be a pleasure to recall our many & intimate talks together ...". When Chamberlain died the following month, the King wrote to Queen Mary: "I know that I have lost a trusted friend. When he was PM he really did tell me what was in his mind, & what he hoped to do. I was able to confide in him."

The King was suspicious of Chamberlain's successor. He would have preferred Lord Halifax. This preference would have been opposed by the Labour Party and by many influential members of the Conservative Party, since as Chamberlain's Foreign Secretary Halifax had been as responsible as he had been for the British government's appeasement policy. Vis-à-vis Germany he had pursued it even more assiduously. There was an objection to him becoming Prime Minister of a different kind: he was a member of the House of Lords. This would not have disqualified him on constitutional grounds, but to have a peer leading the House of Commons from a seat in a different chamber in the twentieth century was deemed impractical.

Though the King sent for Churchill on Chamberlain's advice he had misgivings. He recorded in his diary at the time: "I cannot yet think of Winston as P.M." He had always mistrusted Churchill as a political adventurer, a maverick who had twice changed his party allegiance, a trouble-maker who had been irresponsible in his opposition to independence for India in 1935 – he had called Gandhi "a naked fakir" – and an opportunist who had done his best with

Beaverbrook to allow Edward VIII to marry Mrs Simpson and yet remain as King. He knew that Churchill had discussed with some newspaper proprietors the possibility of Edward transacting a morganatic marriage with Mrs Simpson and remaining on the throne, and that with Beaverbrook he had discussed the formation of a King's party to support the King against the Prime Minister. These events were less than four years in the past, and kept only too fresh in his mind by the Duke's dangerous dabblings in international relations.

He was even more unhappy about his new Prime Minister when he received Churchill's recommendations for posts in his first Cabinet. Lord Beaverbrook was to be included as Minister for Aircraft Production. The King knew that after the Abdication Beaverbrook had continued not only to be a friend of the Duke but to give him favourable publicity in activities which, in the King's view, were a threat to the safety of the country. In January 1940, well before the fall of France, dissatisfied with his post with the British Military Mission at Vincennes just outside Paris, and determined to get something better, the Duke flew to London from Paris without informing the King and had had a meeting with Beaverbrook, at which he expressed the view that France would shortly collapse, and that he would then return to Britain and lead a campaign to end the war. According to others present at that meeting – Monckton among them – Beaverbrook responded with: "Go ahead, Sir, and I shall back you." After Beaverbrook had left, alone with the Duke, Monckton warned him that "he had been speaking high treason".

The King did what he constitutionally could to prevent Beaverbrook's appointment. Using the third of the uses of the Royal Prerogative – the right to warn – he wrote to Churchill saying he thought the names put forward were:

> very good, ... but I would like to warn you of the repercussions, which I am sure will occur, especially in Canada, at the inclusion of the name of Lord Beaverbrook for aircraft production in the Air Ministry. You are no doubt aware that the Canadians do not appreciate him, & I feel that as the Air Training Scheme for pilots & aircraft is in Canada, I must tell you this fact. I wonder if you would not reconsider your intention of selecting Lord Beaverbrook for this post.

The King had been entitled to offer a warning. The Prime Minister though bound to listen to it was not bound to act on it. Beaverbrook became Minister for Aircraft Production.

The King harboured reservations about the Prime Minister for some time, and not all of them had to do with Churchill's friendship with his brother. The King was proud of the knowledge he had acquired of the working man when as Duke of York he had pursued his interest in industrial relations and had earned from his family the nickname of "The Foreman". He remembered the days of the General Strike in 1926 when he and his father had been far more sympathetic to the workers than Churchill had been. In 1942, Lord Woolton, then Minister of Food, a successful businessman who for many years had taken an enlightened interest in industrial welfare, recorded a relaxed conversation with the King in March 1942 on the subject of labour relations. This was a time when Churchill's stock was at its lowest. Several political leaders would have liked to see him replaced, and there were murmurs that he would have to go. Woolton recorded that at his meeting with the King he:

> talked very intelligently about the food situation, and very frankly about my colleagues! ... He said that B [Ernest Bevin, Minister of Labour] had no understanding of the mind of the people, adding "Neither has the Prime Minister." The King has been brought up to do the industrial side of the royal job, and he knows more about it than the Minister of Labour.

Churchill's Private Secretary at the time was "Jock" (later Sir John) Colville, who was in touch with thought and feeling in the Palace since his mother, Lady Cynthia Colville, was Lady-in-Waiting to Queen Mary, and her trusted friend. According to Colville, relations between Churchill and the King (and the Queen) at the outset were not good ... "they are a little ruffled by the off-hand way in which he treats them." Unlike Chamberlain, who arranged his appointments with great consideration for his sovereign's time, Churchill behaved as though he had other things to do. Chamberlain had made a point of going to the Palace regularly once a week, ascertaining well in advance a time convenient to the King, arriving and leaving punctually, and taking the King through the week's events in a careful unhurried and explanatory way. Churchill, according to Colville, was not so accommodating. "Winston says he will come at 6.00, puts it off by telephone till 6.30 and is inclined to turn up for ten hectic minutes at 7.00." The King, a stickler for routine, always nervous when it was broken, did not like this. It was not long before his attitude began to change, partly because the more of Churchill he saw the more he admired, and partly because he soon saw evidence of Churchill's determination, in spite of his affection for the Duke of Windsor, to stand no nonsense from him.

The King's finest hour was in August 1940 when Hitler launched the Blitz on London. These massive bombing onslaughts, to which other cities, such as Coventry, Sheffield and Birmingham, were soon subjected, were intended to soften up Britain's will to resist preparatory to an invasion or to intimidate her into suing for peace. Until then the King felt that he had not really been in the war – once again his elder brother had been nearer the fighting than he had been. He still remembered vividly his frustration and humiliation in the First World War when after he had been invalided out of the Navy he had remained so far away from the sound of gunfire. He said to Mountbatten, then captain of a destroyer, "I wish I had a definite job like yours."

The Blitz changed all of that. As soon as German bombs began to rain down on London night after night he and the Queen had the sense of being in the war. Now, they shared the danger of death as many in the armed forces did not. They could not stop the bombs falling and killing, but at least they could share the risks with their people, and after the German bombers had flown away they could visit the bombed areas and try to comfort those who had survived. The King rapidly became a symbol of the country's will to resist. His morale rose. After a lunch at which the King and Queen were present, Harold Nicolson recorded: "What astonished me is how the King is changed. I always thought him rather a foolish loutish boy. He is now ... so gay and she so calm ... [the two] resolute and sensible."

The worst night of the Blitz was 7 September, when more than 200 German planes dropped bombs on London, most of them falling in the East End. The next morning the King and Queen walked through street after street now reduced to rubble. The following week a German plane flew from east to west along the Mall and dropped bombs directly on Buckingham Palace. At the time the King was working in his study with his Private Secretary, Alec Hardinge. They saw two bombs fall past the window, hit the ground on the opposite side of the Palace quadrangle, explode and open up two craters. The King recorded: "It was a most unpleasant experience, but there was nothing to be done about it, so we got on with our work." The Queen said: "I am glad we've been bombed. It makes me feel I can look the East End in the face."

When mingling with crowds in the devastated streets of the East End the King was completely unselfconscious and totally relaxed. He talked and listened without tension. On formal occasions he might behave very differently. Sometimes his old problems came back. Before reviewing troops, even so small a number as those who formed the nightly guard at Windsor Castle, he could get worked up. On bigger occasions he might become almost unmanageable. In the last few minutes before he went out on parade he would fret and frown, his jaws would become rigid, his face would become ashen. His equerries would wonder if he would go through with the review. Then, at the last moment, screwing up his courage, he would walk out and do the job to everybody's satisfaction, except his own. To be with him at these times was nerve-racking.

The war brought Princess Elizabeth nearer to everyday life than she could ever have in years of peace. German bombs were no respecters of royalty, and when the air raid sirens blew they blew for everybody. The King and Queen usually spent the day on duty in London and came home to Windsor at night. Elizabeth knew that her father practised his rifle shooting in the grounds of Buckingham Palace, that her mother learned to use a pistol there, and that a small hand-picked body of officers and men from the Guards and the Household Cavalry were on duty day and night with armoured cars ready to rush the King and Queen to safety in the event of enemy parachutists trying to capture them.

The King's puritanical sense of duty precluded any kind of privilege for himself or his family. So far as possible, and subject to the direction of the Prime Minister, he and his family would live as his people lived. The use of water was regulated. A depth of four inches only was permitted for a bath, and in hotels and many private houses a line was painted to mark the level. The baths in Buckingham Palace were painted similarly.

In some respects, the war enabled Princess Elizabeth to identify with the people, and share their experience to a degree which had not been possible before. But in other respects the opposite was the case; she and her sister lived a life even more sequestered than before. Need for security confined them to their home. There were far fewer public occasions, far fewer visits from distinguished guests, and far fewer trips. Their parents' duties meant that they saw less of them than they had before, and even more of each other.

Early in the war there was a suggestion that to ensure their safety the King and Queen should leave Britain and take up residence in one of the dominions. They would not hear of it. It was then suggested to the Queen that along with thousands of other children who were being sent there the Princesses should be evacuated to Canada. The Queen replied: "The children won't leave without me, I won't leave without the King; and the King will never leave."

At the same time there was a concern about the girls' security for political as well as personal reasons. At the time the war broke out the royal family had been on holiday at Balmoral. When the King decided that he must come back to London the girls remained there, going to Sandringham for the first Christmas of the war, and at the end of the holiday moving with their parents to Royal Lodge, Windsor. In May 1940, after the evacuation of British troops from Dunkirk, when invasion seemed possible, the Princesses went to live in Windsor Castle, which then became their home for the whole of the war.

Life was very different there from what it had been there before the war. The castle had been made into an armed camp, bristling with anti-aircraft guns, Lewis guns, air-raid shelters and troops. "So depressing," said Queen Mary. In the early days there were no bomb shelters; when the air-raid sirens sounded the Princesses were taken down to the cellars. There was an alarm two nights after they took up residence. They got up from bed and, still half-asleep, began to get dressed. Crawfie told them there was no time to put on their clothes: they must put on coats over their nighties, and hurry to the cellars. When the all-clear sounded the Master of the Household, Sir Hill Child, solemnly walked across the cellar to the Princess, bowed ceremoniously to her and said "You may go to bed, Ma'am". With all their restrictions and discomforts it was these wartime years living in Windsor Castle which led the Queen in retrospect to think of it as her real home. It was from here that she made her first broadcast. Derek McCulloch, "Uncle Mac" of the BBC's Children's Hour, made a series of programmes with children evacuated from London to a "house somewhere in the country". He asked if the Princesses could be included. Elizabeth made a very good job of it, and the recording was broadcast all over the Empire. Her voice was a little more high-pitched than usual – both girls had inherited their mother's high register – but she delivered the text very well. At the end of her stint she called, "Come on, Margaret." Margaret said, "Goodnight, children." It was quite an event.

The fall of France in June 1940 was the signal for more trouble from the Duke of Windsor. The Duke first made for Spain, arriving in Madrid with the Duchess at the end of the month. Churchill told him that he was arranging for him to be brought back to Britain. The Duke said he would do so only if the King would give his wife the title of Her Royal Highness, and find him a suitable post. The King had previously been willing for the Duke to return but now changed his mind. He and Churchill now agreed that the Duke must be kept out of both Britain and the United States. If he arrived in America he would almost certainly try to build up a peace offensive and press for negotiations with Germany, encouraging the Americans to keep out of the war at a time when Britain fighting Hitler single-handed was desperately trying to bring them in. To quarantine the Duke effectively, Churchill now suggested that he should be invited to become Governor and Commander-in-Chief of the Bahamas. The King thought it an excellent idea – the Queen demurring on the grounds that the Duchess was not fit to be the wife of the Governor of a British colony. With Beaverbrook present, Churchill dictated the draft of the invitation to his Private Secretary, Jock Colville, who recorded:

> "I think it is a very good suggestion of mine, Max," said Churchill. "Do you think he will take it?" "Sure he will," said B., "and he'll find it a great relief." "Not half as much as his brother will," replied Churchill.

Before the governorship of the Bahamas was officially offered to the Duke, the Colonial Secretary, Lord Lloyd, sent a telegram to the Prime Ministers of the Dominions telling them what was going to happen and why. The first draft of the telegram included the following passage: "The activities of the Duke of Windsor on the Continent in recent months have been causing HM and myself grave uneasiness as his inclinations are well known to be pro-Nazi and he may become a centre of intrigue." That passage was deleted from the telegram before it was dispatched, probably by Churchill. The King may not have seen the sentence, but he knew about the situation they referred to, as was shown by remarks he made at the time to the Head of the Foreign Office, Sir Alexander Cadogan. The King mentioned the existence of a report on the "quisling activities of my brother", quisling by then having become a word for co-operation with the enemy, after the name of the Norwegian army officer who encouraged the Germans to occupy Norway in 1940. According to Cadogan the King may not have taken the report very seriously, but he certainly knew about it.

Flying boats were sent to Lisbon to evacuate the Duke and Duchess. The Duke sent the flying boats back, and remained in Lisbon. He did not intend to go to the Bahamas if he could avoid it. He and the Duchess saw the appointment to the Bahamas as banishment, as indeed it was and was meant to be. Postponing and prevaricating, he spent several more weeks in Lisbon, during which he had talks with various people, some of whom were agents of the German government, authorised to talk to him by the German Foreign Minister, Ribbentrop, about how the war could be brought to an end. Later, accounts of these talks were to prove embarrassing. After the war German documents dealing with these matters became available, adding to and confirming what was being communicated to the Foreign Office at the time. Not all of what the German agents reported back to Ribbentrop turned out to be true, but nobody knew that at the time, and the fact that so much was being reported, true or false, was significant in itself – and very alarming. According to Ribbentrop's agents, they and the Duke discussed the possibility of the "assumption of the English throne by the Duke and Duchess – Hitler thought she would be an excellent queen" – and, also, the Duke's conviction "that if he had remained on the throne war would have been avoided".

At some stage while these talks were going on the Duke changed his mind about the Bahamas appointment and decided that he would take it. Why he did so is not clear, but according to the German agents who were reporting back to Berlin, he now thought that if he did not comply with the British government's request that he go to the Bahamas his ultimate intentions might become apparent. The German Minister in Lisbon reported to Berlin: "He was convinced that the present moment was too early for him to come forward ... Once things changed, however, he would be ready to return immediately ... He had already initiated the necessary arrangements."

The records suggest that the phrases "the present moment" and "once things changed", and the statement that the Duke "had agreed on a code word, upon receiving which he would immediately come back over" indicate that what was being discussed was the subjugation, or domination of Britain by German force of arms or the threat of it, followed by a summons to the Duke to return so that he could be restored to the throne or otherwise put in charge of his country's fortunes. What was particularly disturbing was that the reports suggested that the Duke was not merely listening to proposals, but was contributing to them. A few weeks after the Duke arrived in the Bahamas he was reported to have cabled one of the agents in Lisbon "asking for a communication as soon as action was advisable", and a year later the same agent reported another similar request from the Duke.

The King's reaction to what he heard about the Duke's behaviour, as it always was to what burdened him most, was either to pretend to pooh-pooh it or to be silent about it, occasionally breaking the silence to vent his fear and anger in explosions of temper. So far as nearly everybody except the King and the Queen was concerned the Duke had been moved not so much into the outer darkness as into a belt of silence. Crawfie recorded that for the Princesses, "The Royal conspiracy of silence had closed about him as it did about so many other uncomfortable things. In the Palace and the Castle his name was never mentioned." However brave and clear-sighted about danger and adversity the King and Queen might be to each other in private, to everybody else they behaved as though they were not aware of any griefs and perils that might exist. Elizabeth, like her father, unflinching in the face of public duty at whatever risk, inherited her father's habit of avoiding or repressing what was unpleasant, or threatening, in her private life, and carrying on as though all was well.

In August 1940 the Duke left for the Bahamas. His decision to accept the appointment may have been influenced by his discovery that if he were to reside in Britain or the United States he would have to pay income tax. It would also have been influenced by a powerful telegram from Churchill, sent to him earlier, shown to the

King and heartily approved by him, pointing out to him that he was a serving soldier and must obey orders: "I most strongly urge immediate compliance with wishes of government." According to Colville, it was at this time that the King saw that however helpful Churchill had been towards his elder brother at the time of the Abdication he was now going to make no allowances for him. "Suspicions which the King and Queen may have had about Winston's support of the Duke of Windsor evaporated when the Duke made difficulties in connection with his appointment as Governor of the Bahamas and the Prime Minister himself sought the King's permission to reply to the Duke's complaints with considerable severity."

The King wrote a letter to the Duke on his appointment as Governor saying that he was glad the Duke had realised that he should not come back to Britain. For three years after that, so far as is known, the King made no direct contact with the Duke. So far as he could he left the Duke and his problems to Churchill.

Churchill did not relish dealing with the Duke. At this time President Roosevelt was striving to get the Lend-Lease Bill through Congress. The Bill provided for the sale of arms and munitions to Britain on credit. After a rough passage, for isolationist sentiment was still strong, the Bill cleared the House of Representatives in early February 1941 and reached the Senate. At that point the Duke gave an interview to the American magazine, *Liberty*, which was re-published in Britain a few weeks later, advocating negotiations for a peace and urging America to stay out of the war. Churchill was alarmed. He sent the Duke an angry telegram, rebuking him for the interview in *Liberty*, reprimanding him for associating himself with policies opposed to that of the British government, and ordering him not to consort with the pro-German and appeasement-monger financier, Wenner-Gren. The Duke, also angry, replied that had it not been for the King and Queen's unreasonable attitude to himself and his wife he and the Duchess would now be in Britain, "proud to share these sad and critical times with my countrymen". He complained with indignation about the treatment of the Duchess by the King and Queen, citing a recent article in *Life* magazine in which the Queen was reported to have spoken of the Duchess as "that woman".

On 7 December 1941 Japanese aircraft bombed American warships in Pearl Harbor. This brought the United States into the war overnight. The activities of the Duke of Windsor could now do little or no damage to British interests. He could no longer hope to set himself up in America as the international peacemaker, and make that a stepping stone to a new career in Britain. From now on he had only one object: to obtain for his wife the title of Her Royal Highness.

He went about this in the worst possible way. In August 1942 his younger brother, the Duke of Kent, was killed in a flying accident on his way to inspect Royal Air Force locations in Iceland. The Duke of Windsor used the occasion to write the King a letter in which he said: "It is, therefore, a source of great pain to me now to think that on account of your 'attitude' towards me, which has been adopted by the whole family, he [the Duke of Kent] and I did not see each other last year when he was so near me in America." Later that year he wrote to Churchill requesting that the King would "restore the Duchess's royal rank" in the New Year's Honours List, as "an act of justice and courtesy [for] her public services in the Bahamas". Churchill felt he had to pass this request on to the King, who responded to Churchill predictably:

> I feel I cannot alter a decision which I made with considerable reluctance at the time of his marriage ... I am sure that there are still large numbers of people in this country and in the Empire to whom it would be most distasteful to have to do honour to the Duchess as a member of our family ... I have consulted my family who share these views.

The King to some extent added to his own unhappiness by continuing to hope that his brother would come to his senses, accept the situation with understanding, make the best of it and behave accordingly. Such a hope was unrealistic, but it says much for the King's goodness of heart that he continued to cherish it. In May 1943 he asked Churchill to convey to the Duke that he continued to be "unhappy over this family estrangement". The result was a letter from the Duke direct to the King, complaining bitterly of "studied insults", and of the King "persecuting me". It was clear, the Duke claimed, that the King had instructed the Foreign Office that "my wife and I are to have different treatment to other royal personages".

Unhappy as he was about the Duke's paranoid state of mind, the

King did not yield an inch of the position he had taken up in 1936. In September 1944 on his way from the Quebec conference to New York Churchill made arrangements to have a brief meeting with the Duke of Windsor there, and asked the King if he would like him to take a fraternal greeting to his brother. The King declined the offer, recorded Colville, sending Churchill "a most cold message in reply". Soon after this Lascelles warned Churchill that "constant harping on this problem might have a really serious effect on the King's health."

For nearly all the reminder of the war period the story of Elizabeth is much the same. How many people she would have met, how many scenes she would have visited, what of the world she would have come to know had there not been a war, it is impossible to say: the fact is that as it was she lived a very restricted life. It consisted almost wholly of her relations with her mother and father, with a sister who was much younger than herself, with a governess and a nanny, and several servants. She was prevented from meeting many people who in normal times might have become her friends. The effect of the war, therefore, was to sweep her from childhood to adulthood without passing through the normal period of transition. Yet in some respects she remained younger than her age. This was partly due to the constant company of her sister. To a great extent they were brought up as though they were of the same age, and since Margaret, of whom less was expected, had an instinctive determination to be and do what she wanted, this meant being brought up at Margaret's age.

This was partly due to the King. One of his unhappy memories of childhood was the gap that developed between him and his elder brother, and the sense of inferiority which he developed as a result. He did not want a child of his to suffer a similar deprivation. He wanted his children to grow up feeling that they were equals. At the age of seventeen Elizabeth was nearly always wearing the same kind of clothes as her sister four years younger – same style, same colours. This may well have accounted for the view many people had at the time that Elizabeth was young for her age whereas Margaret was old her hers.

In the spring of 1942 Elizabeth, nearly sixteen years of age, was confirmed, her preparation being undertaken by the Archbishop of Canterbury, Dr Lang. He recorded that he did not find his candidate "very communicative", but she "showed real intelligence and understanding". The confirmation service, at Windsor, was private, attended by only a few relatives and friends, and by the choristers of St George's Chapel. Queen Mary was there, accompanied by Lady Airlie, who recorded: "I saw a grave little face under a small white net veil and a slender figure in a plain white woollen frock. The carriage of her head was unequalled, and there was about her that indescribable something which Queen Victoria had."

At the age of sixteen Elizabeth was required by law to register for national service, which meant that thereafter she could be conscripted to the armed forces or to industry. She welcomed this: many of her friends were already in war service; her cousin, Lady Mary Cambridge, was a nurse in London. The King refused to let her leave home. Perhaps he thought she would be at too much risk; perhaps he thought she was too immature to be away from her governess; perhaps he was too possessive about her. Three years later, when she was nearly nineteen, he took a different view. On 24 February 1945 she joined the Auxiliary Territorial Service, enrolled as Number 230873 Second Subaltern (the lowest rank of officer) Elizabeth Alexandra Mary Windsor, and began a six-week course on driving and vehicle-maintenance at No. 1 Mechanical Transport Training Centre, Aldershot. She was driven there and back from Windsor every day. On 14 April she qualified as a driver, having passed the standard tests in vehicle-maintenance, learned to drive cars and trucks in convoy, and how to strip an engine.

If she had looked forward to some sort of active service, and getting away from home, she was to be disappointed: the war in Europe was over almost as soon as she had finished her training. The King's last words in his diary on VE Day, 8 May, were about his daughters: "Poor darlings, they have never had any fun yet."

During the war the King had changed his mind about Churchill. He had forgotten Churchill the political apostate, the Churchill who had said his father George V talked "cheap and silly drivel" about the Navy, the Churchill of the Abdication, the Churchill who had helped bring down his friend Chamberlain; for him Churchill was now the greatest war leader ever, the architect of victory, the saviour of his country, his mentor and his personal friend. For the King, therefore, Churchill's defeat in the general election of 1945 came as a great personal as well as political shock. When Churchill arrived at the Palace to submit his resignation the King could hardly speak. In a personal letter to Churchill a few days later he wrote:

My heart was too full to say much ... I was shocked at the result & I thought it most ungrateful to you personally after all your hard work for the people.

In a second letter he paid tribute to what he personally owed to Churchill:

You often told me what you thought of people & matters of real interest which I could never have learnt from anybody else. Your breadth of vision & your grasp of the essential things were a great comfort to me in the darkest days of the War ...

Princess Elizabeth was old enough to see and share the King's concern about the "ingratitude" shown to Churchill, and his initial apprehension about the coming to power of a socialist government. Like her father, and her grandfather, she was a natural conservative. She had read – and heard – enough history to see Churchill the wartime Prime Minister as the symbol of Britain's great past as well as the country's leader in the heroic devoted to the King. She and her father knew from Jock Colville that Churchill was, "as Lady Churchill once said to me, the only surviving believer in the divine right of kings and his respect for the monarchy amounted almost to idolatry". During the war Churchill had lunched with the King privately on around two hundred occasions, and on many of these he and the Princess had met. She had heard that in January 1944 Churchill had wanted to have her declared Princess of Wales when she became eighteen years old the following April – the King opposed the idea. In short, Churchill loomed very large in Elizabeth's perception of the world around her in her teens. Leaving aside her family and a handful of friends he was the person she was most aware of. For her, next to her father, he was the outstanding figure of the war, and the saviour of her country. Next to the King he was the hero of the hour.

The King had now to adjust his mind to the arrival in government of a socialist party with a huge parliamentary majority committed publicly to a highly collectivist legislative programme, led by a man with a personality very different from Churchill's. The King confided to his diary initially that he had found Attlee difficult to talk to, but it seems he coped very well. Attlee recorded of his first meeting with the King after the election: "The King pulled my leg a bit.

He told me I looked more surprised by the result than he felt."
Again, as he had five years previously when Chamberlain whom he
so much admired was replaced overnight by Churchill whom he
did not trust, the King did his duty to his Prime Minister as a
constitutional monarch. Again, it was not long before the King
settled down happily with the new Prime Minister, possibly because
both of them had had a problem with their shyness, partly because
each recognised the other's altruism and integrity. The King soon
found also that his new Prime Minister was no revolutionary. On
the contrary he began to regard him as a bulwark against demogogic
change.

Elizabeth also saw, as she was meant to see, how dutifully her
father behaved towards the new government. The King, Herbert
Morrison, Home Secretary in the first Labour administration,
said in his autobiography, was "meticulously observant of his
constitutional position" in all his dealings with the Labour government, accepting "calmly and willingly the changes of political
outlook and of personality in the kind of minister he had known
throughout his reign ... fair in his observations". On some issues
the King supported Attlee against attacks from Churchill. One of
the most controversial measures which the Labour government
introduced was a Bill to reduce the power of the House of Lords
to veto Bills from two years to one. Churchill assailed the Bill with
immense sound and fury, denouncing it in the House of Commons
as "A deliberate act of socialist aggression!" His effort signally failed
to stop the Bill becoming law, one of the reasons being the knowledge
that after discussion with Attlee the King had decided to raise no
objection to it.

Though it has often been exaggerated, not least by himself, the
influence of Lord Louis Mountbatten at this time was important.
He encouraged the King to make friends with the new government.
He told the King that, far from becoming less influential with the
new administration than he would have been had the Conservatives
come to power, "You will find that your position will be greatly
strengthened since you are now the old experienced campaigner on
whom a new and partly inexperienced Government will lean for
advice and guidance." Mountbatten made no secret in royal circles
of the fact that he and his wife in many respects sympathised with

and supported the Labour government, notably, for instance, in its intention to give independence to India, to establish the Welfare State, and to promote good relations between owners and employees, a cause dear to the heart of a king who was proud of his nickname, "The Foreman". How much Mountbatten's views weighed with the King is still debateable, but certainly the King decided to do many things which Mountbatten had gone out of his way to recommend.

There is still discussion as to whether at his first meeting with the new Prime Minister, on 26 July, the King, by his use of the Royal Prerogative, brought about the appointment of Bevin as Foreign Secretary. After the meeting the King wrote in his diary:

> I found he was very surprised his Party had won & had had no time to meet or discuss with his colleagues any of the offices of State. I asked him whom he would make Foreign Secy. & he suggested Dr Hugh Dalton. I disagreed with him & said that Foreign Affairs was the most important subject at the moment & I hoped he would make Mr Bevin take it. He said he would ...

The King would have heard a great deal about Bevin and Dalton from Churchill. In Churchill's view Bevin was a statesman, "far the most distinguished man the Labour Party have thrown up in my time", and a great patriot. By contrast, Churchill's view of Dalton was very low, and his opinion was shared by the Foreign Office. According to Colville, the Secretary to the Cabinet, Sir Edward Bridges, and Sir Alan Lascelles, the King's Private Secretary, discussed the situation, and then "persuaded the King to suggest to Attlee that Bevin should be Foreign Secretary rather than Dalton who had originally been intended for the post". How much the views the King expressed on the appointment weighed with Attlee we do not know. The morning after Attlee had told the King he was thinking of making Dalton Foreign Secretary he was still talking to Dalton as though he intended to make him Foreign Secretary, telling him that it was so hot in Berlin – whither the new Foreign Secretary would have to proceed in the next few days for the resumption of the Potsdam conference – he should take a lightweight suit with him. However, at teatime that day he told Dalton that Bevin would become Foreign Secretary and that he wanted Dalton to become Chancellor of the Exchequer. Both Bevin and Dalton were disappointed by the switch, and Bevin was very surprised.

In his official biography of King George VI, published in 1958, Sir John Wheeler-Bennett says that after the King's first interview with Attlee a rumour began to circulate to the effect that the King had "insisted" on the appointment of Bevin, "and that Mr Attlee, against his own judgement, complied". Sir John commented:

> This rumour Mr Attlee has most properly and emphatically denied, saying that Mr Bevin was his own choice. (*Daily Herald*, 20 February 1952).

> What is clear from the King's own record, and from the memorandum made by Sir Alan Lascelles (the King's Private Secretary) immediately after the audience, is that His Majesty was exercising what Walter Bagehot has defined as one of the constitutional prerogatives of the Sovereign – the right to advise, and that Mr Attlee, having taken this advice into consideration, doubtless in conjunction with other factors, made his decision of his own wisdom and free will. There is no conceivable evidence of "insistence" or "pressure".

The following year, in the *Observer*, Attlee gave his own account of what had happened. He said that in the hours immediately after the result of the 1945 election was known, the long-term personal animosity between Bevin and Morrison had flared up again. Morrison, though Attlee had already been to the Palace and had accepted the King's commission to form a government, was intriguing to have him removed from the leadership of the Party and at the same time pressing him to make Morrison Foreign Secretary. In the hours which transpired between his talk with Dalton in the morning and his talk with him at teatime Attlee had learned that relations between Bevin and Morrison had become so strained that the position of the new government might be put in danger by them. Bevin had telephoned Morrison and angrily told him: "If you go on mucking about like this, you won't be in the bloody government at all." Though Attlee had, as he says in his autobiography, "hesitated for some hours as to whether Bevin or Dalton should take the Exchequer or the Foreign Office" he now concluded that these new developments had decided the matter – "if you'd put both on the home front there might have been trouble ... it was better that Ernie should operate mainly in foreign affairs."

73

The fact that the King was, as Morrison put it, "meticulously observant of his constitutional position" did not mean that he was without political feeling or, indeed, without political views. The King believed that all citizens of the British Empire and Commonwealth, whatever their colour or creed, were as one. Politicians he could not help dividing into "Us" and "Them". The Conservatives were "Us": the Labour Party was "Them". The Earl of Longford, a minister in Attlee's administration, has recorded that when he met the King for the first time he was greeted with the question: "Why did you join them?" The King did not sound reproachful or censorious, but simply curious. Five years later, life with Labour did not seem to have changed the King's political views. After an overnight stay with the King and Queen at Windsor Castle just before the Budget of 1951, Hugh Gaitskell, then Chancellor of the Exchequer, and the leading member of the right wing of the Labour Party, wrote in his diary that, as he had always assumed they were, "the King and Queen are extremely conservative in their views". Gaitskell thought the Queen was the more "reactionary" of the two:

> The Queen talked as though everybody was in a very bad way nowadays ... I got into an argument with her then and implied that not everybody was quite so miserable and perhaps she did not see the people who were happier. I think she resented this.

As for the King, Gaitskell recorded, "He is, of course, a fairly reactionary person." The term "reactionary" is often used subjectively, having different meanings for different people, and changing with the context. At the time Gaitskell pronounced the King to be reactionary many Labour MPs would have described Attlee and Bevin "reactionary", and Aneurin Bevan and Michael Foot would certainly have used the word to describe Gaitskell.

The King and Queen were certainly "reactionary" in the sense that they saw rapid changes going on in the world they had been brought up in, many of which they would have prevented if they had been able to. But they were philosophical about it. They were professionals.

"Everything is going now. Before long I shall also have to go," the King told Harold Nicolson's wife, Victoria Sackville-West, in 1948, when her family home, Knole, was taken over by the National Trust because the family could no longer afford to keep it up. The

King remembered vividly the fears of his father after the end of the First World War that in the foreseeable future Britain might cease to be a monarchy and become a republic.

Nevertheless in 1945 the King set out to show the world that with a Labour government in power, the monarch would continue to behave as a constitutional monarch should. The monarch would behave in a way that was in line with the general policy of the government and would do nothing to suggest that he was not in sympathy with it. Austerity was the order of the day. Budgets were restricted. Belts could not be slackened. This was the regime over which the government presided: the monarch must support his government with precept and by example. There were many instances of the King doing so. After the end of the First World War substantial grants were made by the State to the military leaders who had led the country to victory. The King made it clear that no such awards would be made after the Second World War. During the war the number of royal feasts and entertainments had been drastically reduced. The King made no attempt to bring back those which had been eliminated. At a dinner in Buckingham Palace for the Shah of Iran in 1948, Queen Mary complained to Hugh Gaitskell "They don't do enough of this kind of thing now." The King may have shared her view, but if he did he had no intention of doing anything about it.

These matters lay in the future. In September 1945, now that the war had been won and his new government had been formed, the King's first objective was to have a family holiday, the first real unrestricted family holiday for six years. The family went up to Balmoral. The King spent a great deal of time with Elizabeth, much of it deerstalking, which he loved and which she had never done before. She took to it with enthusiasm, and kept it up for many years. Later, when the King was no longer there to accompany her, she went out on her own with gillies. It may have been the best holiday the family ever had. Elizabeth shot with her father, fished with her mother, talked with her sister. They walked, went riding, had barbecues, danced reels, and speculated on the future. It was a splendid holiday, the first peacetime holiday, the first adult holiday, and in many ways it began a new chapter in the life of "the family firm".

By now the Princess had made it clear to the family that she was in love with Prince Philip of Greece and that her mind was set on marrying him. She was nineteen. In the six years since her visit to the Royal Naval College he was away in the war. When on leave he visited the royal family a number of times, but his main contact with his wife-to-be was through their letters. These became more and more frequent as time went by. Possibly because she saw so little of other young men Elizabeth's thoughts dwelt more and more on Philip. The relationship grew more from letters than from meetings. By the end of the war, as though to announce to the world that her mind was made up and that she intended to have her way, the Princess had placed a photograph of Philip on her mantelpiece. There was to be a good deal of talk within the family before the King gave his permission for the engagement to be announced. But the more talk there was the clearer it became that the Princess would not change her mind. There was something of a psychological fixation in the way she looked at Philip and spoke of him. She not only loved him but he totally absorbed her capacity for love. He was an idol as well as a loved one. He could do no wrong.

In many marriages, the children come first and the spouse second. That was not to be the case with Elizabeth – or with Philip.

4

South African tour.
Marriage.
Her father's death
1947–52

THE EXTREMELY LONG South African tour of early 1947 was to
have a great influence on Elizabeth. Every day and all day for
four months she was with her father, seeing and hearing the
Commonwealth through his eyes and ears. If there was one single
period in her life which, in retrospect, could be described as her
initiation in her father's conception of the new Commonwealth, and
the monarch's future role in it as Head, it was this one. The tour
also laid the basis for one of the most anguishing problems she
would have to face as Queen. The King's equerry, Group Captain
Townsend, accompanied the royal family everywhere, treated more
like a member of the family than a courtier. The seeds of the fateful
relationship between him and Princess Margaret were planted at
this time.

The winter of 1946–7 was one of the most severe Britain has
ever experienced. An extremely cold period set in well before
Christmas, and continued unbroken throughout the following
month. On 29 January Britain froze, and throughout February the
country endured its worst weather for nearly seventy years. There
was a shortage of fuel throughout most of the earlier winter months,
and in February a fuel crisis. Two million people were put out of
work. Electricity had to be rationed for industrial and domestic use.

Great damage was done to the national morale and to the national economy.

On the first day of February, the whole of Britain still frozen, and no sign of the weather improving, the King and Queen and the two Princesses were to set out from Britain for South Africa. The tour was politically and economically very important. It had been planned for a long time previously. Its main objective was to lend political support to the South African Prime Minister, Field Marshal Smuts, leader of the United Party. Smuts, to whom the King had awarded the OM in the New Year's Honours List, would have to face a general election early the following year. The Opposition parties were gaining strength. Smuts believed that a visit from the royal family would enable his party to win. It was important for the British government that he did so: the United Party were friends of Britain, loyal to the Commonwealth and committed to the valuable trading relationship with Britain. His opponents, the Nationalist Party, were anti-British. In their ranks were many who intended South Africa to become a republic and leave the Commonwealth. The South Africa visit had another object: to give the royal family, and in particular the King, a holiday. The sea voyage preceding the tour would take about three weeks. The royal party would sail in the Navy's newest battleship, *Vanguard*, launched by Princess Elizabeth on Clydeside in December 1944.

As the date for his departure got nearer, the King became more and more reluctant to leave the country. There was no sign of the fuel crisis coming to an end. He wanted to stay and suffer with his people. These feelings he communicated to the Prime Minister, but Attlee and Winston Churchill impressed upon the King that the tour must proceed. The government must above all keep faith with Smuts, to whom Britain owed so much for his loyalty during the war. To call off the tour at this late stage would be a grave political embarrassment to him. It could lose him the election, and open the door to power for the Nationalists. Also, if the King cancelled the tour, the world would jump to the conclusion that Britain's crisis was far greater than it was. This could be economically disastrous.

The King and Queen and the two Princesses sailed from Portsmouth on 1 February as planned. The King fretted throughout the voyage, and continued to worry throughout the tour that followed, complaining every day that he should be back among his people.

The second objective of the tour, therefore, to give him a holiday, was doomed from the start.

The voyage and the tour told the Princess a great deal about her father's health. In the early days at sea the weather was rough, and the King, though previously regarded as a good sailor, spent most of his time in his cabin. When he emerged he was edgy, and sometimes ill-tempered. He found fault with day-to-day arrangements. When he left the ship to begin the tour, instead of being rested and relaxed, he was tense. The prospect of the two-month programme ahead clearly daunted him.

It was an exacting schedule. He spent thirty-five nights on the royal train, and by day covered hundreds of miles by car or train. The Queen wrote to Queen Mary: "This tour is being very strenuous as I feared it would be & doubly hard for Bertie who feels he should be at home ..."

Smuts was delighted that the King had kept his word to come and help him shore up his political position. His opponents were correspondingly disgruntled. They showed their resentment openly. When at Cape Town on 17 February the Senate and the House of Assembly officially welcomed the King and Queen no Senator from the Nationalist Party, and only eleven out of forty-six Nationalist members of the House, were present at the ceremony. Those newspapers which supported the Nationalist Party in so far as they reported the royal tour at all were disparaging about it.

All in all, what with fatigue and a growing sense of how large a proportion of the white population was against him, the King's spirits flagged. To those he could trust he made no secret of it. He was irked by the control of his movements by Afrikaner police; "the Gestapo", he told the Queen. He resented the fact that he met so few black Africans. He chafed under the burden of the timetable. Once again he found himself in a situation which reactivated the psychological pressures which had plagued him in the past.

The King was accompanied on the tour by his equerry, Group Captain Peter Townsend. In his autobiography, *Time and Chance*, published in 1978, Townsend describes an incident which gives an idea of the stress the King was under at times in the course of the tour. On an extremely hot day, accompanied by Townsend, the King and Queen and the two Princesses made a lengthy tour in an open Daimler of the mining towns of the Rand. Thousands of black miners and their families had lined the narrow road, waving and cheering, many of them surging forward to the sides of the vehicle. The atmosphere was of intense excitement.

According to Townsend, because of the heat, the noise, the proximity of the crowd, and his own fatigue, the King became extremely agitated. Unable to contain his anxiety he began to shout instructions to his driver, who soon became unnerved. The Queen and the Princesses tried to calm the King, but he became more and more distressed. Townsend feared the driver would panic and there would be a calamity. He wrote: "I turned round – and shouted angrily – and with a disrespect of which I was ashamed: 'For Heaven's sake, shut up or there's going to be an accident.'"

There was, though not of the kind that Townsend feared. As the royal party entered Benoni they saw a policeman rushing towards them, his staring eyes fixed on something that was happening behind their vehicle. Townsend looked back and saw that a black man was chasing their car. He caught up with them. In one hand he was carrying something, with the other he grabbed hold of the car ...

The Queen, with her parasol, landed several deft blows on the assailant before he was knocked senseless by policemen. As they dragged away his limp body, I saw the Queen's parasol, broken in two, disappear over the side of the car. Within a second, Her Majesty was waving and smiling, as captivatingly as ever, to the crowd.

What the black man had been clutching, they learned later, was a ten-shilling note which he had wanted to press on Elizabeth as a present for her coming birthday. The police had over-reacted. The King knew that he had over-reacted too. Later in the day he apologised to Townsend: "I am sorry about today. I was very tired."

British newspapermen covering the tour saw not only the King's fatigue but his boredom, and his sense of being paraded not for Britain's benefit, but to help Smuts and his government to win the coming general election. His mind, they reported, was not on the tour; it was back in Britain. He felt he should be there. James Cameron, covering the tour for the *Daily Express*, reported that the King "kept saying that he should be at home and not lolling about in the summer sun; never was a man so jumpy ..."

The tour lasted for over two months, ending on 20 April in Cape Town. The following day was Elizabeth's twenty-first birthday. It was marked by a public holiday throughout the country. The Princess attended several public events during the day and that evening made a broadcast to the peoples of the British Commonwealth and the Empire. She ended it with the solemn message of dedication, to be referred to frequently in after-years:

> I declare before you all that my whole life, whether it be long or short, shall be devoted to your service and the service of our great Imperial Commonwealth, to which we all belong.

That night there were fireworks and illuminations, and at a ball at Government House Smuts presented the Princess with a necklace of twenty-one diamonds. Three days later the royal family went aboard *Vanguard*. They arrived back in London in early May.

For Elizabeth it had been an educative experience, and in many ways a sad one. She had met more citizens of the Commonwealth in a few weeks than she had met in the whole of her previous life. She made a contact with black people which was to influence her views on the Commonwealth for the duration of her reign. She saw that whatever they thought of the conditions in which they lived in South Africa there was no limit to their love and loyalty for the royal family. She saw the gap that divided the blacks from the whites. She never forgot what she had learned from this tour.

She learned too that her father's health was becoming a problem. The tour had been a demanding one, but it had aggravated not caused the King's indisposition. The duration of the tour put her more in contact with him than she had been for many years, and she saw him and was able to study him in a way that would not have been possible had they stayed at home. That opportunity would not come again. It was the King's last tour.

Back in Britain Elizabeth's life began to change. On 9 July the King and Queen announced her betrothal to Lieutenant Philip Mountbatten, RN, son of the late Prince Andrew of Greece and Denmark, and nephew of Lord Mountbatten. At once, Elizabeth began to spend part of her time at least in a world of her own.

We have it on the authority of *The Royal Encyclopaedia*, whose publication in 1991 was approved by the Queen, that Elizabeth was in love with Prince Philip of Greece at the age of eighteen. Crawfie thought that the Princess may have been in love with him nearly four years earlier. At Christmas 1943, playing a leading role in the annual family pantomime, the Princess, according to Crawfie, gave the performance of her life. "I have never known Lilibet more animated. There was a sparkle about her none of us had ever seen before. Many people remarked on it." The explanation of this transformation, in Crawfie's view, was that sitting in the front row of the audience, home on leave and looking extremely handsome in his naval uniform, was the fair-haired Viking who had been the last to turn back from his pursuit of the royal yacht when the royal family sailed from Dartmouth in 1939.

The Princess and Prince Philip had been exchanging letters for some time. Early in 1944 Prince Philip began talking to his relatives about his feelings for the Princess, and had speculated candidly on the subject of marriage. In March his older cousin, the King of Greece, raised the matter with the Princess's father. The King's view, according to Mountbatten's official biographer, Philip Ziegler, was: "We both think she is too young for that now as she has never met any young men of her own age . . . I like Philip. He is intelligent, has a good sense of humour & thinks about things in the right way . . . [but he] had better not think any more about it for the present." Harold Nicolson, however, recorded in his diary: "The family were at first horrified when they saw that Prince Philip was making up to Princess Elizabeth. They felt he was rough, ill-mannered, uneducated and would probably not be faithful . . ."

Philip was a member of the Greek royal family, grandson of King George I of Greece and son of Prince Andrew of Greece. His mother, Princess Alice of Battenburg, was a great-granddaughter of Queen Victoria and sister of Lord Louis Mountbatten. Prince Philip was born at his parents' home on the island of Corfu on 10 June 1921. He left Corfu eighteen months later when his father, then serving as a Lieutenant-General in the Greek Army, had been sentenced to perpetual banishment by the Greek Chamber of Deputies for his alleged part in the catastrophic defeat of the Greek army by the Turks at Smyrna earlier that year. Exiled, the Prince's parents settled in Paris. They had virtually no income of their own, and in 1930, when Philip was eight years old, they separated. His father, Prince Andrew, when he died comparatively young in 1944, was living in Monte Carlo, supported financially by friends. His mother, Princess Alice, by that time had become a nun, and had gone back to live in Athens. During the war, when Greece was occupied by the Germans, she did noble work for children's relief.

In 1930 Prince Philip came to England, living partly with his grandmother, the Dowager Marchioness of Milford Haven, granddaughter of Queen Victoria, at Kensington Palace, and partly with his maternal uncle, George Mountbatten, the 2nd Marquess of Milford Haven, at Lynden Manor near Maidenhead. In his first three years in Britain he went to Cheam School in Surrey, after which he spent a year at Salem, Baden, in Germany, a school owned by his brother-in-law, the Margrave of Baden. He then went to Gordonstoun, founded by the former headmaster of Salem, Kurt Hahn, who had left Germany when the Nazis had come to power. Philip had no brothers. His four sisters married German princes. When his uncle, George, died in 1938 his younger uncle, Lord Louis Mountbatten, took over responsibility for his upbringing. The young prince was left much to himself, and, having no money of his own, spent a good deal of his holidays in Germany with his sisters. When the time came for him to think about a career he was advised by Mountbatten to go to Dartmouth, and then into the Navy. Philip followed his uncle's advice. He was intelligent, diligent and ambitious, and had a very successful war career. His heart was set on continuing in the Navy.

Mountbatten was proud of his nephew, and had begun to press for his engagement to Princess Elizabeth as early as 1944. The King wrote to him: "I have been thinking the matter over since our talk, and I have come to the conclusion that we are going too fast." Mountbatten took this in, and wrote to his sister, Princess Alice, urging her not to raise the subject with the King and Queen: "The best hopes are to let it happen – if it will – without parents interfering. The young people appear genuinely devoted and I think after the war it is very likely to occur."

Meanwhile he offered his nephew plenty of advice on how to pursue his courtship. On one occasion Philip protested: "Please, I beg of you, not too much advice in an affair of the heart, or I shall be forced to do the wooing by proxy." Mountbatten also prescribed books which would prepare him for his future role. Again, Philip was occasionally moved to protest. When Mountbatten complained that the reason why Philip had not yet read Shaw's *The Intelligent Woman's Guide to Socialism and Capitalism*, which he had sent him, was that he was "antagonistic to the principles of Socialism", Philip replied that on the contrary his mind was open to all systems. He added: "Don't forget you are attempting to educate me for a certain job, and a little knowledge is a dangerous thing, if not worse than none at all."

Prince Philip's engagement to the Princess Elizabeth was not announced as soon as the two young people had hoped and expected. It was some time before the King decided to consent to the marriage. In the words of Wheeler-Bennett:

> He had always liked Prince Philip and had grown to esteem him highly, but he still found it difficult to believe that his elder daughter had really fallen in love with the first young man she had ever met, and perhaps he also dreaded losing her from that compact and happy family circle which had been his delight and solace since his early married days in Royal Lodge.

Whatever his motive, in the months before he gave his consent to the engagement the King organised a number of parties, in and out of the Palace, at which a number of eligible young men were present, but in which Philip was not included. Some of these young eligibles, the "Body Guard" as Queen Mary called them, joined the royal family for Christmas at Sandringham. Philip was not among them.

As well as not wanting his daughter to get married to the first young man she had got to know at all well the King, though thinking well of Philip, may have had some misgivings about the young man as prospective son-in-law. He had mixed feelings about the prospect of an alliance between his daughter and a nephew of Lord Mountbatten. Nobody was more aware than the King of Mountbatten's admirable qualities, but he was equally aware of Mountbatten's exhibitionism, which the King thought politically dangerous and personally distasteful. He had no wish to consent to a marriage which would encourage Lord Mountbatten to regard himself as a full member of the royal family. There was also the question of Prince Philip's German background. Some of his cousins had fought against Britain during the war; a few of them were Nazis. Public opinion was not altogether in favour of the match. One poll showed 40 per cent against the marriage, mainly because those polled regarded Philip as a foreigner with German and Nazi connections, and without a solid family background. On the other hand, the Prince's suit had some influential supporters. These included the Prime Minister, possibly influenced by his regard for

Mountbatten. Attlee praised Prince Philip, and in letters to his one and only confidant, his elder brother, Tom, expressed his hopes that the marriage would take place.

If the King had ever considered that Prince Philip would be an unsuitable husband for his daughter it was not long before he changed his mind. The main reason that he did so was it became more and more clear that Elizabeth was genuinely in love with the young man and was bent on marrying him. The King and the Prince had a good deal in common. Both were Navy men and loved the Navy. Philip not only had a sense of humour; he shared with the King the same boisterous schoolboyish sense of fun, love of practical jokes, and enjoyment of after-dinner yarns when the women had left the table and were out of earshot. The King loved the kind of entertainment provided by Bud Flanagan and the Crazy Gang, and their blue-tinged jokes told even when the Princesses were present. So did Philip. Both men loved horses and rode well, but did not care for racing – unlike the Princess who already adored it. They loved nature and the outdoors. The King liked the idea of his daughter marrying a man of royal blood: after two world wars it was in short supply.

In early 1947 Philip took British nationality, ceased to be called Prince Philip, and became known as Lieutenant Mountbatten, RN. His surname, Schleswig-Holstein-Sonderburg-Glucksburg, did not appeal to the King, or indeed, to anybody else, and the Royal College of Heralds was asked to supply a new one. The name of Oldenburg loomed large in the Prince's pedigree, and the Royal College of Heralds suggested that he should take the English version, Oldcastle. The Home Secretary, Chuter Ede, who was aware by now that Philip was likely to become the husband of the heiress to the throne, did not favour Oldcastle, and suggested that Philip should take the name of his mother's family, Mountbatten, his uncle of that name now serving as Viceroy of India, and loyally carrying out the government's policy there. Chuter Ede's suggestion was accepted. Though pleased at becoming a British citizen, Philip was not enthusiastic about becoming a Mountbatten: "I wasn't madly in favour ... But in the end I was persuaded, and anyway I couldn't think of a better alternative." Perhaps he felt the name Mountbatten made him look his uncle's man.

Mountbatten was naturally delighted when the engagement was announced. He credited himself with having brought it about, and since it was he who had introduced his nephew to the royal family, in a sense he had. But he was prone throughout his life to believe, or pretend to believe, that he had brought about results which in fact he had not, and this trait was well known to the royal family. They all regarded "Uncle Dickie" with great affection but also with reserve. He was not as respected by them as he assumed he was. The King liked talking about the Navy with him, and did not underestimate his charisma and ability. But he never forgot Mountbatten's once close relationship with his elder brother and his equivocal attitude in the earlier days of the Abdication crisis. He was as aware as anybody was of Dickie's penchant for exploiting the royal connection.

Elizabeth shared her father's view of Mountbatten but was more critical. Being reserved and quiet by nature, and more aware than everybody except her mother of the King's unassuming personality, she did not find Mountbatten's exuberance and egotism always to her taste. With her, a little of him went a long way. She was not conscious of him as a matchmaker. On the contrary, it seemed to her that she had made the match herself, much as her great-great-grandmother Victoria had made hers.

Philip too had reservations. As soon as the engagement was announced Mountbatten started to give Philip his views on arrangements for the wedding and on how the new household should be run. Philip thought it wise to caution him. "I am not being rude but it is apparent you like the idea of being the General Manager of this little show, and I am rather afraid that she might not take to the idea quite so docilely as I do. It is true that I know what is good for me, but don't forget that she has not had you as Uncle *loco parentis*, counsellor and friend as long as I have." So far as is known Philip never expressed a profound feeling of indebtedness to his uncle on account of his marriage or of anything else. In later life when asked about people who had influenced his development he never referred to Mountbatten, and at least one interviewer who had innocently proposed to question the Duke on the general subject of who and what had helped him to form his views was advised in advance to leave Mountbatten out. The only member of the royal family who would say from time to time that he owed something to Mountbatten's advice was Prince Charles.

In November the King conferred the Order of the Garter on them both, and created Philip a Royal Highness and Duke of Edinburgh. The marriage took place at Westminster Abbey on 20 November. The King believed that feeling in Britain against the Germans was such that to invite Philip's German relations, some of whom had fought with the Nazis, to Westminster Abbey would cause serious trouble. Consequently they were not invited. Prince Philip's three surviving sisters, all of whom had married German princes, were left off the list. The Duke of Windsor was not asked, nor were the King's own German relations. Attlee, by now on the best of terms with the King and Queen, and greatly supportive of the match, gently but firmly declined to proclaim the marriage day a national holiday: the country could not afford the loss of production which would ensue. The day was cold and clouded. Coming in the period of severe restrictions and rationing which had followed Britain's first post-war financial crisis in August it took Churchill to pronounce the wedding "a flash of colour".

The King's feelings were mixed. The family which meant so much to him would never be the same again. The daughter in whom he saw so much of the best of himself, of his father and Queen Victoria, quiet, unspectacular but dedicated and rocklike, and the future monarch, his pride and joy, would now leave home and live a life of her own. She was moving away from him. But the family, the "firm", must go on as before. It must stay in business. The business of duty. The wedding over, the King wrote to his daughter:

> Our family, us four, the "Royal Family" must remain together with additions of course at suitable moments!! I have watched you grow up all these years with pride under the skilful direction of Mummy, who as you know is the most marvellous person in the world in my eyes, & I can, I know, always count on you, & now Philip, to help us in our work. Your leaving us has left a great blank in our lives but do remember that your old home is still yours & do come back to it as much & as often as possible. I can see that you are sublimely happy with Philip which is right but don't forget us is the wish of your ever loving & devoted
>
> PAPA

His daughter's happiness cheered the King in a year which had brought him many anxieties. The state of the nation had rarely looked so grim in times of peace. To finance her war effort Britain had sold off most of her overseas investments, and no longer received the annual income they had brought in. Britain was heavily in debt to the United States, and to some of the Commonwealth countries. India and other countries of the old Empire were pressing for their independence, which they would shortly be given, leading to further reductions in Britain's revenues. On his South African tour the King had seen the forces at work to take that dominion out of the Commonwealth. By the time he had got back to London in May the end of Mountbatten's negotiations with Nehru and Jinnah were in sight and the independence of India and Pakistan was planned for the following August. India had meant more than any other part of the Empire to his great-grandmother, his grandfather, his father and himself – it was from India that he drew his title as Emperor. He had had to face the fact that the withdrawal was the consequence not only of India's desire for independence but of Britain's inability to maintain the Raj. The King saw all this clearly, but the break with the past was hard for him to bear.

The future of India, however, opened up the prospect of a new role for Britain in a new Commonwealth. India chose to remain in the Commonwealth and to recognise the King as its Head. This meant a great deal to the King. He recognised the concept of a new relationship between Britain and the Commonwealth countries, and rose to it. The old Empire would be replaced by the new Commonwealth, a free association of self-governing countries linked by voluntary acceptance of the Crown as Head. The concept gave a new lease of life to the old association and a new dimension to the British monarchy. He talked about it to his daughter with enthusiasm. His feeling for it was his chief legacy to her. It became part of her life, and at the right time. She had come of age, had married, and had seen that the decline in her father's strength meant that she must take on more of his duties. She saw herself as the inheritor of her father's conception of the new Commonwealth. This function of her queenship would become the dominant one of her reign, the one she most esteemed and cared for after she had acceded to the throne.

She publicly committed herself to the new hope and faith in the Commonwealth in the speech – quoted earlier – she had broadcast from South Africa on her twenty-first birthday.

Encouraged as they were by hopes for the future of the new

Commonwealth the King and his daughter had to face the fact that some of its former members, once they had achieved their independence, were resolved to leave it. Burma, for which Mountbatten had done so much in the war, became an independent republic in June 1947, and had left the Commonwealth by the end of the year. Nearer home, Ireland severed her last connections in September 1948, declaring herself a republic early in 1949.

Harold Nicolson noted how personally the King took the departure of Ireland, and what efforts he made to try and persuade the government of Eire to remain within "the family". Nicolson records the King as having asked the Irish Minister in London if Eire was leaving the Commonwealth through any fault in himself. He was assured that this was not the case.

India became a republic in January 1949. Nehru was willing to remain within an association with Britain, provided there was mutual agreement on the terms. The essence of these was a change in the status of the King and of Great Britain in relation to the new Republic: the King would no longer be the Emperor of India, and India would no longer owe allegiance to the British crown; but India would remain in the Commonwealth, which it saw as an association of peoples of which the King would be the Head. The headship would have a reality, as was soon to become clear. The relationship with the British monarchy which India accepted became the basis of the arrangement made with other countries as they achieved their independence.

This thinking, and these attitudes, on the part of the King and his daughter, were, happily for both parties, in line with those of the government. Historically the Labour Party had denounced imperialism, deplored the notion of Empire, and was committed to freedom for all men at all times in all places. Nevertheless, Attlee, who in 1927 had spent several months touring India as a member of the Simon Commission, since then had always had reservations about India's capacity for self-government, and these had been accepted by many members of his Party. The Labour governments of the post-war period, while continuing to be committed to self-government for the former colonies, were aware of the dangers of independence coming too quickly. Hence policy with regard to colonies and Commonwealth did not make for conflict between a conservatively minded King and a radically minded government.

The King worried about the future of the monarchy in the

Commonwealth, but he worried too about its future in Britain. His fears, like those of his father after the First World War, centred on the growth of Republicanism. Labour leaders such as Attlee and Bevin were stout defenders of the monarchy, but there was always a doubt in the King's mind that socialist measures introduced by the Labour government, even if its leaders did not wish to, might pave the way to a republic. Various measures of public ownership, including the nationalisation of the Bank of England, and constitutional change, such as reduction of the legislative powers of the House of Lords, might lead in the same direction. The King sometimes wondered if the economic pressures on British society would in time bring about mass unemployment, hunger, discontent and the collapse of law and order, and in their train the downfall of the monarchy.

His fears on this account were aggravated by the latest news of the Duke of Windsor. Since 1945 the Duke had kept relatively quiet. In October of that year the Duke had been given permission to come to London to visit the King and his mother, and the meetings had been amicable. The King, who by now had come to the firm conclusion that the Duke had best make his home in the United States, said again that he did not think the Windsors should return to Britain, but that he would be happy about the Duke having a job in the United States provided it was not an official one. The British government, the King said, was adamantly opposed to the Duke being in any sense a recognised representative of Britain; if he were, it would inevitably embarrass the British Ambassador in Washington. The Duke said that if he could not in some way officially represent Britain in the United States – which would exempt him from paying income tax – he would elect to go to Paris where he could reside tax free. To the King's disappointment – he would have liked the Duke to be much further away from London – the Duke went to Paris.

A year or so later, while the King was in South Africa, there had been a highly secret exchange of views between the British and American Foreign Secretaries on the subject of the Duke's wartime activities. The end of the war had brought many documents to light. On 15 March 1947, the American Secretary of State, General Marshall, at the time in Moscow with Bevin for a conference of Foreign Ministers, sent a top-secret message to Dean Acheson, his Under Secretary of State back in Washington:

Bevin informs me that Department [of State] or White House has on file a microfilm copy of a paper concerning the Duke of Windsor. Bevin says only other copy was destroyed by Foreign Office, and asks that we destroy ours to avoid possibility of a leak to great embarrassment of Windsor's brother. Please attend to this for me and reply for my eyes only.

So far as is generally known the microfilm copy referred to does not now exist. If it does, no member of the public has access to it. It is likely that the microfilm referred to German papers concerning the Duke's talks with German agents in Portugal in 1940 which the King had already seen. These papers were published in 1957 in Volume X of the official *Documents on German Foreign Policy*.

The King would have been most embarrassed if information of this kind had become known in 1947. As it was he was having trouble with his brother already. The Duke was pressing for permission to come to London to see the King and Queen Mary. The King was worried about this. In private the Duke had been venting highly critical opinions about the Attlee administration: knowing his brother the King feared these might reach a wider audience, and further embarrass the monarchy. The Duke had written to Queen Mary "I hope and believe the people of Britain will eventually rebel against the theoretical and ideological socialists they acclaimed and elected to power a year ago ... the Socialist policy towards India is a disaster ..." He wrote to the Chairman of the Great Western Railway sympathising with him on account of "the headaches this railroads nationalization scheme imposed by these crazy and dangerous Socialists must be giving you". To the King he complained that the British government's policies were "as alarming as is the apathy of the people towards all the rules and regulations imposed on them". The Duke told his mother that fifty or so Labour MPs were virtually communists. The King warned her that if the Duke was allowed to visit Britain "we must take the line that he cannot live here." These meetings passed off without turbulence.

Princess Elizabeth's marriage had raised the question of what kind of life she and her husband would live. It was announced that Prince Philip would pursue his career in the Navy. For the Princess the change in her life brought about by the marriage was not great; for her husband it was considerable. His financial circumstances, the way he had been brought up, and his years in the Navy meant that he had lived in a comparatively simple and independent style. Now everything was different. First he and his wife lived in her apartment at Buckingham Palace, then for a short spell in Kensington Palace, after that in well-appointed refurbished and modernised accommodation in Clarence House. Life had become grand, but he was no longer his own man. From now on he would want for nothing, but on public occasions he would have to walk behind his wife. The Prince did not take to this easily, and for several months the staff found him difficult. He was ill at ease, and the short temper which was, and is, a part of his personality, was soon in evidence. He was happier when, the immediate post-wedding period being over, he was able to get back to work, for the time being working in the Admiralty, and attending a Staff course at Greenwich. He assumed that for some years he would be free to serve in the Navy and achieve his ambition, which was to command his own ship. The Princess also assumed that many years would pass before she would be required to change her way of life; that there would be a lengthy period before she succeeded her father in which she could concentrate on being a wife and mother. Prince Charles was born in November 1948. The young couple's life seemed set and predictable for several years to come. Apart from a limited number of public engagements they would live the lives of an up-and-coming naval officer and his wife and family. The following autumn Prince Philip was posted to Malta as first lieutenant and second-in-command of *Chequers*, leader of the first Mediterranean destroyer flotilla. Just before Christmas his wife flew out to Malta to join him.

If ever the Queen-to-be enjoyed a life that was at all non-royal it was in the next three or four months. Though in Malta she lived in style – in the Villa Guardamangia, overlooking the harbour, as guests of Lord Mountbatten, now commanding the first cruiser squadron in the Mediterranean – she had no official duties. Prince Philip, between hours of studying for his next examination – he failed the first time but succeeded at the second attempt – learned to play polo. Elizabeth spent a good deal of her time watching him. The Duke was gregarious and popular, and at parties and picnics she met a good many young people of a kind she had not known before. She seems to have enjoyed herself. In the spring she was pregnant again, and flew back to Clarence House to prepare for her second baby. Princess Anne was born on 15 August 1950.

The same day, the Duke was gazetted lieutenant commander. He was now able to achieve his ambition, and flew out to Malta to take command of *Magpie*, a frigate in the Mediterranean fleet. His wife nursed her new baby, and then flew out to join him. This, too, proved a very agreeable and stimulating experience. Mountbatten, the commander-in-chief, put his dispatch vessel, *Surprise*, at her disposal, and the two ships made a number of visits showing the flag at various ports in the Mediterranean. It could not be said that Princess Elizabeth was living the life of a typical wife of a naval officer, but she was certainly seeing more of the world than she would have seen if she had married a European princeling without a successful professional career.

Their spell in Lord Mountbatten's house was not without its problems. The Duke, as ever, wanted to show that he was his own man and not his uncle's nephew. It took some time for them to work out a viable relationship. Mountbatten wrote to his daughter that he and Philip had had "a heart-to-heart in which he admitted he was fighting shy of coming under my dominating image and patronage". After that they seem to have got on much better.

The prospect of a protracted private life for the young couple soon disappeared. The King's health, in decline for some years, began to deteriorate rapidly. For this more than anything the visit to South Africa in 1947 was blamed. The arduous tour would have been an ordeal for him even if he had been in the best of health, but he began it a sick and unhappy man, and its rigours and tensions took a disproportionate toll. By the time it was over he had lost seventeen pounds in weight. In January 1948 he began to suffer from cramp in his right leg. In November James Learmonth, Regius Professor of Clinical Surgery at Edinburgh University, an expert on vascular disease, was called in and diagnosed early arteriosclerosis. Since gangrene might set in his doctors considered amputation. The King was ordered to bed, with strict orders to cut down his smoking. He had been a heavy smoker throughout his adult life. This did him good; the risk of amputation was removed, but he must continue to take things more easily. The tour of Australia and New Zealand which he had planned would have to be called off. His doctors issued a bulletin which included the statement: "the strain of the last twelve years has appreciably affected his resistance to fatigue."

He was much cheered by the birth of Prince Charles on 14 November. His spirits rose, and before Christmas he was out of bed. In January he had a day's shooting.

Two months later Learmonth performed a lumbar sympathectomy operation. After it the King was better able to move around, but he was warned that part of his trouble was psychological stress, and he must take things more easily. This he did, in terms of appointments and engagements, but he was not able to throw off his anxieties: 1949 was a bad year for Britain. There was a surge of economic and political problems. The country's crucial export trade was dealt a heavy blow by a dock strike in the summer; there were rumours that Clement Attlee was about to be replaced as Prime Minister as the result of a coup within his Party, and that a general election was imminent; in September the pound, ignominiously, since the government had denied the possibility, was devalued from 4.03 to 2.80 dollars. The general election returned the Labour Party but with an overall majority of only five. The concerned and conscientious King found it hard to take things easier.

To his other burdens was added disquieting news about the activities of the Duke of Windsor. In the same year it became known that the Duke was going to publish memoirs which would contain his account of the circumstances leading to the Abdication and its aftermath. At that point the Duke made three consecutive attempts to have his wife recognised as Her Royal Highness. First he approached the Lord Chancellor of the "crazy" Socialist government, Lord Jowitt, who told him that nothing could be done. He then tackled the Prime Minister; Attlee said the same. The King had predicted as much to Queen Mary ... "no one else can change the position except me, and I won't do anything." The Duke then went to see the King, who once again refused to "change the position". This time the King seemed to be struck as never before by the Duke's unwillingness or incapacity to understand why his family had taken up that position in the first place. Perhaps because he now had a presentiment that he would not live for long he followed up the personal meeting with an unusually long and measured letter. More than anything he had said or written before this assessment of the situation should have brought home to the Duke how hopeless it was to pursue the matter. The King described his shock at hearing that his brother intended to marry Mrs Simpson, the "ghastly void" which the Abdication had created for himself and his family, and his ordeal in having to face the Coronation, and assume the responsibilities which his brother had abandoned. He taxed the Duke with his failure to consider anybody's feelings in the matter but his own. The British people and the Empire had taken the view that it was not right for Mrs Simpson to be their Queen. The Duke at the time had accepted this. For the King now to take up a position different from the one he had committed himself to in 1936, concluded the King, "wouldn't make sense of the past".

It seems that at last the Duke accepted the inevitable. Six months went by before he responded to this letter, doing so then only with a brief covering note for four articles he had written about his early years for *Life* magazine. His autobiography, *A King's Story*, was published the following year. By then the King was a dying man. The brothers never met again. The Duke next came to London for the King's funeral, and to do what he could to ensure that he continued to receive his allowances. Before he left, the Duchess warned him to be very circumspect in dealing with the newly widowed Queen, and urged him to undo if he could the effects of the "offending letter" which he had written to his mother in 1937. The Duke did his best. Queen Mary recorded: "He saw E[lizabeth] and the girls, he had not seen them since 1936, so that feud is over." But the Duke was not so sure. According to his account of his meeting with his brother's widow, she "listened without comment and closed on the note that it was nice to be able to talk about Bertie with somebody who had known him so well."

It was not surprising that he failed. The early death of his brother was not a propitious occasion for peace-making with a widow who believed that her husband had died prematurely, a martyr, because duty and loyalty to country and family had forced him to take up in stressful circumstances a task for which he was neither trained by experience nor suited personally. She believed that her husband had been a victim of his brother's selfishness and irresponsibility. Her animosity towards the Duke was the greater for the anxieties he had subjected her husband to from his accession in 1936 to the day of his death, his anguish deepened by the importunities and recriminations, often couched in cruel and unjust terms, culminating in the "offending letter". She was even more opposed to "changing the position" than her husband had been. Knowledge of this situation did not make the new Queen's problems any lighter.

Two years earlier the King, with that determination he had shown throughout his adult life, had regained some of his former health, of mind as well as body. But the writing was on the wall. The winter of 1950–1 dragged him down. Early in the new year he began to cough. There is still some controversy about his doctor's diagnosis of the new symptoms, and whether if it had not been the right one this would have made any difference. As it was, in September the surgeons removed the King's left lung.

Attlee announced a general election for October 1951. He had told the King in the greatest of secrecy earlier in the year that a general election should take place shortly, and that he would hold it before the King embarked on the tour of Australia and New Zealand which had been scheduled for the spring of 1952. In a passage in his autobiography Attlee recorded:

It would, I knew, be a constant anxiety to the King if there were a possibility of a fall of the Government or a General Election during his absence from the country. Clearly therefore there were cogent reasons for having an Election in the autumn and I made up my mind before the House rose for the Autumn Recess. It will be seen that there is no foundation for the silly suggestion of some Tory Members that we had an Election in order to get out of our responsibilities.

Still suffering from the effects of his operation the King was only just well enough to participate in one of the meetings of the Privy Council required to prepare for a general election. It was an unusual meeting. Five Privy Councillors stood outside his bedroom door to hear him pronounce almost in a whisper the single word "Approved".

Two weeks before the election, Princess Elizabeth and the Duke of Edinburgh left for a tour of Canada and the United States. The Princess's Private Secretary, Lieutenant-Colonel Martin Charteris, took with him documents which would be necessary in the event of the Princess succeeding her father while she was away. The King made his Christmas broadcast, though this time it had to be pre-recorded, almost sentence by sentence. Nevertheless, he came over the air with such strength that most of his listeners concluded that all he was suffering from was a heavy cold.

He went to Sandringham for Christmas in good spirits. He felt better. He did not know what the extent of his illness was. His doctors now knew that he had cancer, but the information was kept from him. He believed that his operation was for bronchial trouble. He went on with plans for a trip to South Africa in March. He did a little shooting. When on 31 January Elizabeth and Philip left for the tour of Australia and New Zealand, which he had earlier planned to make, he went to Heathrow to see them off.

Six days later, at Sandringham, he went out with his gun after rabbits and hares, shooting in excellent form. That night he retired to his bedroom in good spirits, and read for about an hour and a half until midnight. At that time a watchman in the garden saw him fastening the latch of his window, looking as though he was about to get into bed. In the early hours of the morning, he died in his sleep, a blood clot having reached his heart.

Princess Elizabeth, on her way to Australia and New Zealand, was 4,000 miles away in East Africa. Her wedding present from the people of Kenya, then a colony, had been a hunting lodge on the Sagana River in the Aberdare Forest game reserve. Near the lodge was the Treetops Hotel, built in the branches of a gigantic fig tree. On the night of her father's death the Princess was among the branches of this fabulous tree looking down at the wild animals that came to the waterhole beneath: elephants, rhinoceros and water-buck. It was a rewarding night for animal-watchers, the Princess did not go to bed until just before dawn.

The royal party were to leave the same day. On his way to lunch, Martin Charteris, the Princess's Private Secretary, walking across the car park of the Outspan Hotel, where the newspaper correspondents had been accommodated, was asked to go to the telephone box in the hotel. Here he found a newspaperman, pale and shaken, who told him that the Reuters news service had just reported that King George VI was dead.

An official announcement was made in London at 10.45 a.m., the time being 1.45 p.m. in Kenya. Charteris waited to hear it, drove back to Sagana Lodge, and gave the news to Michael Parker, Prince Philip's Private Secretary, who immediately telephoned London to have the news confirmed. Parker took the view that before the Princess was informed he should first inform the Prince, who was in his sitting-room, reading a newspaper. Parker entered the room and gave him the news. The Prince listened, then sat silently, as though stunned, staring into the newspaper which he had been holding when Parker came into the room.

That morning the Princess and the Prince had been out fishing. She had caught more than he had, and she was very pleased with herself. She was now about to go out riding. The Prince went into her room and told her what had happened. About a half-hour later, she appeared before her officials and staff, wearing black clothes which she had brought with her as a precaution. She looked pale but perfectly calm. There were documents to be signed and apologies to be cabled, and other small tasks, and she did these quickly and efficiently. Many of these required her signature. She was asked what name she wanted to use. "Oh, my own name – what else?"

Within an hour or so the royal party was on its way to the airport. When Elizabeth got to the top of the steps leading into the plane, she turned and gave a brief wave and a smile. This was her grateful goodbye to the people of Kenya who had looked after her. It could also have been her goodbye to the days of her childhood and youth.

5

Bagehot's ideas on the monarchy. Their influence on the Queen

HOW MUCH DID the Queen know about the role of the monarch when she came to the throne? She had learned a great deal from watching and talking with her parents, from her grandmother, and from what she had observed for herself with that "long cool stare". And she had received some instruction.

From the age of twelve she was tutored by Sir Henry Marten, a famous teacher of history, later Provost of Eton. He gave her lessons, and set her essays, in the history of Britain, the Dominions, in the leading countries of the world, and in the development of the Constitution. Sir Henry also familiarised her, as her grandfather and father had been, with the writings on the monarchy of Walter Bagehot.

Walter Bagehot, a banker's son who became a barrister and an economist, was Editor of *The Economist* from 1860 until his death in 1877. In 1867 he wrote his classic work, *The English Constitution*, which includes a famous section on the monarchy.

Many people think that Bagehot's views about the monarchy are out of date. Others see him still as the most perceptive of all writers on the subject. Serious books about monarchy written today almost certainly will refer to him.

According to Bagehot, any constitution which has been effective over the centuries:

> has two parts ... first, those which excite and preserve the reverence of the population – the signified parts, if I may so call them; and, next, the efficient parts – those by which it, in fact, works and rules ...

In the nature of things, he says, the efficient parts of government, the most useful, do not excite so much reverence as do the dignified parts, the theatrical.

> The elements which excite the most easy reverence will be the theatrical elements – those which appeal to the senses, which claim to be the embodiment of the greatest human ideas, which boast in some cases of far more than human origins. That which is mystic in its claims; that which is occult in its mode of action; that which is brilliant to the eye; that which is seen vividly for a moment, and then is seen no more.

Many people deplore Bagehot's belief that the majority of the people are unintelligent, and therefore recoil from his view that the monarchy is as valuable as it is because it can be understood even by the mass of the people, as unintelligent as they are:

> We have in a great community like England crowds of people scarcely more civilised than the majority of two thousand years ago ... The lowest orders, the middle orders, are still, when tried by what is the standard of the educated "ten thousand", narrow-minded, unintelligent, incurious ... Those who doubt should go outside into their kitchens ... The fancy of the mass of men is incredibly weak; it can see nothing without a visible symbol ... The best reason why Monarchy is a strong government is that it is an intelligible government. The mass of mankind understand it, and they hardly anywhere in the world understand any other.

The people understand the monarchy, said Bagehot, or think they understand it, because in action it looks so simple:

> The nature of a constitution, the action of an assembly, the play

of parties, the unseen formation of a guiding opinion, are complex facts, difficult to know, and easy to mistake. But the action of a single will, the fiat of a single mind, are easy ideas; anybody can make them out, and no one can ever forget them.

On the importance of the royal *family* Bagehot says that it "brings down the pride of sovereignty to the level of petty life". No feeling could be more childish than the enthusiasm of the British people for a royal marriage. It is treated as a great political event. But "The women – one half of the human race – care fifty times more for a marriage than a ministry."

In Bagehot's view, therefore, the first reason why monarchy is the best form of government is that it is so intelligible.

Royalty is a government in which the attention of the nation is concentrated on one person doing interesting actions. A Republic is a government in which attention is divided between many, who are doing uninteresting actions.

The second feature of the British monarchy, says Bagehot, is that it "strengthens our government with the strength of religion". The feeling that the King must be obeyed simply because he *is* King goes back a long way in our history. The cavaliers in the seventeenth century believed that the King ruled by "divine right". The King was the "Lord's anointed". Parliament, the laws, the press were human institutions; but the monarchy was a divine institution. The influence of this feeling was very much reduced as a result of the "Glorious Revolution" of 1689, when James II having fled the country was succeeded jointly by his daughter Mary and his Dutch son-in-law, William of Orange. "All through the reign of William III there was (in common speech) one king whom man had made and another whom God had made." Many recognised that William ruled in fact, but that "The King over the water" *ought* to have ruled. This religious feeling about the monarch returned with Queen Anne, James's daughter, went again with George I and George II, Hanoverians imported and enthroned by Act of Parliament, and returned again in 1760 when George III came to the throne. At that point, according to Bagehot, "The English were ready to take the new young prince as the beginning of a sacred line of sovereigns." Writing in 1867, Bagehot said:

So it is now. If you ask the immense majority of the Queen's subjects by what right she rules, they would never tell you that she rules by Parliamentary right, by virtue of 6 Anne, c. 7. They will say she rules by "God's grace"; they believe that they have a mystic obligation to obey her.

The monarchy by its religious sanction now confirms all our political order ... It gives now a vast strength to the entire constitution, by enlisting on its behalf the credulous obedience of enormous masses ...

The third feature of the monarchy, said Bagehot, was:

The Queen is the head of our society. If she did not exist the Prime Minister would be the first person in the country. He and his wife would have to receive foreign ministers, and occasionally foreign princes, to give the first parties in the country; he and she would be at the head of the pageant of life; they would represent the Government of England ...

In some countries, says Bagehot, this would not matter much. "In a country where people did not care for the outward show of life, where the genius of the people was untheatrical, and they exclusively regarded the substance of things, this matter would be trifling. Who is the showman is not material unless you care about the show." But in his view these considerations very much matter to the British. They do care about the show. "It would be a very serious matter to us to change every four or five years the visible head of our world."

What he calls "the show" is very attractive to the ambitious – the House of Commons, for example – and the ranks of the ambitious include some undesirables. "If the highest post in conspicuous life were thrown open to public competition, this low sort of ambition and envy would be fearfully increased. Politics would offer a prize too dazzling for mankind; clever base people would strive for it, and stupid base people would envy it."

This leads Bagehot to an observation about the Court:

There are arguments for not having a Court, and there are arguments for having a splendid Court; but there are no arguments for having a mean Court.

The fourth feature of the monarchy, in Bagehot's words, is that "We have come to regard the Crown as the head of our *morality*." He points out that George I, George II and William IV were not "patterns of family merit" and that "George IV was a model of family demerit". But:

> The virtues of Queen Victoria and the virtues of George III have sunk deep into the popular heart. We have come to believe that it is natural to have a virtuous sovereign ...

Last, says Bagehot, but most important of all is the continuity, the impression of non-change, which the monarchy represents. The on-goingness of the monarch reminds us that when governments change much that is fundamental remains. "Constitutional royalty ... acts as a *disguise*. It enables our real rulers to change without heedless people knowing it ..." There is another respect, according to Bagehot, in which the British monarchy is a "disguise":

> So, like the Greeks, we have a Republican Government, concealed by the kingship ... we live in a "disguised republic" which suits us.

Bagehot now comes to the part the monarch plays in the "efficient parts" of the constitution. The monarch is not a third estate of the realm, as it once was. The monarch has no legislative power. The Queen cannot veto a Bill; "She must sign her own death-warrant if the two Houses unanimously send it up to her." Nevertheless the Queen has powers, even though there may be some doubt and ignorance, not to say some dispute, about what these are. And Bagehot did not like the idea of anybody trying to find out:

> A secret prerogative is an anomaly – perhaps the greatest of anomalies. That secrecy is, however, essential to the utility of English royalty as it now is. Above all things our royalty is to be reverenced, and if you begin to poke about it you cannot reverence it. When there is a select committee on the Queen, the charm of royalty will be gone. Its mystery is its life. We must not let in daylight upon magic. We must not bring the Queen into the combat of politics, or she will cease to be reverenced by all combatants; she will become one combatant among many. The

existence of this secret power is, according to abstract theory, a defect in our constitutional polity, but it is a defect incident to a civilisation such as ours, where august and therefore unknown powers are needed, as well as known and serviceable powers.

Not everybody agreed with Bagehot even in his own day about the importance of secrecy for the monarchy. Lord Acton, famous for his dictum, "Power tends to corrupt and absolute power corrupts absolutely", also said: "Everything secret degenerates: nothing is safe that does not show it can bear discussion and publicity."

Bagehot never for a moment in all his praise of the monarchy expressed admiration for any particular incumbent of that exalted office. On the contrary:

A constitutional sovereign must in the common course of government be a man of but common ability. I am afraid, looking to the early acquired feebleness of hereditary dynasties, that we must expect him to be a man of inferior ability. Theory and experience both teach that the education of a prince can be but a poor education, and that a royal family will generally have less ability than other families ... Probably in most cases the greatest wisdom of a constitutional king would show itself in well-considered inaction.

Bagehot dwells on the fact that the monarch has certain rights. He must be kept informed by the Prime Minister – there is no law which says he must, but established constitutional convention almost dictates that he must – about the important decisions made by the government, about the important votes in Parliament, and about the problems facing the country. He has a duty to tell her everything that she ought to be told. The monarch has the right to complain if he or she is not kept informed of anything which the government proposes to do while there is still time to consider it, and to prevent it being done.

This brings Bagehot to the Royal Prerogative, and to the most important observation in his book, the dictum which is most quoted today, and which has never been effectively disrupted:

The sovereign has, under a constitutional monarchy such as ours, three rights – the right to be consulted, the right to encourage, the right to warn.

Bagehot points out something about the monarch which, since he wrote in 1867, has been mentioned many times since:

> In the course of a long reign a sagacious king would acquire an experience with which few ministers could contend. The king could say:
>
> "Have you referred to the transactions which happened during such and such an administration, I think about fourteen years ago? They afford an instructive example of the bad results which are to attend the policy which you propose.
>
> "You did not at that time take so prominent a part in public life as you now do, and it is possible you do not fully remember all the events. I should recommend you to recur to them, and to discuss them with your older colleagues who took part in them. It is unwise to recommend a policy which later worked so ill."

Bagehot stressed the fact that unlike a Prime Minister, who might be here today and gone tomorrow, and might crave for sudden fame and act on "burning ideas (such as young men have)" which come to nothing or do harm, the monarch takes a different perspective:

> But a wise and great constitutional monarch attempts no such vanities. His career is not in the air: he labours in the world of sober fact ..,

The great advantage of a constitutional king, says Bagehot, is "the permanence of his place". This gives him the opportunity of acquiring a consecutive knowledge of even the most complex affairs of state. "But it gives only an opportunity. The King must use it." The monarch must do his homework. Nor does Bagehot extol all constitutional kings who do their homework. George III was "a meddling maniac".

Bagehot had a view on the age at which the good constitutional monarch should take up his duties. It would be a bad thing all round if the heir came to the throne too young,

> but the case is worse when he comes to it old or middle-aged.

He is then unfit to work ... it is unnatural to expect him to labour ... The only fit material for a constitutional king is a prince who begins early to reign – who in his youth is superior to pleasure – who in his youth is willing to labour – who has by nature a genius for discretion. Such kings are among God's greatest gifts, but they are also among his rarest.

Nothing made more impact on George VI than what Bagehot wrote about the moral role of the monarch:

We have come to regard the Crown as the head of our morality. We have come to believe that it is natural to have a virtuous sovereign...

Given the new Queen's regard for her father, and for what he believed in, it is certain that she, like him, came to the throne imbued with Bagehot's views on "all principles of Monarchy", and on the moral responsibilities of the sovereign in particular.

6

Elizabeth II is crowned
Princess Margaret and
Peter Townsend
1953–5

IF QUEEN ELIZABETH II had come to the throne a middle-aged lady or even a youthful frump, the mood in which the public greeted her would have been very different. It would have been respectful, sympathetic and loyal, but it would not have been romantic. As it happened in 1952, a likeable, glamorous and very young woman came to the throne, prematurely because of the early death of her father. The circumstances inspired sympathy as well as admiration for her. Moreover, the new Queen was the wife of a handsome dashing husband, mother of two charming children, and daughter of the very popular Elizabeth the Queen Mother.

Even if the Queen's name had not happened to be Elizabeth there would have been in the political context of the early fifties a good deal of talking and writing about a "New Elizabethan Age". In the year she succeeded her father, and in the following year, in which she was crowned, there was much comment and speculation about what might be achieved in her reign as though it was capable of reproducing in the twentieth century successes, if not glories, comparable to those of the era of her illustrious ancestor.

The government created, fostered and exploited these hopes. The Conservatives had ousted the post-war Labour government in October 1951, just four months before the Queen came to the throne, having promised to end austerity, root out socialism, rescue free enterprise and restore Britain's power in the post-war world. With a Parliamentary majority of only seventeen they found themselves facing an uphill task. They soon discovered that problems they had claimed had been brought about by the Labour government's doctrinaire socialism were of deeper origin and would not disappear overnight. Less than three months after the general election, the Chancellor of the Exchequer, R. A. Butler warned the country that it faced "a major calamity for sterling".

The outlook was grim. People wanted to escape, to be distracted, to be given a new hope. Talk and writing about the New Elizabethan Age was an expression of this. The original Elizabethan age was a time of great bold private enterprise, conducted by the likes of Drake, Raleigh and John Hawkins, inspired by the greatest entrepreneur of them all, the first Queen Elizabeth. Talk about her was good political propaganda for the Conservative government. The Coronation would signify more than the crowning of a new monarch; it would mark the beginning of a new chapter in British history, one ushered in by the Tory Party. The government prepared to capitalise on it. Apart from the entertainment it would provide, the Coronation would generate great national and international publicity. Delegations from all the countries of the Free World would come to Britain for the occasion. There would be a valuable opportunity to "sell Britain" to them. After the ceremony the Queen would make many visits overseas: she would be Britain's prime saleswoman. The government saw the events which would precede and follow the Coronation as opportunities for reforging economic and financial links with the countries of the Commonwealth, and forming new ones with markets for British exports, such as the United States. The huge influx of visitors from abroad would create vast trade for the British tourist industry. A few republicans deplored the fuss which was to be made of the crowning of the new Queen; many monarchists complained of the waste of money and the interruption in production which would be incurred. Churchill was asked: "How do you justify such great expenditure on the Coronation of the Queen, when England is in such financial straits?" His reply was: "Everybody likes to wear a flower when he goes to see his girl." Most people welcomed the Coronation for one reason or another.

In the great rush to exploit the young Queen in one way, and for one reason or another, not enough attention might have been paid to the fact that she already had responsibilities to her young family, to her husband and to herself. In the process of making her into a combination of a national symbol, an international saleswoman and a world-famous film star, the need for her to have enough time and quiet to be a good mother and to learn more about what being a good mother required might have been given less thought than it deserved. This was a young woman who had been precipitated into her royal vocation many years before the appropriate time. There was a consensus of demand on her potential which did not make for a balanced development of her education or her marital experience.

There was no more enthusiastic a New Elizabethan than that old Victorian, Sir Winston Churchill, and certainly nobody so eloquent about it. His hopes were most succinctly expressed in a speech he made on the eve of the Queen's departure on her Commonwealth Coronation Tour. "It may well be", the Prime Minister declared, "that the journey the Queen is about to undertake will be no less auspicious and the treasure she brings back no less bright than when Drake first sailed an English ship around the world."

Always a romantic monarchist, to some degree still living in the reign of the present Queen's great-great-grandmother, and, now, nearly eighty, more sentimental and less realistic than was good for the government which he headed, Churchill was nevertheless shrewdly aware of what might be achieved politically by hitching its wagon to the royal star. "All around we see proof of the unifying sentiment which makes the Crown the central link in our modern changing life." In his case personal feeling went hand in hand with political calculation. He used the "gleaming figure" of the Queen to distract the people's minds from their everyday problems. To best serve that purpose, he believed, she must remain a mysterious almost religious presence, a being above the mundane world of political and economic striving, her dazzling radiance obscuring the hard realities of the times.

Churchill's view of how the monarchy should be presented was shared by most of the prominent courtiers at Buckingham Palace. Nobody was more committed to it than the Queen's Private Secretary, Sir Alan Lascelles. The "mystic" view of the monarchy, however, was not shared unreservedly by the second most important person in the royal family, the Duke of Edinburgh. In his view the monarchy should be not "mystic" but "modern". From his earliest days as consort, Prince Philip had made it clear by many things he said and did that if the monarchy was to survive it must *de*-mystify itself, and relate more effectively to the modern world. With that belief went his plans for his own career. He had no intention of becoming a lackey to his wife, a figure who would only be seen in public walking a dutiful half a dozen paces behind her. On the contrary, he meant to do things and say things on his own account. Between 1949, when he became President of the National Playing Fields Association, and 1951 when he was President of the British Association for the Advancement of Science, he made many speeches, in which the ideas and language were clearly his own. Some of his remarks were controversial, and in the view of some leading politicians bordered on political comment. The older generation at Court, headed by Lascelles, became apprehensive. They were unhappy about his views on how the monarchy should behave, and about his clear intention to do what he had to do in his own way. They saw that Prince Philip had a great deal of influence on the Queen. Since the death of the King, she looked up to him as something of a father figure. She listened to him. She had a mind of her own, but where she was faced with a choice of advice she was more likely to act on Prince Philip's than on anybody else's.

The courtiers were not happy about the Duke's choice of Private Secretary, Commander Michael Parker. The Prince had met him in the Navy in 1942, and they had become great friends. Parker was an Australian, boisterous, extrovert and irreverent. He liked having fun; he enjoyed parties. Some of the courtiers thought him a raffish figure, with some dubious friends, who introduced the Duke to bohemian company, which included journalists, artists, actors, photographers, and others not normally encountered in royal circles.

Prince Philip had been on excellent terms with Attlee, the Labour Party's Prime Minister, whom he had met through Mountbatten. His uncle had been a friend and supporter of the Labour government: Attlee thought highly of Mountbatten, and had been in favour of Philip marrying Elizabeth from the moment he had met him. Philip did not have a similar relationship with Churchill.

One of the issues on which they differed was whether on the death of the King the name of the royal family should be changed from Windsor to Edinburgh. A few days after the Queen had come to the throne, Jock Colville, then serving again as Churchill's Private Secretary, was asked to see Queen Mary. He found her most upset. She had been told by Prince Ernst August of Hanover that he had just come back from Lord Mountbatten's house in the country, Broadlands, and that at dinner, in the presence of many royal guests, Lord Mountbatten had said that in Britain "the House of Mountbatten now reigned". This was technically correct: on her marriage Princess Elizabeth had taken her husband's name, so when she succeeded to the throne her name was still Mountbatten. Churchill, and the Court, however, had been for some time planning to restore the family name of Windsor. There had already been some gossip that Mountbatten was "moving in on the monarchy", and Colville's account of his conversation with Queen Mary lent colour to it. Churchill accordingly urged the Queen to issue a proclamation announcing that the name would become Windsor again. At this point Philip sent the Prime Minister what Colville described as "a strongly but ably worded memorandum protesting against a proposed Proclamation", and arguing that the name of the royal family should now become Edinburgh. Churchill took umbrage and consulted the Lord Chancellor and the Cabinet, the result being a flat rejection of Prince Philip's proposal. When Philip was informed he is reported to have said that in that case he was nothing but "an amoeba – a bloody amoeba". On 9 April, the proclamation was issued: "The Queen today declared in Council her Will and Pleasure that She and Her Children shall be styled and known as the House and Family of Windsor ..."

Churchill was kept well informed about the Prince's ideas and conduct by his contacts at Buckingham Palace. Colville, as a result of his foot in both camps – he had served as Princess Elizabeth's Private Secretary in 1947–8 – was a valuable go-between. Whether the Prime Minister feared that the Prince might take the monarchy too far down the populist road for it to play its historic role in the British political system, or whether he thought Philip a bit of a maverick, he seemed determined to give him no latitude.

They had not seen eye to eye on other matters. At the time of the King's death Elizabeth and Philip, and their two children, had been living in Clarence House. They had had it modernised, redecorated, furnished to suit them, and they were happy and comfortable there. It was a home. When the King died it was expected of them that they would move to Buckingham Palace. The Prince resisted this. He and the Queen knew what living in the Palace was like. The building was vast, the rooms impersonal, the plumbing out-of-date, the electric wiring inadequate, the heating

spartan, and internal communication between royal family, secretaries and staff depending on notes borne by liveried footmen on
silver salvers.

Prince Philip urged Churchill to let the royal family go on
living in Clarence House. It was so much more comfortable. Let
Buckingham Palace continue to be the office block of the monarchy:
even on foot it could be reached from Clarence House in less than
five minutes.

Churchill would not entertain the idea, and told Prince Philip so
in uncompromising terms. Buckingham Palace was the official
London residence of the sovereign, had been since Queen Victoria
had made it so in the mid-nineteenth century, and must remain
such. The new royal family must move into it as soon as possible.

When with reluctance the royal family complied, the Prince
examined every aspect of life at the Palace, from protocol to
plumbing. On the day-to-day living level he found many anomalies.
One of the most quoted was the practice of putting an unopened
bottle of Scotch in the Queen's bedroom every night, in spite of
the fact that everybody knew she did not drink spirits. The Prince's
enquiries revealed that this practice had begun in the previous
century when Queen Victoria, suffering from a heavy cold, had
asked for some Scotch to be supplied to her bedroom. The following
day the bottle was taken away, and was replaced by another,
unopened, and the practice had continued. The Prince found that
if he wanted to have a sandwich delivered to his room at least four
people would be employed before he got it. As a result of making
these initial discoveries he decided to conduct a massive personal
inspection of the Palace, going into nearly every one of its 600
rooms, and walking the underground corridors to the kitchens.
When en route he encountered people, he asked them what they
were doing and why. As a result, a number of changes were made.
The kitchens were updated, an internal telephone system installed,
the plumbing modernised, and the Palace rewired for lighting and
heating. The Prince was not only interested in better equipment
for the Palace but in better administration: experts were brought in
to advise on a reorganisation of its business. He was shrewd enough
to try to avoid giving any impression that here was a new broom.
Some of the Palace officials admired what he was doing; some did
not. There was some resistance to his reforms, some due to
habit, some to laziness, some to fear of change. The Prince,

characteristically, having set his hand to the plough, ploughed on. From time to time his impatience showed.

The many meetings between the Queen's representatives and the government's to discuss the arrangements for the Coronation soon revealed that on one very important topic there was a significant division of opinion: were television cameras to be admitted into the Abbey to enable the Coronation ceremony to be broadcast live? The modernists said Yes, and the mystics said No. Such questions were meant to be dealt with by the Coronation Commission, of which the Chairman was Prince Philip, appointed by the Queen. Her decision to entrust the job to him had been much criticised in some quarters, notably by the Old Guard at the Court.

The Prince took the view that the ceremony should be televised live, and said so with his usual force. Though as Chairman of the Commission his view carried considerable weight this was not a matter which the Commission could decide on its own. Important personages outside the Commission became involved. Churchill opposed live television because he thought it would destroy the solemnity of the occasion and, also, would impose too much strain upon the young and inexperienced Queen. The Archbishop of Canterbury, Dr Fisher, was opposed to it because he thought the presence of live cameras would turn a sacred service into a public spectacle. Lascelles opposed live transmission because he thought it would let in the light of common day and dissipate that mystique of the monarchy, which, he believed, was the secret of the institution's strength and charisma.

The issue came up at a meeting in May 1952. Jock Colville attended as the Prime Minister's representative. The majority of those present were opposed to televising the Coronation ceremony, and recommended that the Queen be advised against it. The Duke of Norfolk, who as the Earl Marshal was responsible to the Queen for the organisation of State occasions, and the Archbishop of Canterbury reported that the Queen was already personally opposed to it. Colville reported all this to Churchill, who then advised the Cabinet to tell the Queen that they too were against it. The Queen, thereupon, was so informed.

To the surprise of Churchill and the Cabinet the Queen declined to take their advice. They received a message from her stating that she wanted the television cameras in the Abbey. She wanted the ceremony to be televised live. She wanted everybody to see and hear the service, with the exception of that part of it in which she took holy communion. Churchill, bewildered, but clear about his duty, told Colville that plans for live television must go ahead. "After all it was the Queen who was to be crowned and not the Cabinet. She alone must decide." The Cabinet met and decided to withdraw their earlier recommendation. "Thus it was", recorded Colville, "that the new twenty-six-year-old Sovereign personally routed the Earl Marshal, the Archbishop of Canterbury, Sir Winston Churchill and the Cabinet, all of whom submitted to her decision with astonishment, but with a good grace."

According to Leonard Miall, historian of the BBC, for a long time it was rumoured within the Corporation that the Queen's decision to televise the ceremony live had been urged on her by her aged grandmother, who realised she was too frail to get to the Abbey yet was determined to witness the proceedings. Later, Jock Colville, who used to visit Queen Mary every week, told Miall this was not the case. "I am sure that if she had been keen on the Coronation being televised she would have told me. I rather doubt if she even had a set."

Queen Mary died five weeks before the Coronation. When the Duke of Windsor heard that she was at death's door he was in New York, and by the time he had flown to London she was dead. He told his wife: "My sadness was mixed with incredulity that any mother could have been so hard and cruel towards her eldest son without relenting a scrap. I'm afraid the fluids in her veins have always been as icy cold as they are now in death ... What a smug stinking lot my relations are ..."

The decision to televise the ceremony was applauded by the newspapers, mainly because they were initially under the impression that it was the power of the press which had brought about the change of plan. Earlier, hearing that there was opposition to the idea, they had campaigned against what they described as a plot on the part of the Court to keep the cameras out of the Abbey. The *Sunday Express*, briefed, it was rumoured, by Mountbatten, inveighed against "the tight-knit group of palace officials whose determination to keep the people as far as possible away from the throne never diminishes". The *Daily Express* declared: "The sooner Mr Churchill can announce the ending of the ban, the sweeping aside of the ruling of the palace officials, moved only by protocol, the sooner the nation will be able to express its gratitude." The

Daily Express pointed to that phrase in the Coronation Service which enjoined the sovereign to take the Coronation oath – to rule according to law, to exercise justice with mercy, and maintain the Church of England – "in the sight of all the people".

The Queen's decision that the ceremony should be televised live was a victory for the modernists over the mystics. But time was to show that it had created some problems. To allow television cameras into the Abbey was to range her with the modernists: but her conduct, her comportment, the image she projected during and via the ceremony placed her with the mystics. The idea of showing millions of people what went on in the Abbey was very modern, but what the millions saw was most archaic. The Queen revealed herself as devout and dedicated. Her attitude to monarchy seemed sacerdotal. She was consecrating herself to her duty. She behaved not like a priestess, she was too unassuming, but like a vestal virgin. The image she projected was what might have been expected from words she had used in her first Christmas broadcast as Queen: "Pray for me on that day," she said. "Pray that God may give me wisdom and strength to carry out the solemn promises I shall be making." She had carried out a programme of prayer and meditation for several weeks before the day of the ceremony.

The key to her decision to let the millions into the Coronation ceremony was her wish that every citizen of the country and the Commonwealth would share the mystical character of her queenship. The essence of the monarchy was to be preserved by being shared. This way the great family of monarch and people could be kept together. The miracle of television had made it possible.

The tone of what might be called the mystico-monarchist view of the Coronation was exemplified by the main leader in *The Times* on the morning of Coronation Day:

Today's sublime ceremonial is in form, and in common view, a dedication of the state to God's service through the prayers and benedictions of the Church. That is a noble conception, and of itself makes every man and woman in the land a partaker in the mystery of the Queen's anointing. But also the Queen stands for the soul as well as for the body of the Commonwealth. In her is incarnate on her Coronation day the whole of society, of which the state is no more than a political manifestation. She represents the life of her people ... as men and women, and not in their limited capacity as Lords and Commons and electors. It is the glory of the social monarchy that it set the human above the institutional.

The morning after the ceremony, even the *Daily Mirror*'s famous columnist, the iconoclast Cassandra, was enthusiastic: "I have heard the beating heart of England ... Who can doubt our strength and dignity and power?"

Forty years later, in the anniversary year of the Coronation, the *Guardian* asked the question: if the *Sun*, which had not existed at the time – "it was not until 1969 that it transformed into the tabloid we all know" – had existed in 1953, what would it have said on the morning after the Coronation? For an answer to the question it sought out a former *Sun* journalist and former editor of the *Mirror*, Mr Roy Greenslade, to "turn back the clock". Mr Greenslade wrote as follows:

G'DAY MA'AM AND GOODBYE

SORRY to spoil your big day, ma'am, but *The Sun* has a duty to speak the truth. Even when it's unpalatable.

You looked terrific yesterday – every inch the queen you officially became – and we are proud to join the chorus in praise of your beauty, charm and grace.

But the sad fact is that from today you'll be using those gifts in the service of an out-dated institution ...

Maintaining a monarchy and all its trappings is preserving a system of inequality and privilege which has no place in the 1950s.

Mr Greenslade's hypothetical article, had it been written at the time, would have gone on to point out that Britain was rapidly falling behind Americans, French and Germans, industrially and socially. Why?

Because unlike Britain these countries don't have the dead weight of the old aristocracy on their backs. They encourage talents from all classes to help their country in a spirit of enterprise. Meritocracy is their watchword.

According to Mr Greenslade in 1993 the *Sun* of 1953, had it existed, would have gone on to say that the British aristocracy was kept in place by the monarchy. The monarchy was about "keeping the lucky few at the top of the heap". The 1953 *Sun* editorial would have concluded:

> So, ma'am, now you've had your fun, ridden in the coach, waved from the balcony, tried on the crown, why not do something really useful for Britain:
> ABDICATE TOMORROW

The *Sun* that exists today did not exist in 1953, and if it had, it might have expressed views more like those of the *Mirror* at the time and less like those of Mr Greenslade, looking back from forty years later. Notwithstanding the non-existence of the *Sun*, however, Britain's need to face the reality of how to earn a living was not neglected. It was urged, for example, by an editorial article in *The Times* which appeared the day after the Coronation. Now that the ceremony had come and gone, said *The Times*, the people of Britain should start doing what was necessary to save itself from the economic adversities which would otherwise lie ahead:

> The British people have had a holiday from reality long enough ... Even in a welfare state facts must be seen penny plain. Britain's economy still always on a knife-edge ... The main reason why Britain has not yet prospered sufficiently to lift herself above the safety line is that the British people as a whole have not yet had the will to prosper ... A country made great by resourcefulness and energy is slowly strangling itself with restrictive practices ... by a plain disinclination for hard work.

In terms of public relations the televising of the ceremony was a huge success, a peak, if not a watershed, in the history of the medium. Nearly a quarter of the population of the world were said to have seen the programme. In Britain, where only a small minority owned television sets, hundreds of thousands of people watched in the homes of relatives or friends, thus setting up new records for television viewing. The effect on the sales of television sets, and thus on the influence of the medium, was dramatic. Almost overnight television took on a new dimension in the national consciousness.

What the effect of the televising of the ceremony had on the monarchy is not so clear. Even in the short term opinions were divided. Many people had been deeply moved by what they had seen and heard, and by the erudite commentary of the BBC's expert on royal affairs, Richard Dimbleby, delivered in reverent and necessarily hushed tones, but all the more effective for that, explaining the significance and meaning of the various stages in the ritual. Others saw not mystery, mystique, religion and the divinity of kingship but picturesque if not artistic mumbo-jumbo with no relevance to real life in the twentieth century. They saw orbs, ampoules, sceptres, swords of state and relics of kings dead a thousand years; they heard solemn promises, vows of allegiance, citations of virtues, invocation of saints, and the swearing of historic oaths. They saw that a large proportion of the people assembled in the Abbey were lords and ladies wearing coronets and ermined robes, the sole reason for their presence there being that their ancestors had been there before them. For many viewers the televising of the Coronation deepened many people's sense of the mystical and religious aspects of the monarchy: for many it revealed the interdependence of the Crown and the class system, and gave unprecedented confirmation of their opinion that the monarchy was a harmful anachronism. Many viewers objected that an excess of historical and religious content had related the ceremony too much to the United Kingdom and not enough to the other countries of the Commonwealth. However, most people agreed that the television programme had done great good to the personal image of the Queen, and that for her personally it had been an unqualified success.

The long-term effect of the televising of the Coronation would be even harder to assess. To many viewers the television programme would have given them their first sense of contact with the wearer of the crown. For some it would have made the royal figure more mysterious and more remote. For others it would have made the monarch more human, more like themselves, and therefore the royal figure nearer. For many television viewers it had placed the Queen among the stars of stage and screen. The Minister of Works, Sir David Eccles, the member of the Cabinet responsible for the public arrangements of the Coronation, on one occasion spoke of the Queen as his "leading lady". He was taken to task for this, but in fact he had said what millions of people had thought. He had pointed, whether conscious of it or not, to an aspect of the monarchy of which the public was only just becoming aware – the monarchy as entertainment. The monarchy had long possessed its mystique; ever since Edward VIII had become King in the thirties it had been making terms with modernity. Now it was being seen as something out of Hollywood. Mystique, modernisation, and the make-believe of Hollywood: the question arose of how – and if – these three aspects would combine. Whatever the televising of the Coronation might have done for the Queen and the monarchy it had certainly created a problem for the government. This was presented to the Prime Minister by the Secretary to the Cabinet, the sagacious Sir Norman Brook, in the following prophetic terms:

> What arguments will remain for refusing T.V. facilities of e.g. royal funerals or weddings, religious services, or even proceedings in the House of Commons? . . .
> Television has come to stay and unless it is fully used on an occasion like this it will be said that we are not moving with the times.

In the previous twelve months the Queen had had plenty on her hands: the death of her father, her accession, the death of her grandmother, preparations for the Coronation, and for the Commonwealth tour by which it would be followed. Now, almost before the ceremony at the Abbey had come to an end, she had to deal with the love affair between Princess Margaret and Group Captain Peter Townsend.

After a brave and brilliant career as a fighter-pilot in the RAF, for which he had been awarded the DSO and the DFC, in 1944 Group Captain Peter Townsend had been appointed equerry to the King. Townsend says in his autobiography that before he went to be interviewed at Buckingham Palace he had been warned about the King's short temper: the King, he was told, might raise his voice or even shout, but there was no need to be alarmed.

Townsend was a man of character and charm, and of high intelligence. Like the King he, too, stammered. He got the job, and soon established a notably good relationship with the King, who, it was said, in time came to treat him more as a son than an equerry. Townsend had a soothing influence on the King. There were times when this needed to be brought into play. When the King became "irked or rattled", wrote Townsend, "the steady regard in his blue eyes [became] an alarming glare ... Then, he would start to rant noisily, and the Queen would mollify him with a soothing word or gesture; once she held his pulse and, with a wistful smile, began to count – tick, tick, tick – which made him laugh, and the storm subsided. In those moments he was like a small boy, very lovable."

Previous to the appointment of Townsend the King's equerries were chosen on a personal basis, their family or regimental connections being a major consideration. The King decided to "widen the net", in Townsend's words, and appoint temporary equerries chosen for their fighting record. Townsend was the first of these. His appointment, he was told, would be for three months; in fact he was to be a vital part of Buckingham Palace life for the next nine years.

The King very much enjoyed and learned from talking to Townsend about his experiences on active service. Listening to his equerry made the King feel closer to the fighting which to his regret he had had little opportunity to see, let alone take part in, in both world wars. Nearly all the courtiers came from the aristocracy; Townsend came from the middle class. Conversations with Townsend widened the King's experience. They brought back happy memories of his days as "the foreman". In some respects the King learned more from Townsend than from the Prime Minister or his Private Secretary. He became closer to him than he had been to anybody since his elder brother in their childhood.

Townsend's intimacy with the King brought him close to the three women in the family. They liked and admired him on his own account, but as well they were grateful for the good influence they saw he had upon the King. "So charming and thoughtful was this family, whom I hardly knew, that they made me feel more of a guest than an aide."

However, he soon learned that the Queen-to-be, although hospitable, knew her place and expected everybody else to know theirs. Talking of her grandfather, George V, the Princess said one day:

His manner was very abrupt; some people thought he was being rude. Townsend said, "I rather like people like that because if they are rude to you you can be rude back at them." "Yes, but you can't very well be rude to the King of England," retorted the heir to England's throne.

Townsend commented: "I took note to be more wary in future of what I said." Townsend's comments, and the glimpse of the Queen-to-be which they afford, have been echoed by many people since.

Townsend does not seem to have become a particular friend of Prince Philip at any stage in their acquaintance; such evidence as there is suggests that there was some distance between them. The situation is easy to understand. At a time when Townsend was established as the King's adviser and confidant, Prince Philip was an occasional visitor, seeing the royal family only when invited to when home on leave, and well aware of the King's disinclination to hasten his suit for his daughter's hand.

In 1947, as mentioned in an earlier chapter, Townsend accompanied the royal family to South Africa. He was then thirty-three, and Margaret was sixteen. It seems that it was at this time, when he and the royal family lived closely together for several weeks, that Margaret began to feel drawn towards him. In 1950 Townsend was appointed Master of the Household. The King was sick, Elizabeth was married: Margaret saw more and more of Townsend. After the death of the King, Townsend was elevated to the post of Controller of the Royal Household. There were many raised eyebrows. At this time Townsend was in the process of divorcing his wife. The royal family had previously frowned on divorce, and for the Queen Mother to give such prominent employment to a person who had been involved in one, though the innocent party, was generally thought to be uncharacteristic of her.

Some time before the Coronation was to take place the situation of Princess Margaret and Townsend took a new turn. He described this in his book as follows:

At all events we wished the Queen to know of our feelings, and these Princess Margaret confided privately to her sister. A few days later, at Buckingham Palace, Her Majesty invited us both to spend the evening with her and Prince Philip. Both were in good spirits and the evening passed off most agreeably. From it there stands out in my memory one unforgettable impression: the Queen's movingly simple and sympathetic acceptance of the disturbing fact of her sister's love for me. Prince Philip, as was his way, may have tended to look for a funny side to this poignant situation. I did not blame him. A laugh here and there did not come amiss. That evening we had several. But, as I sat there with them, the thought occurred to me that the Queen, behind all her warm goodwill, must have harboured not a little anxiety.

Townsend goes on to describe how the Queen Mother reacted when she was told how he and the Princess felt about each other:

Princess Margaret also told her mother, who listened with characteristic understanding. I imagine that Queen Elizabeth's immediate – and natural – reaction was "this simply cannot be". But thoughtful as ever for the feelings of others, for her daughter's above all and for mine as well, she did not hurt us by saying so. Without a sign that she felt angered or outraged – or, on the other, that she acquiesced – the Queen Mother was never anything but considerate in her attitude to me.

The time had now come, Townsend thought, for him to talk about the situation to the Queen's Private Secretary, Sir Alan ("Tommy") Lascelles.

I entered his sombre but spacious office. When, first, Air Chief Marshal "Peter" Portal, then the King, had initiated me to my job of equerry, both had received me, at my own level, standing. Now that I was on the point of leaving it, Tommy remained seated, regarding me darkly while I stood before him and told him, very quietly, the facts: Princess Margaret and I were in love. Visibly shaken, all that Tommy could say was: "You must be either mad or bad." I confess that I had hoped for a more helpful reaction.

Townsend told Lascelles that he was quite ready to face the immediate consequences and leave the Queen's household. "Lascelles wanted more – to banish me, forthwith, abroad." But nothing was done: the situation was kept secret. Townsend afterwards recorded that if he had been told what foreign newspapers were saying at the time he would have left his employment at once. But, he said, though foreign newspapers were reporting rumours of the situation between him and the Princess, and though Lascelles and the Press Secretary to the Queen were aware of these, neither of them made these reports known to the Queen, nor did they tell Townsend about them. "Had they only taken me into their confidence and alerted me to the danger, I would have got out of the way fast, dutifully, for the sake of the Royal Family, and selfishly, for my own sake." But, he said, they did not. So when the Queen Mother asked him to stay on and continue his duties at Clarence House he did so.

Within the Palace nothing was said to anybody about the relationship between the Princess and the Group Captain. Lascelles would have had painful memories of what divorce proceedings had done in the events leading up to the Abdication crisis of 1936. He may have feared that if rumours of the Princess's love affair were to leak out at this time the preparations for the Coronation would be compromised. The mystical and religious significance of the event would be lost in a flood of stories in the newspapers about the Queen's sister wanting to marry a commoner employed in looking after her mother's household.

Lascelles was more concerned to have the problem concealed for the time being than he was to have it solved. He advised the Queen that under the Royal Marriages Act of 1772 Margaret was not free to marry without the Queen's permission until she was twenty-five – the Princess was then twenty-three. He also pointed out that since the Queen was Head of the Church of England, which did not recognise divorce, for innocent as well as guilty parties, she could not consent to the marriage without the agreement of the Cabinet. For Lascelles so to inform the Queen was natural. Yet, though he thought such a marriage should be prevented at all costs, and, as his subsequent actions show, though he was determined to do everything he could to stop it, at the time he did not say so to the Queen. When the Queen asked him if a marriage might be possible he either said "Yes" or refrained from saying "No". One explanation of this is that he may have thought that to rule out the possibility of marriage then and forever might have provoked the Princess into some precipitate action. This might give rise to public controversy, which in turn would ruin the prospects of a glorious Coronation. This he was determined to avoid. He might also have thought that to behave as though a marriage could take place later would give time for the Princess to grow out of what might be an infatuation. Whatever his motives he did not tell the Queen or anybody else at Court that the marriage would continue to be opposed. Many years later Princess Margaret said that if she had been given this information at the time she and Townsend would have parted.

According to Jock Colville whatever Lascelles said or did not say to the Queen at the time he took a somewhat different line with the Prime Minister. He visited the Prime Minister at his home in the country and with Colville present appraised Churchill of the situation. Such a marriage, Lascelles said, could not possibly take place. "The Prime Minister's first reaction after Lascelles had left," recorded Colville, "was to say that the course of true love must always be allowed to run smooth and that nothing must stand in the way of this handsome pair. However, Lady Churchill said that if he followed this line he would be making the same mistake that he made at the abdication." According to Colville she went further: "Winston, if you are going to behave like that again I shall leave this house and go and live in Brighton."

When Churchill had had some time to reflect on the problem, he acted swiftly. He called a meeting of the Cabinet, as a result of which the Cabinet made it known to the Queen that they could not approve a marriage between the Princess and the Group Captain. This was communicated to the Princess, but she was also told that when she reached the age of twenty-five she could reopen the subject. Nobody told the Princess, or, so far as we know, told the Queen, that the answer would have to be the same in 1955 as in 1953.

Townsend remained at his post. Neither the Queen, nor the Queen Mother, wanted him to leave, and Lascelles probably did not wish for him to make a departure which might arouse comment and question before the Coronation had taken place. According to some accounts, only Prince Philip faced the fact that a marriage would never take place; he advised Margaret and Townsend "to forget it". After the Coronation service in the Abbey had ended, while members of the royal family were standing around the entrance waiting for the coaches to take them back to Buckingham Palace, an American newspaper reporter observed Princess Margaret go up to Group Captain Townsend, and, as she stood talking to him, looking up into his face, raise her hand to his chest and brush a bit of fluff off his uniform. "Next day," wrote Townsend, "that charming little gesture made the headlines in the New York press." Eleven days later the British Sunday newspaper, the *People*, ran a story: "It is high time for the British public to be made aware of the fact that newspapers in Europe and America are openly asserting that the Princess is in love with a divorced man and that she wishes to marry him ... Every newspaper names the man as Group Captain Townsend." The *People* sought to cover itself by treating the foreign newspaper reports as unfounded and irresponsible speculation. "It is quite unthinkable that a royal princess, third in line of succession, should even contemplate marriage with a man who has been through the divorce courts." At this point Lascelles advised the Queen that Townsend should leave the country.

Several stories appeared in British newspapers over the next few days – including opinion polls urging the Princess to ignore "the stuffed shirts at the palace" and get married to the man of her choice. Princess Margaret and the Queen Mother then left the country for a previously planned visit to Rhodesia. The Princess and Townsend parted for the time being, expecting to see each other again when she returned on 17 July. While she was away Lascelles informed Townsend that the post of air attaché to the British Embassy was vacant at three capitals, and that he should take his pick of them and be out of the country by 15 July, before Margaret returned. Townsend chose Brussels, and left: "I had been with the Royal Family for nine years. Now I was being booted out." That, for the time being, was that.

Meanwhile, the Queen was confronted with a political and constitutional problem which was all the more difficult for her as a result of the leading members of her government wishing her and her secretaries to conceal it from the public: the fact that both her Prime Minister and her Foreign Secretary were seriously ill, were unable to discharge their duties, and that the country was being run by the Chancellor of the Exchequer and a secret committee without proper authority.

Two weeks after the Coronation, Churchill suffered a stroke. In the first few days it looked as though he would not recover from it. The Foreign Secretary, Eden, generally supposed to be his successor, was in a clinic in the United States recovering from an unsuccessful operation on his bile duct. He was expected to be out of action for several months. Butler, as the next senior minister in the government, took over the running of the country, assisted by Lord Salisbury, who was Leader of the Conservative Party in the House of Lords, with a seat in the Cabinet as Lord President of the Council.

What Mary Soames, Churchill's daughter, later described as a "conspiracy" was immediately organised. "After discussion with, and the collusion of, two Conservative press proprietors, Lord Beaverbrook, who owned the *Daily Express*, and Lord Camrose, who owned the *Daily Telegraph*, the Cabinet decided to withhold a full account of Churchill's condition, then believed to be mortal, and to state publicly only that he was over-fatigued and needed rest. Lascelles was told the truth, but it seems that he did not pass it on to the Queen, who in a letter to Churchill at the time said that she was sorry to hear he "had not been well" and that she hoped his illness was not "serious".

There was more to the "conspiracy" than the misrepresentation of Churchill's state of health. Lord Salisbury was a longstanding political ally and personal friend of Eden. With other Conservative leaders he wished to ensure that Eden and not Butler would be the next Prime Minister. This powerful group accordingly formed a plan: in the highly probable event of Churchill's death in order to keep Butler out Lord Salisbury would go to the Queen and ask her permission to form a caretaker government. As soon as Eden was well enough to accept the Queen's invitation to form a new government the caretaker government would resign.

Since Churchill soon rallied, and remained Prime Minister for another two years, there was no need to put this plan into effect. But the fact that it existed raised a grave constitutional issue. Had it been carried out, a young and untried Queen would have become accessory to a Conservative Party plot to deny the premiership to the acting leader of the majority in the House of Commons, and to make a member of the House of Lords the temporary Prime Minister. The Opposition would have opposed such expedients tooth and nail, and a political crisis might have ensued. The question arises: did the Queen know about the plot? If she did, she should not have acquiesced. If she did not, she was seriously misled by her Private Secretary. It could be said that to justify her prerogative to decide who should be Prime Minister she should have made more enquiries about what was going on.

As it happened Churchill made a remarkably swift recovery. The fact remains that for several months the country had had no authorised Prime Minister or Foreign Secretary. The day after the stroke Churchill was taken down to Chartwell. Forty years on, his daughter, Lady Soames, told the *Observer* (14 February 1993): "He was there for six weeks and somehow Christopher [Soames; her husband, later Lord Soames] and John Colville between them kept the machine turning over ..." Information about the stroke and the Prime Minister's incapacity was withheld from the country. On the face of it the Queen connived at this deception, and at an extraordinary flouting of the constitution.

The Commonwealth Coronation Tour, which began on 23 November was, as the name implies, intended to do for the countries which the Queen was to visit what the Coronation had done for the people of Britain. On the whole it succeeded. It was the last tour a British monarch made before demands for self-government and independence began to bring about a change in the climate of opinion in the Commonwealth countries. The tour lasted for several months, and in the course of it the Queen travelled more than 40,000 miles. Apart from spreading the Coronation experience throughout the countries of the Commonwealth the tour was intended to achieve three objectives: to carry out the late King's wish to thank in person the peoples of the Commonwealth for their support in the Second World War; to strengthen the political and social links between the United Kingdom and the Commonwealth countries at a time when these were being threatened by the movements for independence, republicanism, and withdrawal; to promote trade and financial interests between London and the Commonwealth capitals. The tour had a profound personal significance for the Queen. As was described earlier, her father had imbued her with a sense of the crucial importance of the Commonwealth not only to the United Kingdom but to the royal family. She saw the Commonwealth, especially the new Commonwealth, which George VI understood well, as the embodiment of her devotion to her father and her duty to her peoples. To have to make such a tour in his stead and so soon after his death was a moving and in some ways saddening experience.

To what extent the long and glamorous tour conveyed the three aspects of the monarchy to the Commonwealth countries – its mystique, its function and its film-star attraction – would have been difficult to assess even at the time. Its effects would have varied from one country to another. But the down-to-earth secular aspects of the preparations were certainly in evidence before the tour began. There were practical discussions between the British government and some of the Commonwealth governments about how the financial burden of this vast and unprecedented enterprise was to be shared. The new royal yacht, *Britannia*, in fact a small liner, was not ready in time for the opening stages of the tour, and it was necessary to charter the liner *Gothic*. The expense of maintaining a small royal household on board the vessels was much publicised. Some people were critical of the Queen being out of her own country for so long a period, and for being away from her small children. But on the whole the tour was accepted as worth while, and monarchists rejoiced in the good publicity it received and in the accounts of the Queen's success which came back to London from every place she visited.

The Queen opened seven Commonwealth parliaments. The keynote of her addresses to her Commonwealth peoples was in her most-quoted remark:

> In the wider sphere of world affairs the British Commonwealth and Empire have shown to the world that the strongest bonds of all are those which are recorded, not in documents, but in the hearts of the people who share the same beliefs ... bonds of human friendship and unity which come from sharing the same heritage and aspirations and the same loyalty.

The tour ended on 15 May 1954, at Westminster Pier. Churchill had gone out into the Thames Estuary to board *Britannia* and sail back to shore with the Queen. At a lunch given for her by the City of London at the Mansion House she said:

> I set out to learn more of the peoples and countries over which I have been called to reign, and to try to bring them the personal reality of the monarchy. The structure and framework of the monarchy could easily stand out as an archaic and meaningless survival. We have received visible and audible proof that it is living in the hearts of the people.

It could be said that this was the peak of the Queen's reign: after the darkness of her father's death, a glamorous and spectacular Coronation of unprecedented colour and publicity, came a vast tour of the countries of the Commonwealth which by traditional standards had been a brilliant success. The mystique of the monarchy, given an audience as never before through the power of the media, radiated through the Western world as it never had before and never would again.

The Queen returned to a realm now restless with the symptoms of a country having to make a long-term adjustment to the pressures of the post-war world. The main problem was to export enough to pay for essential imports of food and raw materials, when traditional markets overseas had been lost in hitherto backward countries, now able to manufacture and sell their own products. Britain was suffering increasingly from industrial unrest – low productivity, absenteeism and strikes. The Queen had not come home to a happy country, or a country to which the future seemed to beckon.

Her Prime Minister had no intention of resigning in favour of a younger man. He was now eighty-three, and had been in the House of Commons for fifty-three years. Eden was becoming more and more frustrated by the old man's determination to hang on to power. Many Conservative MPs felt that Churchill was not only too ill and too old to remain in charge, but that he had been out of touch with modern problems for many years, and that the public knew this. Many Conservatives believed that if a more contemporary figure than Churchill had led the party into the 1945 election it would have won. Others believed that if he had not been leader in the 1951 election the Conservatives would have won by a much larger majority. It was widely known that Churchill now did not bother to read papers on subjects which he did not find interesting, a category which included the key issues of domestic policy – industrial strife, trade, finance and production. His mind was fixed on the restoration of Britain's pre-war position in the international balance of power, which he was set on obtaining by means of a grand summit conference which the United States and the Soviet Union would attend and over which he would preside. To this end, which both the American State Department and the British Foreign Office opposed, he wanted stability on the domestic front. He instructed his Minister for Labour, Sir Walter Monckton, never to allow a dispute between workers and employers to erupt in a strike; before that point was reached he must meet the strikers' demands and get them back to work as soon as possible.

Early in 1953 there was a concerted movement to try and persuade

Churchill to announce that he would resign immediately after the Coronation. He did not commit himself, and when the Coronation had come and gone the renewal of attempts to speed his departure were forestalled by his stroke. As soon as he had recovered he announced that it was his duty to remain at his post until the Queen had finished her Commonwealth tour and had returned to the United Kingdom. Throughout 1954 and early 1955 the state of his health worried all who knew about it, among them being the Queen: Colville was in the closest touch with Lascelles. Colville recorded in his diary that Churchill was becoming "less reconciled to giving up office" and complained that "he was to be hounded out of office merely because his second-in-command wanted the job". Meanwhile the old man was "ageing month by month" and becoming increasingly "reluctant to read papers". It was becoming "an effort to sign letters and a positive condescension to read Foreign Office telegrams". Colville predicted that before Churchill agreed to make way for Eden there loomed the prospect of "a terrible and painful struggle". For the young and inexperienced Queen, brought up to revere Churchill as her country's saviour, the spectacle of this old man now part senile, stubbornly standing in the way of the firm and forceful leadership the country clearly needed, must have been a harrowing sight and a disturbing problem.

It is a pity that in the first few formative years of her reign the Queen did not find herself working with a Prime Minister much younger than Churchill, more in touch with public opinion, less archaic and romantic, more in tune with the modern world, much more knowledgeable about the social and economic problems of the day, and not only more aware of the profound changes the Commonwealth would have to experience to survive but equipped psychologically as well as by knowledge to direct them instead of stubbornly resisting them. The extent to which Churchill the fanciful old man attempted to maintain out-of-date notions in the young Queen's head we shall never know. But we do know that he tried to impose the burdens of the worn-out past on other people.

Early in the new reign Churchill had said to Colville about the Queen: "I don't know her. She's a mere child. I knew the King so well." Colville, who had been Private Secretary to her from 1947 to 1949, responded: "You will find her very much the reverse of being a child." Churchill, according to Colville, soon abandoned his view of the Queen as "a mere child". After his first audiences with her he would return to Downing Street and greet Colville with "what a very attractive and intelligent young woman!" They got on very well, though in the early days the Queen confessed to being frightened of him, so gigantic a hero had he seemed to her as a child in the depths of the war.

It was not long before she felt at ease with him. She had learned about her father's little game with members of the Cabinet, described among others by Herbert Morrison:

> On occasion [The King] enjoyed trying to trip up his ministers by asking about some detail of which he had good knowledge but of which they might be ignorant despite the fact that it affected their office ... I got into the habit of checking up details of such people and matters as I surmised might be the subjects of this friendly contest of knowledge.

The King always enjoyed telling his wife and daughters when he thought he had scored off one of his ministers. So when she became Queen, Elizabeth was familiar with these ploys. Colville relates that before one audience he made a point of advising Churchill to study an important telegram that had just reached the Foreign Office from the British Ambassador in Baghdad. Churchill neglected this advice. During the audience the Queen raised some of the points made in the Baghdad telegram. Churchill did his best to conceal the fact that he had not read the telegram, but left the Palace with the feeling that his responses to her questions had not impressed the Queen. When he got back to Downing Street he took Colville to task: "You should have made me read it." According to Colville, Churchill's audiences with the Queen got longer and longer, and his accounts of what had transpired at them shorter and shorter. Sometimes he would come back to Downing Street and say nothing about what had passed, and if Colville ventured to enquire into what they had talked about might reply, vaguely, "Oh – racing."

Pressures for Churchill to resign mounted throughout the summer of 1954. He still talked of little but restoring Britain's rightful place alongside the other two great powers, and doggedly pursued the idea of a summit conference which would guarantee the long-term stability of the international order. A general election would almost certainly take place in the first half of 1955. Several Conservative leaders, including Butler and Macmillan, suspected that Churchill had made up his mind not to step down much before that election. Some believed that he intended to stay on, and lead the party into it. Either prospect, the party leaders thought, could be very damaging to the Party's chances of winning.

Eden was aware that Butler, several years younger than himself, could afford to wait to become leader of the Party whereas he himself could not. He decided to force the issue. Churchill agreed to give up the leadership in April 1955.

On the eve of the announcement of his resignation Churchill gave a grand party for the Queen at Downing Street. In his last speech before her as Prime Minister he presented himself as a devoted and aged servant of the monarchy, born half-way through the reign of the Queen's great-great-grandmother, and growing up in the great days of her Empire. He had fought as a subaltern in the last charge ever made by British cavalry. He had served the present Queen's grandfather in the Cabinet during the First World War, and he had been her father's Prime Minister in the Second. Now he had come to "the wise and kindly way of life of which Your Majesty is the young and gleaming champion". When all the guests had gone home, Colville relates:

> I went up with Winston to his bedroom. He sat on his bed, still wearing his Garter, Order of Merit and knee-breeches. For several minutes he did not speak and I, imagining that he was sadly contemplating that this was his last night at Downing Street, was silent. Then suddenly he stared at me and said with vehemence: "I don't believe Anthony can do it." His prophecies have often tended to be borne out by events.

The relationship between Churchill and the Queen was a warm one. A letter she wrote to him early in her reign illustrates the human relation side of it, and, also, shows that the Queen could function as an informal non-political support system if a Prime Minister wishes her to. Martin Gilbert provides some examples of this in his biography of Churchill. "On December 27 Churchill received a hand-written letter from the Queen who was at Sandringham, thanking him for the 'beautifully bound' copy of Volume IV of his War Memoirs. She also congratulated him on the success of his horse Pol Roger at Kempton Park on the previous day, and hoped that after his visit to the US he would have a 'peaceful time in the sun' in Jamaica. The Queen ended her letter with best wishes for the New Year, 'which I think will see us surmount many of our difficulties successfully'."

In his correspondence with the Queen Churchill followed Disraeli's advice: he laid on the flattery with a trowel. But his admiration for her was clear and unfeigned: "Today I have the belief that the New Year starts well and good hopes that its end may be better still. If this should prove true it will be largely due to the sparkle, youth and unity which the amazing exertion of your majesty and the Duke are making for the sake of us world-wide ... My only misgiving is lest too much be drawn from You by the love and admiration of your subjects in so many lands."

The Queen reciprocated. On his resignation she wrote to him as follows:

It would be useless to pretend that either he [Eden] or any of those successors who may one day follow him in office will ever, for me, be able to hold the place of my first Prime Minister, to whom both my husband and I owe so much and for whose wise guidance during the early years of my reign I shall always be so profoundly grateful ... you have had to face the cold war and with its threats which are more awe inspiring than any you have had to contend with before, in war or peace ... For my part I know that in losing my constitutional adviser I gain a wise counsellor to whom I shall not look in vain for help and support in the days which lie ahead. May there be many of them.

In his reply, Churchill again stressed how important he felt the Queen had been to him:

I deem myself extremely fortunate to have been Your Majesty's adviser in the first years of what, I pray, may be a long and glorious epoch in our history. I have tried throughout to keep Your Majesty squarely confronted with the grave and complex problems of our time. Very soon after taking office as First Minister I realised the comprehension with which Your Majesty entered upon the august duties of a modern sovereign and the store of knowledge which had already been gathered by an upbringing both wise and lively. This enabled Your Majesty to understand as it seemed by instinct the relationships and balances of the British Constitution so deeply cherished by the mass of the nation and by the strongest and most stable forces in it. I became conscious of the Royal service as well as rule, and indeed to rule by serving. I felt the impact of a new personality on our unfolding history. Our Island no longer holds the same authority or power that it did in the days of Queen Victoria. A vast world towers up around it and after all our victories we could not claim the rank we hold were it not for the respect for our character and good sense and the general admiration not untinged by envy for our institutions and way of life. All this has already grown stronger and more solidly founded during the opening years of the present Reign, and I regard it as the direct mark of God's favour we have ever received in my long life that the whole structure of our new found Commonwealth has been linked and illuminated by a sparkling presence at its summit.

These letters, quoted from Martin Gilbert's monumental biography of Churchill, reveal a relationship between monarch and Prime Minister to be compared only with the relationship between Victoria and Lord Melbourne.

On the resignation of Churchill the Queen used her prerogative in deciding who would become the next Prime Minister. There has been some controversy about it. Most people at the time thought that she would invite Eden, and would do so on the advice of the outgoing Prime Minister. She did indeed invite Eden, but not on the advice of Churchill. According to Colville, she got no advice from Churchill on the subject, since he believed it was not constitutionally correct for the outgoing Prime Minister to mention a successor unless the monarch asked him to, and the Queen did not ask him to. Colville adds that Eden's name was not mentioned at the final audience.

At the time both Butler and Macmillan thought that they rather than Eden might be sent for. It is highly probable that the Queen chose Eden on the basis of information collected by the whips. They would almost certainly, and by a substantial margin, have favoured Eden. Their views would have been conveyed by Salisbury and others to the Queen's Private Secretary. The monarch is free to consult anybody he or she likes about the succession, and is free to use the prerogative as to who it is to be. The Queen appointed Eden.

Eden called an election for 26 May, and won it with a majority of fifty-eight seats. His eighteen months as Prime Minister were not an easy time for the Queen. At the time of the election a dock strike was in progress and two days later a railway strike was to begin. On 31 May Eden asked the Queen to proclaim a State of Emergency. A special meeting of the Privy Council was held at Balmoral, and the Queen signed the Proclamation. Eden announced his concern in a BBC broadcast: "I am not going to leave you in any doubt as to the deadly seriousness of what is happening to our country." Behind closed doors Conservative leaders put the blame for industrial unrest on that laxity towards the militant unions which Churchill had imposed on the Ministry of Labour so that he could pursue his foreign policy uninterrupted.

The strikes ended, but the prospect of trouble with the unions increased. The cost of living was rising and the unions were demanding higher wages. Chronic inflation had begun, and Eden declared that the first priority of the government must be to contain it. Feeling grew that problems of trade, industrial production, the balance of payments and the increasing power of the trade unions, were now the main problems the country had to face, and that the Eden government seemed unable to cope with them. In the summer of 1955 the mood of the nation was restless.

On 21 August Princess Margaret would reach the age of twenty-five, at which she would be free to marry without the Queen's permission. For the past two years there had been many photographs of her in the newspapers, creating an impression of her as more a popular film star than a member of the royal family. She was often photographed at smart nightclubs in the company of eligible young men, and there was speculation that she might marry one or another of them. But no newspaper took its eye from what might happen when she became twenty-five.

The general opinion seemed to be that she and Townsend would be reunited. His divorce was written and spoken about as though it were no bar. The Prime Minister and two senior members of the Cabinet had been through the divorce courts. Nobody with any authority in the matter had spoken publicly against the prospect of a marriage. Public opinion seemed in favour of it. Two days before Margaret's birthday the *Daily Mirror* carried the banner headline: "Come On, Margaret! Please Make Up Your Mind."

Two months went by. Speculation in the popular newspapers

mounted. Townsend returned to London from Brussels on 12 October. He stayed with friends of Princess Margaret, the Abergavennys', in Lowndes Square, within walking distance of Clarence House, to which the following day Princess Margaret returned with her mother from Balmoral. Townsend, followed everywhere by newspapermen, then moved to the house of the Lycett family in Berkshire. Mrs Lycett was a cousin of the Queen. Princess Margaret was invited to the Lycetts' for the weekend. To judge by the newspaper stories it seemed that the whole nation was asking only one question: when would the engagement be announced? Most people, according to the newspapers, were all in favour of a marriage.

The Queen was still at Balmoral. Eden flew to see her. He told her that the Cabinet would not approve of the marriage. If consent for it were given, some members of the Cabinet would resign, including Lord Salisbury. The key issue was the relation of the royal family to the Church of England. The Church did not recognise divorce. The royal family, at the head of the Church, could not recognise divorce. If Margaret married Townsend she could not remain a full member of the royal family: she would have to give up her right to succeed to the throne, and lose her income from the Civil List. She would have behaved in a way which cut across the royal family's obligation to the Church of England.

A leading article in *The Times* opposed the marriage but on different grounds. The central issue, said *The Times*, was not constitutional or theological but social: the Queen was a symbol throughout the Commonwealth of the ideal of family life; millions of citizens of the Commonwealth would not regard a marriage between Townsend and Margaret as acceptable. This view was attacked by the *Daily Mirror*.

Townsend met the Princess at 4 p.m. the day the article in *The Times* appeared. According to his autobiography before the meeting took place he drafted a statement for the Princess to make announcing that there was no question of a marriage taking place. When he met the Princess at Clarence House "I gave her the rough piece of paper and she read. Then she looked at me and very quietly, too, said, 'That is exactly how I feel.'"

A few days later Margaret went to see the Archbishop. There are some accounts which agree that she said something like this to him, "Put your books away, Archbishop. I have come to give you some information, not to ask for it," and then told him that she was not going to marry Townsend. In 1959 the Archbishop gave the author a different version of what had happened. "The Princess came to me as her spiritual advisor and I told her what the position was. She went away and made up her own mind as to what she would do."

Margaret published a statement which read:

I would like it to be known that I have decided not to marry Group Captain Townsend. I have been aware that, subject to my renouncing my rights of succession, it might have been possible for me to contract a civil marriage. But, mindful of the Church's teaching that Christian marriage is indissoluble, and conscious of my duty to the Commonwealth, I have resolved to put these considerations before others ...

In this decision and the events that led up to it can be seen, again, the growing conflict between what was required by the mysticians of the monarchy and what was advocated by its modernists, the difference in approach between the traditionalists and the radicals. *The Times* saw the situation as one in which the Princess could do one of two things, give up the man she loved and preserve the place the royal family held in the life of the nation – and in the Commonwealth – or. marry him and damage it. The *Guardian* said that the course she had taken

will be regarded by the masses of the people as unnecessary and perhaps a great waste. In the long run, it will not redound to the credit or influence of those who have been most persistent in denying the princess the same liberty as is enjoyed by the rest of her fellow citizens.

The Princess Margaret/Townsend episode was over. Once again the Group Captain left London for Brussels, but this time never again to be the subject of speculation on the part of the British newspapers.

But the effects of the episode were ineradicable. Once again a leading member of the royal family had wanted to have a love life which the man and woman in the street were free to have but which members of the royal family were not. Members of the royal family could not have things both ways. Princess Margaret recognised this, and decided which way she wanted. But the fact that she had had to make the decision heightened the public's appreciation of the fact that such a decision had to be made – and conceivably could have gone the other way.

7

Suez crisis. Some criticisms of the Queen. Her sister marries 1956–60

THE YEAR 1956 OPENED with strikes, low productivity, and acceleration in the rise of the cost of living. There was an atmosphere of unease and frustration. Only six months after the Eden administration had come to power its standing was very low. Many people were wondering how Eden, most of whose long experience in politics had been confined to foreign affairs, would cope with the burden of leadership at a time when the country's most pressing problems were domestic. Doubts about whether he was physically fit enough to carry out his responsibilities were voiced in public and in private. Many members of his own party regretted that Butler, with great experience on the home front, and expertise in economic affairs, had not succeeded Churchill. At the end of the first week in January, the Prime Minister felt compelled to take the unusual step of denying a rumour that he intended to resign in the course of the next few months.

In January the influential Conservative *Daily Telegraph* published an editorial article on its leader page expressing deep misgivings about the government's management of the nation's affairs and declaring the urgent need for "the firm smack of government". Delivered so soon after the Conservatives had won the general election this article was a severe blow to Eden's position. No longer was there talk of the New Elizabethan Age of which so much had been expected only three years previously.

The Queen and Prince Philip were about to set out on a three-week tour of Nigeria, the largest of the remaining British colonies, the largest African territory in the Commonwealth, and the leader in Britain's African trade. Nigeria was demanding independence, though so far was not threatening to leave the Commonwealth. As the date for independence approached tensions mounted between the different tribes and religious communities within the territory. Though few people foresaw the degree of violence and bloodshed which would erupt in Nigeria four years later, it was clear to all that the three regions into which the country was divided would be in conflict with each other as soon as the British regime had come to an end. The Queen's visit, it was hoped, might do something in the meantime to calm the country, mute internal rivalries, and get independent Nigeria off to the best possible start.

The Queen did her best. Her time in Nigeria was packed with engagements in every significant part of the regions. Whenever she stopped, she spoke, the theme being the same, best expressed in her plea for understanding and toleration, which were necessary "not only in religious matters but also towards those whose views and traditions differ. It is by this spirit of understanding that the people of various races and tribes will be brought together." The tour was given great coverage, especially by the now rapidly expanding television services. Later tours were to be more extensive, but none was to seem as colourful as this one. The Nigerian tour was the last in which the monarch appeared as the Head of an Empire, rather than of a Commonwealth, and in which the image of the monarch recalled the great days of Queen Victoria.

Before six months had passed Empire and Commonwealth were in the throes of the Suez Crisis. General Gamal Abdel Nasser, dictator of Egypt since his coup in 1952, had counted on British and American aid to complete the building of the Aswan Dam, essential to the economic development of his country. When the Americans decided not to give it to him, he nationalised the Suez Canal, dispossessing the Anglo-French company which had managed it by virtue of the international treaty of 1924, and taking it into Egyptian ownership. This flagrant violation of international law immediately antagonised opinion in the West. Eden had long believed that Nasser was a threat to peace in the Middle East, and had made up his mind that he should be "toppled". When Nasser announced the nationalisation of the canal on 26 July, Eden denounced his coup as an act of aggression and compared him to Hitler. In the early days of the crisis, the leader of the Labour Party, Hugh Gaitskell, used much the same language about Nasser and took a similar position.

The French government was equally concerned about the threat of Nasser's rise to power to Western interests in the Middle East – especially oil. The Israeli government were even more alarmed: for them, Nasser, now the leader of the Arab States, was a threat to the existence of Israel. They, too, wanted Nasser toppled. Out of the interests of these three powers developed the "collusion" which led to the plot to destroy Nasser's government. The plan was simple: Israel, claiming the right to self-defence, would launch a pre-emptive air strike against Egyptian airbases. When Nasser retaliated, Israeli forces would cross the frontier and occupy the Canal area. Citing the 1924 treaty, which gave them the right to protect their legitimate interests in the canal area, British and French forces would move in under the pretext of separating the combatants. Once in, the three invaders would take care not to get out until Nasser, one way or another, had been neutralised or eliminated for good.

Eden's motives in participating in this plot are still debated. Some say that his analysis of the situation in the Middle East, and the course of action he consequently adopted, were a response to his fear that unless he did something spectacular and impressive, something which put him in the centre of the international limelight, his days as Prime Minister were numbered. Some say that he had always nostalgically looked back to the greatest period of his political life, in the late thirties, when he had resigned his post as Foreign Secretary as a protest, and a warning, against the attempts of the Prime Minister to appease Hitler and Mussolini by giving way to their territorial demands. Nasser gave him the chance to live that role again. Some say that he had become a mentally sick man, and that his judgement was already impaired.

On 2 August, Eden set in train a chain of events which were to create difficulties for the Queen in more ways than one. She was down near the Sussex coast, a guest of the Duke of Norfolk at Arundel Castle, where she was staying to attend the racing at nearby Goodwood. While she was sitting in the private box of the Duke of Richmond, waiting for the races to begin, an urgent message arrived from the Prime Minister. Eden said that he wished to inform the House of Commons later that afternoon that in view of the dangerous situation in the Middle East the Queen had signed a Proclamation which authorised him to call up reservists. He could not make that statement to the House unless the Proclamation had been signed.

The Queen's behaviour at that point is not easy to explain. She did not sign the Proclamation – though she read it – but she had a telephone message conveyed to the Prime Minister which assured him that she would sign it if he wished. The Prime Minister consequently informed the House later that day that he had the Proclamation in his hands, and he proceeded to read it out. A special meeting of the Privy Council was held at Arundel the following day, and the Queen signed the Proclamation.

Constitutionally the Queen could not have refused to sign the Proclamation if her Prime Minister asked her to, but she was equally constitutionally entitled before signing it to ask questions about what the Prime Minister intended to do about the Middle East, and, having been consulted, to encourage or to warn. Did she refrain from signing the day before because before doing so she wanted to have the opportunity of using that prerogative? Did she use it the following day? If so, with whom and how? Eden was not present at Arundel. Did she talk with him on the telephone? The documents dealing with this peculiar episode are still on the secret list.

Another question which continues to be asked is: how much was the Queen told about the preparations for the invasion of Suez? According to Eden she was kept "fully informed" about what was going on. Eden did not disclose what the information consisted of. According to Philip Ziegler, Mountbatten's biographer, the Queen knew about the preparations for Suez, but constitutionally was powerless to do anything about it. We know that the Americans were suspicious of Eden's intentions, and that the United States Secretary of State, John Foster Dulles, between whom and Eden there was no love lost, complained that Eden was "deliberately keeping us in the dark". Did the Queen ask Eden if the Americans, Britain's loyal allies, were being kept properly informed? And if she did, what was his answer? It would be interesting to know if the Queen had any communication on the subject with Lord Mountbatten, who at the time was acting Chairman of the Chiefs of Staff Committee. Mountbatten was opposed to the Suez venture from the start. She could not discuss the situation with Prince Philip: on 15 October he had left the country on a five-month tour of the Commonwealth. Did Mountbatten tell the Queen that he was opposed to the Suez project? If so did the Queen ignore him, and refrain from using the prerogative to be consulted and to warn? Did the Prime Minister keep the monarch ignorant of the facts of the situation; or knowing them did the monarch choose to support a Prime Minister who used her acquiescence to lead the country into a disaster? What is so far known about this episode suggests that in some situations the use of the prerogative by the sovereign, manipulated by the Prime Minister, could be a danger to the safety of the realm. If the Commons, or the Cabinet, or the Queen had known what the Prime Minister knew and intended about the preparations for the Suez Operation it is most unlikely that they would have supported the use of the prerogative in the calling up and use of the armed forces. This could have led to a constitutional crisis. One way of avoiding such a crisis was to keep the monarch in the dark.

The Suez crisis erupted into international war. Hostilities began with French and Israeli planes attacking Egyptian airfields. The Egyptians retaliated by bombing land and sea communications on Israeli territory. On 29 October Israeli tanks crossed the Egyptian frontier. As planned in advance, but in what was now claimed as action to separate the contestants, British planes began to bomb airfields in the Canal area, preparatory to landing troops being brought by sea from Cyprus. The Americans were outraged. The United Nations demanded an immediate ceasefire. Eden and Selwyn Lloyd, his Foreign Secretary, who had represented him at all the secret meetings at which the plot had been worked out, wanted to continue the hostilities, but ordered a ceasefire when the Chancellor of the Exchequer, Harold Macmillan, warned them that the Americans in order to coerce Britain into halting the invasion had begun a run on the pound which if allowed to continue would land Britain in a financial disaster.

Strong and circumstantial rumours that Eden had involved Britain in collusion now abounded, repeated in some sections of the press and confidently alleged by the Labour Opposition. Eden strenuously denied them. His stock fell. The country was torn with controversy. Seventy Conservative MPs dissociated themselves from the government. Some junior ministers resigned in protest. The position of the Queen in all this was much discussed. She was not only Queen of the United Kingdom but Head of the Commonwealth, and nearly every country in the Commonwealth denounced the Suez venture. On 19 November it was announced that Eden was suffering from strain and would fly to Jamaica for a rest. Butler took over the government. When Eden returned to London, on 14 December, opinion continued to harden against him. On 8 January he visited the Queen at Sandringham, and told her that his doctors had advised him to resign. The Queen accepted his resignation.

No documents are in the public domain concerning the Queen's role in the Suez crisis, but it is possible to speculate. The initial consideration for her would have been the reaction of the Commonwealth countries, especially of India, Pakistan and Canada. Once British troops had been sent into action she would have to have supported it, but knowing the feelings of the leading opinion-makers in the Commonwealth she would have had deep reservations about what was being done. It must have been a relief to her that Eden wished to resign. Nevertheless, she was generous with her sympathy. There had been considerably less flower and flattery in his communications to her than in Churchill's, but the relationship between Eden and her had generally been good. She wrote a supportive farewell to him: "Much has been said and written during the last week about your record in the House of Commons and as a statesman; I am only anxious that you should realise that that record, which has indeed been written in tempestuous times, is highly valued and will never be forgotten."

Eden's reply might be thought to throw further light on the role the Queen plays in her relationship with her Prime Ministers. He said he wanted

to try to express what my Sovereign's understanding and encouragement has meant at a time of exceptional ordeal. It is the bare truth to say that I looked forward to my weekly audience, knowing that I should receive from Your Majesty a wise and impartial reaction to events which was quite simply the voice of our land. Years ago Baldwin told me that the post of Prime Minister was the most lonely in the world. That may be true in respect of colleagues. That I have not found it so is due to Your Majesty's unfailing sympathy and understanding.

Eden did not advise her who his successor should be but recommended to her Private Secretary, Sir Michael Adeane, that a senior minister should be asked to obtain, unofficially, the views of the members of the Cabinet. It was decided that the informal soundings should be taken by Lord Salisbury and the Lord Chancellor, Lord Kilmuir. They did so, and reported that the choice of the Cabinet would be Macmillan. The Chief Whip also took soundings through his assistant whips of opinion among Conservative MPs. The result pointed in the same direction. The Queen, availing herself of her prerogative to consult anybody she liked about the succession, also consulted Winston Churchill, Lord Chandos and Lord Waverley. They favoured Macmillan. The Queen asked Macmillan to form a government, and he accepted.

The choice of Macmillan came as a great surprise to the general public. The majority of the newspapers had predicted Butler. There is no doubt that Butler had expected to be summoned. Many Conservative MPs, including several who had hoped to get Macmillan, believed that it would be Butler who would be invited to take over. At once there was a political storm, in which the Queen was involved. Taking it for granted that the Conservative Party in the House of Commons wanted Butler – they were wrong – the Labour Party protested that the Queen and the Constitution had been manipulated to produce a Prime Minister who was the democratic choice neither of elected Conservative MPs nor of the people. In the words of the *Daily Mirror*:

At the age of thirty, after less than five years on the Throne, the Queen had to decide who was going to be the next prime minister. And she had to do this against a background of crisis, in a tense and perplexing political situation, at a time when she was deprived of the support of her husband. No wonder many Conservative MPs argue that it is wrong that the young Queen had to make the decision on such limited advice.

The *Daily Mirror*, like many other critics of the Queen at this stage, were not aware that she had been given much more information to go on than the views of the Lord Chancellor and Lord Salisbury. But what the *Daily Mirror* said was read by millions of people, who believed that not only had the Queen used her prerogative to select the wrong man but that it was wrong that she possessed such a prerogative in the first place.

Another aspect of the Queen's choice gave rise to criticism, some of it from members of the Conservative Party. Macmillan, though he made much of the fact that his grandfather had been a Highland crofter, was married to a sister of the Duke of Devonshire, Lady Dorothy. The mother of Lady Dorothy, the Dowager Duchess of Devonshire, was a veteran courtier. She had been a senior and trusted figure in court circles for many years, and currently held the post of the Queen's Mistress of the Robes. Lady Dorothy Macmillan's sister was married to Lord Salisbury, who was a close friend of the Queen Mother. For those who were so inclined to do so it was not hard to represent the selection of Macmillan as Prime Minister as another victory for the Tory aristocracy over the progressive middle class Conservatives such as R. A. Butler.

Prince Philip did not arrive back in Britain until well after the Suez crisis was over. He had been out of the country for nearly five months. Whatever success he may have had in promoting good relations with various countries of the Commonwealth his absence, through no fault of his own, had given rise to newspaper stories which did not enhance the standing of the royal family. The lengthy tour had come about as a result of an invitation he received in early 1956 from the organisers of the Olympic Games which were to be held in Australia in November of that year. Out of this came the idea of a longer trip on board the *Britannia* in which as well as visiting Australia the Prince would call in at various places in that quarter of the globe which had previously been thought too out of the way and not important enough to merit a royal visit, such as the Seychelles, Ceylon, Malaya, Papua and New Guinea, the Falklands and Antarctica, the return section of the trip ending at Gibraltar. It was quite clear that the idea for the long trip came from the Prince. Questions were asked as to whether it was justified – such a lengthy trip would cost a great deal of money – and on what political, diplomatic or constitutional basis the trip could be explained. But nobody who was in a position to do so put any obstacle in its way. On 15 October the Queen went to Heathrow to send the Duke on his way to join *Britannia* at Mombasa.

It was not long before newspaper reports about the progress of the Duke's trip began to raise some eyebrows. Some of the articles created the impression of an absentee Prince reverting to a bachelor life with no responsibilities and having a good time while his dutiful wife with all the cares of the kingdom on her shoulders worked grimly away at home – alone. A series of articles appeared in the *Daily Express* entitled "The Woman of the World with an Absent Husband". Some newspapers reproduced earlier gossip about the Prince's private life at home in Britain – parties for fun-minded people at the home of his friend Baron, then the court photographer, for example, and his membership of the Thursday Club at which he and a few congenial companions would foregather to relax, have fun, and generally let their hair down. He had always, the stories implied, been a bit of a lad, never averse to getting out of the Palace for a night out, ever ready for festivity, and had always had an eye for the girls. Meanwhile, there were references to speculation in American and Continental newspapers that the marriage of the Queen and the Prince was in troubled waters.

At the beginning of 1957, Mrs Eileen Parker, the wife of Commander Mike Parker, the Duke's Private Secretary, aboard the *Britannia* with him, decided that she would start proceedings to get a separation from her husband as a step to obtaining a divorce. Before she did so, she went to see the press secretary at the Palace, Commander Colville, and told him of her intention. She explained that for years she and her family had suffered from Commander Parker's long absences from home on duty with the Prince. She had now learned that her husband had become involved with another woman, and therefore wanted to end the marriage.

Colville was horrified. Eden had just resigned. The country was in the middle of a political crisis. The Queen had enough on her hands. He urged Mrs Parker to change her mind, and, when she refused, begged her to stay her hand. To this she agreed. She would do nothing until her husband was back in Britain. Colville's respite was short-lived. The *Sunday Pictorial* heard about the Parker story, and reported it.

American and Continental newspapers immediately drew parallels between the situation of Mrs Parker and the situation of the Queen. Mrs Parker was miserable and lonely: the marriage had failed. The Queen must be miserable and lonely; that marriage had failed too. Parker had been seeing women other than his wife; Prince Philip had been seeing other women too. The old stories about him were given a new lease of life.

As soon as the news that he was being sued for divorce reached

Parker he announced his resignation from the royal service. He meant well, but the news only added to news and speculation. There were hints that Parker's resignation was designed to draw attention from the situation between the Duke and the Queen. The Queen had two children, but there had been no additions to the family: did this mean that the love-match had long since come to an end? Little notice was paid to the fact that the illness of the Queen's father, his funeral, her Coronation, her extensive travels, had left her with little time to have more babies.

It was soon clear that as well as concern about the personal life of the Queen there were misgivings about the role and achievement of the monarchy. Gone were the hopes and aspirations of 1953. "Is the Elizabethan Age Going To Be A Flop?" demanded the *Daily Mirror*. It renewed the criticisms of the Queen's advisers which it had made during the discussion of whether the Coronation ceremony should be televised or not, and those it had made later when there was talk of Princess Margaret marrying Peter Townsend. "The Circle around the throne is aristocratic, as insular and – there is no other word for it – as toffee-nosed as it has ever been." The *Mirror*'s competitor, the *Daily Express*, weighed in: the royal family were philistines: "none of them patronise the arts or opera". These, and other, newspapers complained about the amount of money which the royals spent, and had spent on them; there was more criticism of the Duke of Edinburgh's cruise; it was "useless", "unnecessary", a "luxury" and had cost the nation "at least two million pounds".

In this climate of opinion various groups began to voice criticisms about the royals. The Lord's Day Observance Society complained about the Queen holding meetings with political leaders on the Sabbath, then going off to watch her husband play polo. The League Against Cruel Sports protested against the Duke's shooting and the Queen's deerstalking.

It was unfortunate that at a time when this climate of criticism was growing the British Foreign Office published those official documents mentioned in an earlier chapter which described the Duke of Windsor's relations with Nazi agents in Portugal in 1940. The royal family had viewed the prospect of these disclosures with apprehension. As it turned out, public reaction to the publication of the documents was comparatively mild. The Duke said little about the documents that appeared, issuing a statement that attempts had been made to persuade him to disobey the British government's instruction that he proceed to the Bahamas as Governor but that "at no time did I entertain any thought of complying with such a suggestion which I treated with the contempt that it deserved". He dismissed the documents as "in part complete fabrications and in part gross distortions of the truth". The Foreign Office supported him: the Duke had "never wavered in his loyalty to the British cause". The Duke's meticulous biographer, Philip Ziegler, has recorded:

> The papers show that the Duke felt the war could and should have been avoided, that he was defeatist about the prospects of victory in 1940 and 1941, that he preached the virtues of a negotiated peace. He had been indiscreet and extravagant enough in what he said to give the Germans some grounds for believing that he might be ready to play an active part in securing such a peace and returning to the throne after it had been negotiated. That is bad enough. What they do not show, and cannot show since no evidence exists, is that the Duke would ever have contemplated accepting such an invitation if it had been issued.

If the Queen had deduced from the sensible behaviour of the Duke on the occasion of the publication of the 1940 documents that he had come to terms with the ranklings and recriminations with which he had plagued the royal family in the past she would have been wrong. The Duke had heard that Sir John Wheeler-Bennett had now completed his official life of King George VI, commissioned by the Queen, and was about to publish it. He wrote to Sir John, asking if he could see the manuscript, since obviously there would be much about himself in the book, and since he had been interviewed by Wheeler-Bennett when he was in the course of researching it. The Duke knew that Wheeler-Bennett would have relied greatly on Lascelles for material, and feared that Lascelles would have done his best to see that "I am shown in as bad a light as possible". Wheeler-Bennett told the Duke that he was not free to show the book to anybody unless he had the Queen's permission to do so. The Duke thereupon addressed himself to the Queen. She promised that he could see the book when it had arrived at the proof stage. She kept her word. The Duke read the book, made a few tiny corrections, and left it at that. But the incident brought back to the Queen unhappy memories of the anguish the Duke had caused her parents in the past.

Early in the year arrangements were made for the Queen to make an official visit to Canada and the United States. The purpose of the visit was to try and heal the breach which had been opened up between Britain and the United States as a result of the Suez crisis. The feeling in America was that the Eden government had behaved abominably in the first place by launching the invasion, an act of aggression which flouted the principles of the United Nations, and in the second place by deliberately keeping the American government in the dark about it. The other purpose of the visit was to try and enhance trade links with the Americans, particularly tourism, assistance from which the British economy was badly in need.

It was unfortunate that the American visit took place at a time when the royal family and the monarchy, having been roughly treated by the British press over Philip's absenteeism and the Queen's deerstalking, came in for criticism from another quarter. Up until now the monarchy had continued to retain some of the radiance it had acquired in the year of the Coronation. Now much of this was wearing off. Malcolm Muggeridge, journalist, broadcaster and a future editor of *Punch*, wrote an article for the *New Statesman*, entitled "The Royal Soap Opera". This article was widely regarded as an attack upon the Queen. Many of the things Muggeridge said were sensible perceptions but expressed in exaggerated not to say provocative language, the tone of the article as much as its content offending many loyal monarchists.

Muggeridge claimed that most of the criticism of his article came from people who had not read or had mis-read what he had written, and that he was not criticising the Queen but simply pointing out that the monarchy had now taken the place of religion in the minds of the masses. Certainly, the most anti-monarchical feature of the article was its title, and Muggeridge was complaining not about the monarchy but of the mentality of those who drooled over it. The extent and virulence of the public reaction to the article is much more interesting than anything said in it. Muggeridge was subjected to much obloquy, indignity and some persecution. Foul communications reached him through the mail and by hand via his letter-box. His elegant flat was broken into and vandalised, and there was a move to have him expelled from his distinguished London club. More serious was the banning of Muggeridge by the

The christening of Princess Elizabeth: a group showing (*standing, l to r*) the Duke of Connaught, King George V, the Duke of York (later King George VI), the Earl of Strathmore; (*seated, l to r*) Lady Elphinstone, Queen Mary, the Duchess of York (later Queen Elizabeth) with the baby Princess, the Countess of Strathmore, the Princess Royal. 'It was a good match, a happy marriage. It was into this self-sufficient world that their first child, Elizabeth, was born and in which she grew up, the child of a dutiful and loving man, and a brave, unselfish and devoted woman. The life of the Queen to be was to reflect that breeding from the start.'

At the age of two. Winston Churchill encountered Elizabeth at this time, and wrote to his wife describing her as, 'a character. She has an air of authority and reflectiveness astonishing in an infant.'

At the age of eleven. Asked what she would like to do when she grew up, Elizabeth replied, 'Live the life of a country lady, with lots of horses and dogs.'

Her Uncle David, at the time of his accession to the throne as King Edward VIII. Had he remained on it she would probably not have become Queen.

Elizabeth, aged thirteen, and her parents with Lord Mountbatten and Prince Philip at the Royal Naval College, Dartmouth in 1939. 'There's a fair consensus that this was the day that romance first struck.'

The King and Queen inspecting bomb damage o Buckingham Palace, in 1940. The Queen aid, 'I am glad we've been bombed. It makes ie feel I can look the East End in the face.'

Elizabeth broadcasting to the Empire on the BBC's Children's Hour in 1940. 'At the end of her stint he called, "Come on, Margaret." Margaret said "Goodnight, children".'

Peter Townsend, the King's Equerry, and Princess Margaret during the royal tour of South Africa of 1947. 'The seeds of the fateful relationship between him and Princess Margaret were planted at this time.'

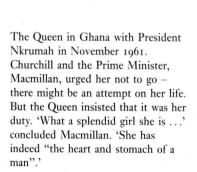

The Queen in Ghana with President Nkrumah in November 1961. Churchill and the Prime Minister, Macmillan, urged her not to go – there might be an attempt on her life. But the Queen insisted that it was her duty. 'What a splendid girl she is ...' concluded Macmillan. 'She has indeed "the heart and stomach of a man".'

The Queen immediately after her
Coronation in June 1953. Prince
Philip 'has loved her, revered her and
has supported her from the earliest
days of their marriage.'

The Queen on a 'walkabout' in
Australia. The term is a misnomer: it
was traditionally applied to the
wanderings of the aborigines who
wanted to get away from people.

The Prince of Wales being interviewed by the author in 1974 at Broadlands. 'A woman not only marries a man; she marries into a way of life, into a job ... She's got to have some knowledge of it, or she wouldn't have a clue whether she's going to like it, and if she didn't have a clue it would be risky for her, wouldn't it?'

When being interviewed by the author at Gatcombe in 1980, Princess Anne asked *him* a question, 'you've never met me before, but I daresay you've read about me in the newspapers. Am I like what you expected?'

The Duke of York with the Duchess aboard his ship, HMS *Campbeltown* in 1991.

Prince Edward, arriving for work at the stage door of the Palace Theatre in London when working as a production assistant for Andrew Lloyd Webber's Really Useful Company.

The Prince and Princess of Wales had been married only a year or so when this picture was taken during a visit to the Training Centre of the Cammell Laird Shipbuilders. (*Below*) Ten years later on the South Korean tour, which publicly failed to bring them together again.

The Queen at the scene of the destructive fire at Windsor Castle in 1992, the calamity which brought a ghastly end to her 'annus horribilis'.

And the future?

BBC. He was then a star of *Panorama*. The Director-General, Sir Ian Jacob, instructed the BBC television service to drop Muggeridge, personally reprimanded him, and when Muggeridge leaked this information to the press informed his colleagues: "This chap will never go on the air as long as I am Director-General", which turned out to be the case. The most interesting thing about the episode was that nobody seemed to be on the side of Muggeridge but everybody seemed to be on the side of the Queen.

It was much the same two years later when John Grigg, known as Lord Altrincham before he renounced his peerage, wrote an article about the Queen in his small circulation highbrow magazine, the *National and English Review*, of which he was proprietor and editor. Whereas Muggeridge, whose political opinions had varied a good deal, and by now did not carry any weight, was dismissed by many people as a publicity-seeker, John Grigg had been born and bred a Conservative, had remained a thoughtful and consistent Tory, albeit an independently minded one of liberal tendencies, and was taken seriously. Altrincham's criticisms were quoted extensively in the popular press, not because the popular press was impressed by them but because editors knew these remarks would bring a reaction from their readers. They had given little publicity to changes made at Buckingham Palace since the Queen had come to the throne – for instance to the fact that the Duke had persuaded the Queen to end the practice of presentation at court for the season's débutantes.

Unlike Muggeridge, Lord Altrincham made remarks which were taken to be criticisms of the Queen personally, though like Muggeridge he claimed that what he had written had been misunderstood or misreported, and in fact what he had criticised was the Queen's personal image.

Among his other complaints was the tone of the Queen's voice when she spoke in public, at the opening of Parliament or to deliver her Christmas Day message. Her speeches were "prim little sermons", and her style of speaking was "a pain in the neck". The words which were being put into her mouth were appropriate to "a priggish schoolgirl, captain of the hockey team, a prefect, and a recent candidate for Confirmation". Altrincham went on to say that the Queen's training for her job had been "woefully inadequate" since she had never been to school, had mixed with few of even her mother's upper-class world, and had hardly any first-hand knowledge of how the mass of the people lived. Altrincham said that many of the people around her at Buckingham Palace, not all, encouraged her to protect the image she did, the rationale for this, presumably, being that "the magic of monarchy would be threatened if her words and actions, in public, were ever to be those of an ordinary mortal of her age". The Coronation, Altrincham said, "had emphasised the priestly aspect of her office, and in the ensuing period she had continued to appear more sacerdotal than secular". This, in his view, was not good for the monarchy or for the country.

Many people, including loyal monarchists, and, it has been said, a few of the Queen's friends, thought that much of what Altrincham had written would do the monarchy more good than harm. But the general reaction was hostile. He received furious letters, and on one occasion he was attacked in the street. Most people were not yet ready to listen to criticisms of the monarchy, which they regarded as attacks. Part of their resistance came from their feeling that the monarchy should be regarded as above reproach. Part came from the feeling that to criticise the monarchy was to damage Britain's reputation and power in the contemporary world. Just as those who had opposed the Suez adventure had undermined Britain's standing, had drawn attention to her declining power, her loss of Empire, those who demeaned the Queen were doing the same thing. The majority reaction to Altrincham, therefore, was that he was another of these troublemakers who on various fronts and in various fields were "pulling Britain down". His message was not popular.

John Grigg wrote about the Queen again in 1992. What he said then will be dealt with in a later chapter.

In 1959 Harold Macmillan called a general election, the theme of it being his famous advice to the people of Britain, "You've never had it so good." Documents are now available in the Public Record Office which throw an interesting light on how on that occasion the Queen exercised one of her most important prerogatives – the Dissolution of Parliament.

When Macmillan began in August to plan for a general election in October he saw that there would be a problem about this with the Queen. The sovereign would have to be in the country to grant the dissolution, and when the ensuing election was over, to preside over the opening of the new Parliament. But the Queen was due to visit Ghana, and she wanted to go in October, partly because the weather would be more bearable at that time, and partly because by then she would have had her summer at Balmoral. How would these requirements fit in with plans for an October election? When was the Prime Minister going to ask for a dissolution? Could it be done by letter? If the Queen's movements changed how could the press and the Opposition be prevented from speculating about an election? As it turned out the Queen was not destined to visit Ghana at this time; she was soon to discover she was pregnant. Prince Andrew was born the following February. But that was not known in the summer of 1959, when the Private Secretaries of the Queen and the Prime Minister began to discuss matters connected with the election.

On 21 August Macmillan informed the Queen in his regular weekly letter that an election was likely in the very near future:

Madam,
Mr Macmillan with his humble duty to the Queen ...

He goes on to report on arrangements being made for the coming visit of the President of the United States, General Eisenhower, and then surveys the international situation. Negotiations of various kinds now lay ahead and it was important for the British Prime Minister to go into these with the greatest possible authority:

I have, therefore, come to the conclusion that it would be right for me to advise the dissolution of this Parliament in the early autumn. After all, the Parliament is now in its fifth year ...
   Your Majesty will understand that I have not yet reached a firm view on the detailed programme. I shall need to seek your approval to the dates of Prorogation, Dissolution, and the first sitting of the new Parliament. I hope I may be allowed to give further thought to this matter ... I am, of course, entirely at Your Majesty's disposal and could, if you so command, make the submission at an Audience; but I rather shrink from the publicity involved in a visit to Balmoral. If Your Majesty is agreeable I would, therefore, prefer to make my final submission by letter ...

The Queen's Private Secretary, up at Balmoral with the Queen, wrote back to the Prime Minister, thanking him on behalf of the Queen for his letter and the information in it: "... sorry though she is that this will not provide an occasion for you to come to

Balmoral, she agrees with you that this might result in undue publicity and she will most certainly be glad to accept your final submission in the form of a letter."

The Prime Minister's Private Secretary conveyed this information to him in a "Note for the Record" in which he also said:

> Our feeling [is] that she ought to come to, or be near, London for the dissolution of Parliament. This is in accordance with the precedent of this century, and is anyhow what the public would expect. If The Queen wishes to hold the Council meetings in Balmoral that will be a little inconvenient for the Privy Council, and would certainly mean that the prorogation and dissolution could not be on the same day, and indeed if there was any fog about and transport became difficult it might be impossible to get the documents down from Balmoral in order to prorogue or dissolve Parliament as planned.
>
> If, however, The Queen decides to come to London just for the Council meetings and dissolution, and is then planning to return to Balmoral, it would clearly be more convenient to Her Majesty if the Council meetings could all take place on the same day. Whether The Queen will do this depends to some extent on the date. Clearly if the dissolution were to be towards the end of September or beginning of October she might choose to make that the end of her Scottish holiday, but we know from correspondence that she is thinking of having a Council in Balmoral on about September 25.

The Queen seemed quite happy about this. The Prime Minister was informed by his Private Secretary:

> Sir Michael Adeane rang me from Balmoral this morning and said that The Queen thought She could come down to London for the Prorogation and Dissolution of Parliament. This is very satisfactory.
>
> The Queen has taken note that you have not yet decided whether to recommend Prorogation and Dissolution on two consecutive days or on the same day. She has asked that if all else were equal and you were balanced in your mind on this matter you should arrange for them to be on one day. She would then come down on the overnight train on Thursday night and

would be able to do her two Councils on Friday. She will of course do whatever the public service requires of her. I think that if you do decide to go for the two consecutive days it would be useful to explain why this was being done, in the formal submission you will be making to The Queen on the actual dates.

Macmillan minuted this note: "I fear we *must* have two days."

The ancient ritual of the dissolution proclamation having to be put under the Great Seal and the summoning of the Privy Council caused further logistical problems. Both sides went into these with great care and courtesy towards each other. Records going back to 1873 were checked to see if prorogation and dissolution could take place on the same day and if this could be done from Balmoral. There was also a check into whether the Prime Minister could request and be granted a dissolution by letter: Attlee had done this in 1950, but the circumstances were such that it could not be clearly said that a precedent had been created. In the end the Prime Minister decided to change his plans. He asked the Queen to let him come up to Balmoral, for the prorogation to be announced from there, and for her to come to London for the announcement of the dissolution. His Private Secretary explained these changes in plan to the Queen's Private Secretary:

... The PM's view [is] that the dissolution of Parliament is perhaps the most important of the Royal Prerogatives, certainly so in the minds of the Public. He all along felt that The Queen should manifestly be seen to be exercising Her own will on the question of the Dissolution of Parliament. The Prime Minister had always thought that the acceptance of this by the public would be enhanced were the Queen to be present in London for the actual Dissolution proclamations. Whereas in the first instance he had not considered it to be a matter of importance in this context that he should visit the Queen personally but that it would be perfectly proper to follow precedent and make his formal submission by letter, he came to the view that nothing should be done at all which might in any way seem to be tending towards a diminution of the Royal Prerogative, and he therefore thought it was right for him to seek an audience.

In reply the Queen's Private Secretary thanked him for his explanation, agreed with all points he had made in it, and especially welcomed what had been said about the dissolution:

> ... It is certainly correct that The Queen should be seen to be exercising her own will in dissolving Parliament as well as in granting the Prime Minister his request for a dissolution.

This exchange of letters and telephone calls, and changes in arrangements seem to have been conducted to everybody's satisfaction. The Queen's Private Secretary ended his letter: "Please do not think that anything to do with this audience is ever a trouble to me or anyone here, it is what we are here for and we enjoy it."

Mr Macmillan won the election with a handsome majority. This was an electoral record: the Conservatives had won three elections in a row, increasing their majority every time. Early in the new year the engagement of Princess Margaret to Mr Antony Armstrong-Jones was announced,

Five years had gone by since the Princess had declared that she would not marry Peter Townsend, and the Group Captain had returned to Brussels. Very little of him had been heard since, and the story of Princess Margaret was of many appearances in public places, including night clubs, with one or another of the same group of young eligibles none of whom seemed to last in the headlines for long and to none of whom did she seem at all attached. Frequently there was a sad expression on her face, and she seemed little interested in the world around her. She was so often seen in the company only of her mother that a feeling had grown that she was destined to live the rest of her life a spinster.

The news that she had fallen in love therefore came as something of a surprise, and even more surprising was the news that the young man in question was a professional photographer. Armstrong-Jones had gone to Cambridge University to study architecture, had coxed the University boat against Oxford, had failed his examinations and after leaving the University had turned to photography. He had served his apprenticeship in the studio of Baron, a close friend of Prince Philip. Baron had taken many photographs of the royal family. Armstrong-Jones had established himself at the top of his profession long before he started taking pictures of members of the royal family. He was introduced to the Princess by one of her oldest friends, Lady Elizabeth Cavendish, daughter of the Dowager Duchess of Devonshire, the Queen's Mistress of the Robes. The Princess found him very different from the type of eligible young men who had escorted her around town for the previous five years or so. He was well read, well informed, moved in many different circles, and was extremely amusing company. The Princess and he soon became friends, and the friendship rapidly developed into something deeper. It was kept remarkably secret for more than a year, the Princess paying many visits to his flat on the river in the East End of London.

When the engagement was announced in February 1960, *The Times* said that it would be "enthusiastically welcomed throughout the Commonwealth on the simple assurance that Her Royal Highness is following her own heart and the Queen is delighted with her choice". Some of the gossip columnists commented on the many colourful and exotic friends the husband to be had in the world of show business and the theatre, but there was no opposition to the marriage. Students of the monarchy commented that the marriage would take the royal family one step further away from the mysterious and mystic world which it had traditionally occupied, and a step nearer the world of the present day. On the whole, public opinion seemed to welcome the match as a movement of the monarchy in the right direction.

The marriage, in Westminster Abbey in May, took it in the direction of Hollywood. The Princess at the top of the Christmas Tree had suddenly stepped down and married not the woodcutter's son but a lad with a camera. The ceremony was the most spectacular event since the Coronation, seven years before, but it was, perceptibly, in spite of the same impresario, the Duke of Norfolk, and same BBC commentator, Richard Dimbleby, more of a film wedding than a religious event. To some extent this was inevitable – Princess Margaret was not going to ascend the throne, she was not going to reign over the kingdom, she was not going to be the Lord's anointed. There was no question of investing her with symbols or requiring her to swear solemn and arcane oaths. The ceremony reflected the rapidly growing expertise of television in projecting the royal family by means of techniques well tried in Hollywood.

Three hundred million viewers saw the marriage on television, and newspapers all round the world covered the event in depth.

But, unlike the televising of the Coronation, the event did not seem to confer any positive benefit on the standing of the monarchy. Many people were reminded of the Princess's earlier romance, which had ended in tears, they said, only because stuffy out-of-date courtiers had set out to sabotage it from the start. Many people felt that somehow there was something inappropriate about a sister of a Queen who so strenuously maintained the tradition of remoteness and mystique marrying a man so much of the ordinary commercial everyday world as a professional photographer. It was not that people thought that there was something wrong about it so much as there was something odd about it. The relaxed and easy-going royal families of the Scandinavian countries walked around the shops and rode bicycles in the park, but they did not marry cameramen.

The event also revived complaints about the expense of maintaining a royal family. To many people it seemed reasonable, for huge sums of public money to be spent on marriages of British royals to foreign royals, and for film spectaculars to be provided free out of which commercial television companies, and their advertising clients would make vast sums of money. It did not seem so reasonable to spend money on the same scale when a member of the royal family married a British tradesman.

Complaints were voiced about arrangements for Princess Margaret's honeymoon recalling those made about the Duke of Edinburgh's tour. Why should the newly-weds spend so long cruising in the Mediterranean in the royal yacht at a cost of about £10,000 a day? Why should the nation pay nearly £60,000 to do up an apartment in Kensington Palace for the young couple when they should pay the cost themselves? What use was "Tony Jones" going to be to the British people who would now, without being consulted, have to pay for him to be kept up in the manner to which his wife was accustomed? Such questions were asked in stately homes as well as pubs. Nevertheless, the marriage was welcomed. There was still a great deal of affection for, and sympathy with, Princess Margaret. People hoped that she had at last got over her star-crossed love affair with Townsend and had found happiness.

8

Some winds of change
1960–70

IN THE LATE 1950s clouds were forming above some of the Commonwealth countries, above all South Africa. Here the white-dominated government was introducing more and more apartheid measures to control the huge black majority, which was becoming more and more restive. The British government, while trying to show sympathy to the predicament of the whites in South Africa, continued to profess the relatively liberal sentiments which had brought about a steady continuing policy of granting of independence and self-government to the one-time colonies. This policy conflicted with the first principles of the South African government, and fuelled the aspirations of those who wanted South Africa to become a republic and leave the Commonwealth.

Having got the election over Macmillan felt he must visit South Africa forthwith, and in January 1960 began an extensive tour which lasted into February. The atmosphere was tense. He and Dr Verwoerd, the South African Prime Minister, exchanged frank views about the situation in public, and spoke even more candidly in private. On 3 February, in a speech in Cape Town to the South African Houses of Parliament, Mr Macmillan made his historic statement: "The most striking of all the impressions I have formed since I left London a month ago is of the strength of this African national consciousness ... The wind of change is blowing through this continent ... and whether we like it or not this growth in national consciousness is a political fact." As though to rebuke this realistic view Dr Verwoerd had responded with the statement: "There has to be justice not only for the black man in Africa but also for the white man." Behind closed doors Verwoerd warned Macmillan that a significant section of white public opinion was opposed to the Queen continuing as Head of the Commonwealth, and that he had already decided to bring this highly charged issue up at the next meeting of the Commonwealth Prime Ministers due to take place in London the following May.

Events overtook Verwoerd's decision. What came to be called the Sharpeville Massacre took place at the town of that name the following month. Police fired on demonstrators, of whom fifty-six were killed. Several resolutions in protest, including general ones demanding the outlawing of apartheid, were tabled at the United Nations, and at once the Commonwealth was subjected to a new divisive pressure, tension between the older and the younger members. Australia wanted Britain to support South Africa, and called on Macmillan to use Britain's veto against any moves the United Nations might make against the Verwoerd government. The Australian Prime Minister, Sir Robert Menzies, publicly took the view that to apply or not apply apartheid was a question for South Africa and South Africa only, and that no Commonwealth country should interfere in the domestic affairs of another. Though it did not say so in public, the British government took the same view, and behind the scenes encouraged Menzies to continue to express it.

The conflict of opinion between the older and white members of the Commonwealth and the younger black ones intensified. It could bring about "a crisis" within the Commonwealth, said Macmillan in April, and he warned the Queen that when the Commonwealth Prime Ministers met in May such was the intransigence on both sides that the association might break down. The conference assembled in an atmosphere of tension and suspicion, which lifted for a brief spell when the Prime Ministers adjourned to participate in the celebration of Princess Margaret's marriage, but returned as soon as the happy event was over. The South African government representatives talked openly of South Africa becoming a republic, of renouncing the Queen as Head of State, and leaving the Commonwealth altogether. Nigeria, Sierra Leone and Uganda, were about to become independent. Ghana, having already become a republic within the Commonwealth, was now in a turmoil the outcome of which was hard to predict. In these circumstances it was clear that if Britain publicly sided with South Africa several members of the Commonwealth would secede.

That the conference ended as well as it did was in great measure due to the Queen. With obvious grasp of the problems and of what was at stake she behaved with charm, tact, and shrewdness. She said little in public but much in private conversation with her Prime Ministers. Much too was achieved by Macmillan's announcement that the Queen would shortly visit India, Pakistan and Malaya, all members of the Commonwealth, but also republics. The British government continued to refrain from criticising the South African government. This silence did not please the majority attending the Conference, and did not please South Africa either since there was no expression of support. Shortly afterwards, the Verwoerd government held a referendum asking the electorate whether South Africa should become a republic or not. The answer was Yes. Before May was out black leaders in Commonwealth countries publicly backed a United Nations Security Council resolution condemning apartheid. The resolution was passed. This was the signal for South Africa to leave the Commonwealth.

The withdrawal of South Africa from the Commonwealth was particularly poignant for the Queen. It was to South Africa that she had made her first Commonwealth tour, in 1947. She had visited it with her father at a time when he was thinking deeply about the future of the Commonwealth, the transformation of the collection of countries which formed the old Empire into an association of free and equal members sharing the same principles and values, and standing for stability and peace in a world of change and disorder. It was during and after the massive South African tour that Elizabeth, listening to her father, had come to believe that the preservation and nourishing of the Commonwealth must be her first duty. To witness the departure of South Africa, therefore, was to experience a great sense of loss; and to some degree to feel that she had failed.

But there was a gain. The continued association of the monarchy of Britain with a country in which a small number of whites continued to rule a vast number of blacks and openly practise and propagate the doctrine of apartheid would have soon undermined Britain's relations with the many black Commonwealth countries. Many of them might have entered the embrace of the Soviet Union. In most of the countries of the Commonwealth which had achieved their independence, or were on the verge of doing so, there were groups which favoured alignment with the Soviet Union rather than with Britain and her American ally, and preferred communist to capitalist systems.

It was with this in mind that the government arranged the Queen's next tour, to last six weeks, beginning in Cyprus, proceeding through India, Pakistan, Nepal, Turkey and Iran. These countries were on the rim of the Soviet Union; in all of them were groups more interested in close relations with the Russians than with Britain and the United States. It was significant that on this tour the Queen was accompanied by the British Secretary of State for Foreign Affairs, Lord Home. Her greatest success was in India, where millions of people turned out to cheer her on her way. They cheered her not as subjects of a crown but as citizens of a republic, but this was all to the good: it showed that the Queen continued to be the Head of a Commonwealth which could include republics. The words the Queen used in her speeches reflected her sense of the importance of registering the change: what had been an Empire in the past she said had now become "a free association of equals".

It was a sign of the times that the feature of the tour which attracted most press coverage in Britain was the shooting of a tiger by the Duke of Edinburgh at a shoot in India which the Queen attended. There was much criticism of them both. Later, there was a shoot in Nepal. The Prince did not take part in this one, giving as his reason for not doing so that he had "an infected trigger finger". The Foreign Secretary, and the Queen's Private Secretary, Sir Michael Adeane, participated in the shoot, and between them killed a white rhinoceros. This animal belongs to a particularly scarce species. The killing of the rhinoceros by the Foreign Secretary and the Queen's Private Secretary evoked even more indignation in the British press than the slaying of the tiger by the Duke.

The demand for royal tours increased. The government continued to watch carefully the development of relations between the Soviet Union and groups within Commonwealth countries, especially those accessible from the Russian borders. Visits from the Queen were an innocuous way of giving encouragement to the anti-communist elements in these countries without being provocative. The Berlin Wall dividing East from West Berlin had now been built by the Russians and had heightened tension between East and West in 1961. Russian diatribes against the Americans and their friends mounted to an unprecedented level.

At this time there was growing concern in the West about what the Soviet Union might try to do in Ghana. The Queen, as mentioned earlier, had to postpone a tour there in the autumn of 1959 on becoming pregnant. The visit had been rescheduled for late 1961. Much had happened to Ghana since it had become independent in 1957. Remaining within the Commonwealth as a republic acknowledging the Queen as Head of the Commonwealth, it had suffered prolonged bitter and bloody civil strife. President Nkrumah's government was a one-party dictatorship. To preserve his regime he had imprisoned many of his political opponents. His life was in constant danger. Macmillan was for some time undecided about what to do about the projected royal visit. On the one hand he wanted the Queen to go because he thought this might help to stabilise the country, and would at any rate show the anti-communist flag; on the other hand he feared that if the visit took place there might be an attempt on the Queen's life, or, more likely, on Nkrumah's life while she was there. After reflection, consequently, he advised her not to make the tour. The Queen demurred; she said that she would call off the visit only if the government officially advised her to do so; otherwise she would use her own discretion, which she made it clear, would mean going ahead with the Ghana visit as planned.

The projected visit to Ghana became a political issue, with several Conservative MPs demanding cancellation, not only because of the danger to the Queen but to show British disapproval of Nkrumah's government. Churchill wrote a long letter urging Macmillan to advise the Queen not to go on account of the danger. Eden, now Lord Avon, supported him. Soon after the matter was aired in Parliament bombs exploded in the Ghanaian capital, Accra. Meanwhile it became known that a Russian military mission was about to arrive, and it was equally well known that if the Russians moved a military mission into a country they would try to leave it there permanently.

Macmillan now made careful enquiries into the state of security in Ghana. Duncan Sandys, Commonwealth Secretary, who had only recently returned from a visit to the country, was sent back with a mission to travel around several danger zones in the company of President Nkrumah, and report his conclusions. With characteristic bluntness Sandys assured Macmillan that the Queen would be safe. The political situation at home was eased for Macmillan when the Leader of the Labour Party, Hugh Gaitskell, told Macmillan that the Opposition would do nothing to prevent the Queen from carrying out a mission which she considered her duty to perform. The Queen's view of the situation remained consistent throughout. She put it to Macmillan at an audience that it was her duty to go, and although she would bow to his wishes if he, as Prime Minister, advised her not to, they would cut poor figures in the world if she did not visit Ghana and Khrushchev did. Macmillan decided to advise her to go.

After the audience Macmillan drove to a function in the City, accompanied by his press secretary, Harold Evans, who recorded in his *Downing Street Diary*:

To and from the Grocer's Hall in the car he talked almost solely of the Queen. "What a splendid girl she is." She had been indignant at the audience just before we left at the idea of having the trip called off. The House of Commons, she thought, should not show lack of moral force in this way. She took very seriously her Commonwealth responsibilities, said the PM, and rightly so for the responsibilities of the UK monarchy had so shrunk that if you left it at that you might as well have a film star.

So the Queen visited Ghana. No harm befell her. After her return, Macmillan wrote in his diary: "The Queen has been absolutely determined all through ... she is impatient of [being treated] as a *woman*, and a film star or mascot. She has indeed 'the heart and stomach of a man'."

In her Christmas broadcast the Queen spoke of her visits to Commonwealth countries that year: "In Asia and Africa we were made aware of the great volume of goodwill and friendship that exists between all the varied peoples who profess different faiths and who make up our Commonwealth family." She made a plea for peaceful and patient attitudes to current problems. "Angry words and accusations certainly don't do any good, however justified they might be ... 'Oh hush the noise, ye men of strife, and hear the angels sing.' The words of this old carol mean even more today than when they were first written."

The year 1962 being the tenth anniversary of the Queen's accession to the throne inspired a spate of speeches and newspaper articles. There were many displays of affection, loyalty and gratitude towards the monarchy. and much praise for the Queen personally. About Prince Philip there were two schools of thought: he won praise for making statements on matters of public interest and for participating on television; but there was criticism that his contribution to the national interest fell far short of that of Queen Victoria's consort, Prince Albert.

As to the monarchy as an institution the degree of reappraisal and criticism would probably not have been anticipated by the "New Elizabethans" of ten years previously. There were several references to the writings of John Grigg and Malcolm Muggeridge. Most of the criticism alleged that the monarchy remained out of touch with the realities of the modern world. The protocol of the Queen's household was still archaic and rigid; the entourage, the number of servants, ushers, ladies-in-waiting, were excessive. Ministers of the Crown having on official occasions to wear court dress, knee breeches and silk stockings was an anachronism. According to one complaint the scale and character of royal visits to cities and townships caused great and unnecessary expense to local authorities. The Queen's Press Secretary replied, saying that the Queen did her best to prevent that happening. "Some local authorities spend fantastic sums painting up the town before the Queen visits them, or holding up all the trains for five hours to let her through, or something ridiculous like that ... when we are consulted by the local people beforehand we do try to suggest that they don't go crazy over extravagant entertainment or redecorating ... The Queen is horrified to think that people who can't afford it are spending large sums of money on her visit which could be better spent on other things."

Several commentators pointed out that there had been a great increase in publicity for the royal family in the ten years since the Queen came to the throne. Some said this owed much to the attraction of the royal family: they looked good, and did much to dispel pessimism about the decline of the value of the family in the life of the nation. Others said that this was due partly to the increase in the influence of the mass media, more than ever addressing women readers and viewers, and therefore using more and more human interest material. This, they claimed, not a rise in pro-monarchy feeling, was the cause of the royal family now receiving more attention than the most prominent of Hollywood film stars.

Sir Harold Nicolson, then seventy-six years old, recognised as an authority on the subject, was interviewed about the standing and the future of the British monarchy. "There is no doubt", he said, "that there is a lot of criticism of the Monarchy today. This is nothing new. The Hanoverians, George IV especially, were heavily criticised. But whereas they were criticised as men, there are now some doubts about the value of the Monarchy as an institution." He thought these doubts "belong mostly to a young intellectual minority. Older intellectuals see the Monarchy as an emblem of continuity." Asked how long he thought the monarchy would last, he answered: "If we get a bad monarch it would go very quickly. Otherwise I would give it a hundred years."

The tenth anniversary of the Queen coming to the throne coincided with much discussion about how the position of the Queen and the sovereignty of the British Parliament, and relations with the countries of the Commonwealth, would be affected in the event of Britain's current application to join the European Economic Community being successful. These questions had been asked since August 1961 when the British government had formally applied for admission to the EEC. In 1962 the national debate was going strong. The Labour Opposition was against joining, as were many Conservative MPs, and there had been much opposition in the Commonwealth, particularly in New Zealand and Australia whose trade in dairy produce with Britain, a prime feature of their economies, was bound to be diminished.

Again, for political and diplomatic reasons a royal tour seemed desirable in the near future. The British government expected to be told that Britain's application to join the EEC would be accepted very early the following year. Consequently, they scheduled a royal tour of Canada, Australia and New Zealand for February 1963, calculating that when the announcement was made the Queen would be in Australia, the country most hostile to the EEC, and that her unmatchable presence would alleviate the angry reaction which would inevitably greet the news.

As it turned out, weeks before the Queen arrived in Australia General de Gaulle had used his veto to have Britain's application rejected. He justified this on the grounds that the United Kingdom's relationship with the countries of the Commonwealth made her ineligible for membership. He made it clear that he would continue to veto Britain's entry so long as that relationship existed. Though the reception of the Queen in Australia would have been worse if de Gaulle had said "Yes" instead of "No" in many places she got an angry reception, partly because Edward Heath, who had led Britain's attempt to join the EEC, had announced that in due course the government would make another application.

Soon after the Queen returned to Britain news of the Profumo scandal broke. The Secretary of State for War, John Profumo, married to a glamorous and gifted actress, Valerie Hobson, was reported to have been sleeping with a call-girl, Christine Keeler, who was also sleeping with a Russian diplomat, part of whose duty was to acquire information on defence matters. In order to give Profumo a chance to clear his name on the Prime Minister's instructions he was questioned in private by a small committee of Conservative MPs, including the Chief Whip and the Attorney General. As a result of the grilling, the Chief Whip reported to the Prime Minister that Profumo was "clean". Macmillan consequently allowed Profumo to make "a personal explanation" to the House of Commons, a very rarely used privilege which enables an MP to deny an accusation or correct a misrepresentation without his remarks being subject to questions or comment, the matter being then regarded as over and done with. Profumo made his personal explanation, but the newspapers immediately showed that much of it was false. To lie to the House in a personal explanation is heinous; Profumo resigned at once. These events reflected very badly on Macmillan's judgement, and he further damaged himself with the lame excuse: "I am not in touch with what young people do today."

The Profumo case not only reduced the Prime Minister's standing; it occasioned another flutter of gossip about the private life of Prince Philip. A prominent figure in the Profumo case was a fashionable osteopath called Stephen Ward. A bohemian man-about-town with many contacts it was Ward who had introduced Keeler to Profumo. As a result of enquiries in the Profumo case, Ward was put on trial also, charged with living off immoral earnings. It transpired that in his possession had been some photographs taken several years previously in which Prince Philip appeared with his old friend Baron. These photographs had passed into the hands of the *Daily Mirror*. The newspaper ran a front-page story containing the statement: "The foulest rumour being circulated about the Profumo Scandal has involved a member of the royal family. The name mentioned is Prince Philip." The rumour, the *Mirror* stated, was "utterly untrue". The Press Council pronounced the story to have been in bad taste: the *Daily Mirror* said no more. Stephen Ward was a talented artist. At the time he was to appear at the Old Bailey a selection of his drawings was exhibited at a public gallery for sale to raise funds for his defence. Some of these were of members of the royal family, among them Prince Philip and Lord Snowdon. These drawings had originally been commissioned by the *Illustrated London News*. Soon after the exhibition opened the royal portraits were purchased and removed by a representative of that magazine. On the last day of the trial Ward was found unconscious, having taken an overdose. He was found guilty of the charge, and died three days later. It seems that much was done to conceal some of the relationships he had previously had with many distinguished people, relationships which might have been harmless enough but knowledge of which might have led to embarrassing speculation.

Gossip about how much time Prince Philip spent with the Queen abated in the autumn of 1963 when Buckingham Palace announced that the Queen was "cancelling all future engagements for the time being", and it became known that she was pregnant. She returned to London from Balmoral. On her arrival she had to deal with another political crisis in which her use of the Royal Prerogative was to be brought in question.

This one was precipitated by the Prime Minister himself. For several months there had been speculation that he might have to resign in consequence of the political aftermath of the Profumo scandal, particularly his admission about not being "in touch with what young people do today". Not only young people but many of their elders, including Conservative MPs, had come to regard Macmillan as indeed out of touch, his Edwardian appearance, manner and choice of language making him seem almost comically anachronistic in the "swinging" sixties. When it transpired that Profumo had lied to the House, Macmillan who had given him the opportunity to do so, looked particularly foolish and incompetent. In the summer of 1963 the chairman of the Conservative Party, Sir

Oliver Poole, made a tour of the country to find out what the Conservative voters thought about the standing of the Prime Minister. Poole's report was not wholly reassuring, but having weighed it up, Macmillan decided that he would "soldier on".

Fate took a hand. In October 1963, on the very eve of the annual conference of the Conservative Party at Blackpool, the Prime Minister was stricken with an acute prostate condition. On the basis of the medical advice he was given he decided to resign immediately. He was determined to choose his successor. He took advantage of the fact that if asked by the sovereign to do so, but only if asked, the outgoing Prime Minister could suggest who his successor should be, his recommendation to be based on information supplied to him by members of the Cabinet, soundings taken by the Leader of the Party in the Lords, and above all by the Chief Whip transmitting the reports of the junior whips on opinion in the group under their charge. Once again the general opinion outside the House of Commons and reflected in the national press was that Macmillan's successor would be Butler. One newspaper poll gave him a rating of 39.5, the nearest runner-up 21.5, and Macmillan's own candidate, Lord Home, only 9.5.

The Queen was now to be faced with a problem which she had not had in 1955, had had to a small degree in 1957, but had to a much greater degree in 1963. In 1955 the obvious successor to Churchill was Eden; in 1957 the choice was between Butler and Macmillan; but in 1963 opinion within the Conservative Party was much more divided. Therefore the Queen, who had chosen not to consult her outgoing Prime Minister in 1955 or 1957, decided in 1963 that she had better do so. She visited Macmillan in hospital. He made it clear that constitutionally it would not be proper for him to recommend a successor unless she asked him to do so. The Queen asked him to. Macmillan then read out to her a memorandum he had written for the occasion, proferring the document for inclusion in the royal archives as a record of his views. While still Prime Minister, and with the constitutional authority of the Prime Minister, Macmillan advised the Queen that his successor should be Lord Home. He then formally handed her his resignation, which she accepted.

It was the end of an outstandingly good working relationship, extremely effective and influential to the last. Throughout Macmillan's memoirs there are frequent references to his briefing of the

Queen, especially on foreign trips, but there are many instances too of him asking her advice, especially on foreign and diplomatic questions. Churchill's and Macmillan's obvious esteem for the Queen cannot be explained simply by saying that they followed Disraeli's policy of flattering the monarch. Their communications to her employ much courtly language but they convey genuine admiration and respect. The Queen's feelings towards Churchill displayed in the letter to him on his resignation have been quoted earlier; similar feeling is reflected in the letter she wrote to Macmillan when his turn came to give up office. After some words of praise for Home, the incoming Prime Minister, the Queen went on to say:

> Nevertheless, it is you who have held the highest office continuously for nearly seven years ... For me it means that for the greater part of my reign you have been my guide and supporter through the mazes of international affairs and my instructor in many vital matters relating to our constitution and to the political and social life of my people. During these years you have had to unravel a succession of major and intricate problems affecting the peace of the world and the very existence of Britain and the Commonwealth. History will witness to the masterly skill with which you have handled them ... There have also been, I am afraid, a number of problems affecting my family – lesser perhaps in scope but not always in intricacy – which must have occupied a great amount of your time. I should like to put on record my appreciation and gratitude for the unstinting care which you have taken in giving me your advice about them and helping me to find a solution.

Macmillan was duly moved: "It is difficult to conceive a more gracious and generous tribute from a sovereign to a subject."

Critical questions were asked about the behaviour of Macmillan and about the behaviour of the Queen. Iain Macleod, who had succeeded Oliver Poole as chairman of the Conservative party, was also the editor of the *Spectator* and therefore in a position to command a considerable public for his views. He made the most of it. He wrote that it was wrong for the Prime Minister to be appointed simply on the basis of a recommendation from the outgoing Prime Minister to the monarch, a process which led to the Queen deciding not only who was to be the new Prime Minister but also who was to be the new Leader of the Conservative Party. Enoch Powell, a senior Cabinet Minister who had openly supported Butler for the premiership, ranged himself with Macleod saying that in not supplying the Queen with all the relevant information about views being held within the Party when she exercised the Royal Prerogative to appoint a new Prime Minister she had been prevented from making proper use of her prerogative.

It soon became clear that the Queen had chosen as Prime Minister a man who did not have the backing of the senior members of the Cabinet, may not have had the backing of the majority of Conservative MPs, and may not have had the backing of the Conservative Party up and down the country. Once again, therefore, the Royal Prerogative, or, at any rate, the use of it, came under scrutiny.

The choice of Sir Alec Douglas-Home – he had renounced his peerage on becoming Prime Minister so that he could take a seat in the House of Commons – was very controversial at the time, and became more so as opinion grew that he was not the man for the job. Criticism of that choice came to a peak a year later when in October 1964 under Douglas-Home's leadership the Conservative Party lost the general election. At that point it could be argued that the previous year the Queen had used her prerogative to appoint as Prime Minister a man who at the time would not have been able to form an administration unless it was known that she wanted him to do so, a man who was foisted on her by an outgoing Prime Minister who had ignored the views of the senior members of the Cabinet, a man who probably did not have the support of the majority of the Conservative Party in the House of Commons, a man who then went on to lose the election and let in the Opposition. The question was asked: was this unfortunate outcome a reflection of the dangers inherent in the existence of the prerogative, or of the Queen's political incapacity to make proper use of the prerogative, or of both?

Misgivings about the use of the prerogative in relation to the choice of a Prime Minister were expressed vigorously by the Labour Opposition. They were in a strong position to do so: they elected their leader annually, so that in the event of the party coming to power as the result of a general election the sovereign would have no doubt as to whom she would invite to form a government. But misgivings were voiced about the Queen's decision by many Conservatives, some of whom were shortly to lose their Parliamentary seats in consequence. As a result of the discussion which ensued, the Conservative Party decided on a drastic change in the procedure by which they chose the leader of their party. Early the following year, Sir Alec Douglas-Home agreed that the Conservative Party should devise a system, quite similar to that of the Labour Party, whereby the leader of the party, and therefore the party's candidate for the office of Prime Minister, should be elected annually by a secret ballot of MPs.

This new procedure established in 1965, substantially reduced the scope of the Royal Prerogative. Up until this change the monarch had been free to choose the next Prime Minister without asking anybody's advice. From now on a Conservative Prime Minister would in effect have been chosen by Conservative MPs. The Queen's role in the appointment of Douglas-Home as Prime Minister was sadly highlighted when in the year in which he had introduced the new system he was deposed from the leadership of the Party to be replaced by Edward Heath.

Bagehot, who had written with such eloquence about the accumulated wisdom of a monarch who had occupied the throne for several years, may have turned in his grave at the thought of what the Queen had done in 1963. She had listened to the advice of a sick old man who by his own admission was out of touch with contemporary opinion; she had not obtained the views of the most senior men in the Cabinet; she had appointed as Prime Minister a man who had no chance of being elected according to the opinion polls, and who then went on to lose the general election, and soon after that the position of leader of the party which she had been instrumental in obtaining for him. To cap it all, as a consequence of these events the Conservatives decided to adopt a system for the election of the leader which virtually took the right to choose a Prime Minister out of her hands, and the Queen lost one of the most important remaining parts of her prerogative.

The mid-sixties brought the Queen her first significant experience of growing anti-monarchical feeling in Canada. The object of her visit, timed for October 1964, was for her to be in Canada for the centenary of the Quebec conference which had decided on the confederation of the French and British provinces, leading to the British North American Act of 1867 which provided for the federation of Canada with the status of a Dominion – it would have been called the Kingdom of Canada had not the Americans objected to having a monarchy established on their border. Quebec, with a large proportion of citizens of French descent, never happy with the British connection, had displayed strong anti-British and pro-republican feeling. There had been demonstrations, and some shooting. Once again the question came up: "Is it safe for the Queen to go?" She decided that it was, and went. The stories and speculations in British newspapers in the weeks before she left caused some apprehension. The danger was the feeling in French-speaking and French-thinking Quebec. The people of Quebec had made it clear that they saw the Queen's visit as the federal government's attempt to impose its authority upon them. The Queen could take some consolation from knowing that local resentment was directed at the government of Canada rather than at herself, but this did not affect the atmosphere in which she found herself. On the day she toured Quebec the city seemed full of police armed with riot helmets and clubs. There was some booing, in most places there was silence. The Queen was not seen to smile much, indeed her face was grim. But Quebec, however important, was only Quebec. In Ottawa the following day the atmosphere was different; the Queen laughed and joked. But even in the most pro-British parts of Canada the response to royalty seemed not to be what it would have been ten years before.

She returned home to receive her first Labour Prime Minister, Harold Wilson, victor in the general election of 15 October by an overall majority of only four seats. Some of the leading men in the new administration were if not republican at heart at least critical of the role and influence of the Crown. Richard Crossman and Tony Benn, for example, disapproved of the pomp and mystique with which, they thought, the monarchy tried to surround itself, and believed that much about it stood in the way of progress. But though in their diaries Crossman and Benn occasionally wrote mockingly about the trappings and pretensions of court life and royal etiquette publicly they accepted the existence and function of the institution without complaint or demand for change. The Wilson governments of 1964–70 coexisted as comfortably with the monarchy as Attlee's governments had in the years between 1945 and 1951.

But the advent of the Labour government, if it did not change the monarchy, had some effect on the way the monarchy was perceived. After winning the election, Harold Wilson records, he received a civil service brief telling him to be ready to go to the

Palace with "morning coat and striped pants". In fact he wore a "short black coat" to the Palace. "It turned out that no constitutional issue was raised." At the Palace:

> I was conducted to the Queen's private apartments. She simply asked me if I could form an administration despite the narrowness of my majority. I was in no doubt that a government could be formed and I was made PM on the spot. Strangely to me and contrary to all I had understood about the procedures, there was no formal kissing of hands such as occurs with the appointment of all other senior ministers. It was taken as read.

In his *Diaries* Crossman recorded many criticisms of what he considered to be the archaic and pompous role of the monarchy. He found the people and the practices of the court "snobbish" and "dreary". He felt a good deal of government time – and taxpayers' money – was wasted in out-of-date ceremonies and conventions. He thought the number of meetings of privy councillors in attendance on the Queen, particularly when busy ministers had to journey up to Balmoral for them, was an unnecessary drain on the government's time and the country's finances. But there is a noticeable lack of edge to his strictures, and there is never any personal criticism of the Queen. "It was perfectly simple and straightforward to get on with her. Indeed she puts one at ease immediately ... has a lovely laugh ... is a really very spontaneous person." His regard for her comes out in an entry about a rushed twenty-four-hour visit he was required to make when she was up at Balmoral:

> If this is necessary to the magic of monarchy, I accept it as fair enough. But surely there must be a limit to which busy Ministers are compelled to sacrifice their time to suit royal private engagements. It's only fair to add, however, that I am pretty certain that the Queen knows nothing about all this ... (members of her secretariat changing dates to suit changes in her personal arrangements).

Crossman saw much of the Queen since as Lord President of the Council it was part of his duties to visit the Queen accompanied by other Ministers and acquaint her with Orders in Council which the government wished to issue and for which therefore they required her assent. His attitude to her is encapsulated in an entry in his diary for October 1964, immediately after the Labour Party won the general election and Crossman with other Ministers had to be sworn in as Privy Councillor. They entered the great drawing-room:

> At the other end was this little woman with a beautiful waist, and she had to stand with her hand on the table for forty minutes while we went through this rigmarole. We were uneasy, she was uneasy. Then at the end informality broke out and she said, "You all moved backwards very nicely," and we all laughed. And then she pressed a bell and we all left her.

Harold Wilson used the honours list to award many people in vocations and professions which had not previously been noticed by the honours list, or not been noticed to great extent – among them actors and actresses, cricketers and footballers, broadcasters, journalists and social workers. The award of the MBE to each of the four Beatles evoked a storm of protest. Many people already holding honours complained that their awards had been debased. Nine people sent their decorations back to the Palace. People complained: "Winston Churchill would never have done this."

Churchill died in January 1965 at the age of ninety-one. The contrast between how he viewed the Queen and the monarchy and how the Labour government did was clear. Wilson and his colleagues did not revere it, love it and celebrate its mystique and romance as Churchill did, but they showed no sign of wanting to abolish it. When Harold Wilson extended the honours list to contain the names of people known to the masses some people suspected a Machiavellian ploy to get rid of the honours list by making it look ridiculous. In fact Wilson could be said to have preserved the system by popularising and democratising it. Wilson's lists were a sign of the times. This was the era of the swinging sixties, of the pop group and the mini-skirt. There was no question of the Labour Party manipulating the honours list for political purposes, except in the sense that they distributed honours in new places into which they believed the people wanted them to go.

In February 1965 the Duke and Duchess of Windsor arrived in London. His health was not good – he had recently had an abdominal operation in Houston, Texas – and now a serious operation on his eye was necessary. He was given treatment at the London Clinic.

The Duke sent a message to the Queen via Lady Monckton, widow of his old friend and legal adviser, Sir Walter, suggesting that they might meet. Pictures of the Duke looking old and frail, and wearing dark glasses, had appeared in the newspapers. It seems that the Duke on his side and the royal family on theirs, conscious perhaps of the passing of the years and the easing of old wounds, were in a mood if not to forgive at least to feel less aggrieved about the past. Accompanied only by her Private Secretary, Sir Michael Adeane, the Queen visited the Duke and Duchess at the clinic. She had last seen her uncle when she was ten years old. After the Queen had broken the ice other members of the family followed, including the Duke's sister, the Princess Royal, Princess Marina and Princess Alexandra. After the operation the Duke moved to a suite in Claridges. The Queen visited him again, this time staying for tea. The Queen Mother, however, did not visit the Windsors. A few weeks later, *A King's Story*, a film based on the Duke's autobiography, was screened in London. Like the book, the film gave an account of the events leading up to and following the Abdication as the Duke had seen them. The film, therefore, could hardly have given any pleasure to the royal family. It seemed, however, that some kind of a bridge had been constructed. It did not look very firm, but previously there had been no bridge at all.

In 1965 the Queen was drawn into the activities of MI5. This did not become known to the public until about fifteen years later, when its disclosure led to some controversy, but it must have created some problems for the Queen at the time. In 1965 MI5 learned that "the fourth man", the unidentified individual who had warned first Burgess and Maclean, and later Philby, that they were known to have been Russian agents and were in danger of arrest, was Sir Anthony Blunt, Surveyor of the Queen's Pictures, an appointment he had held for thirty years. Before taking action against Blunt, the head of MI5, Sir Roger Hollis, conferred with the Home Secretary and with the Queen's Private Secretary, Sir Michael Adeane. It was decided that Blunt should be offered immunity in exchange for confession and complete silence on the matter.

This course was adopted to prevent Blunt making public information which would uncover information about the Duke of Windsor's relations with Nazi agents in Portugal before he left to become

Governor of the Bahamas in 1940. It seems that Blunt came by this information when, immediately after the Second World War had ended, King George VI had sent him to Germany to bring back certain documents said to concern the relations of the Duke of Windsor with the Nazis at that time lodged at the home of the Hesse family, Wolfgarten Castle. Whether the documents existed, and what was in them if they did, has not been made public. Nor is it known how much the Queen was told about the situation. What is known is that after being questioned in 1965 Blunt remained a free man, and carried on with his job at the Palace. This story has to be taken up again later.

Politically, Wilson and the Queen got on well together. He spoke glowingly of her knowledge of the world, of political affairs, her attention to business, her concern for good government, and her prodigious memory. He put it about that the relationship between the Queen and himself was excellent. Far from conflict between Prime Minister and monarch it was their apparent closeness which dismayed and angered good Conservatives. What they feared was not that the Labour Party would diminish the power of the Crown but nourish it and turn it to its own advantage.

Wilson's first major problem of policy very much involved the Queen, personally as well as constitutionally: democracy in Southern Rhodesia, now Britain's only colony on the African continent. For some time the British government had been discussing terms on which the black population of Rhodesia could be given representation in the new Rhodesian Parliament. Their attempts to reach agreement had failed, and the Rhodesian Prime Minister, Ian Smith, was now threatening to make a unilateral declaration of independence (UDI), taking the country out of the Commonwealth entirely and breaking off all links with the United Kingdom. In the view of the British government UDI would be illegal, and if he carried out his threat and declared UDI Smith's administration would no longer be the lawful government of the colony. In that case it would be necessary for the Queen to govern the colony directly through her representative the Governor, Sir Humphrey Gibbs. Mr Smith challenged this: in the event of UDI, he argued, precipitated by a dispute between his government and Her Majesty's government, the Queen would continue to be Head of State but his administration would continue to be the rightful government of the country.

The last thing Wilson wanted was to resort to force, or to

precipitate a breakdown in relations between the two countries. He advised the Queen that he should go to Salisbury, the capital of Southern Rhodesia, armed with a letter from her to Smith, written in her own hand, to emphasise the personal concern she had in the matter, urging Smith to accept the proposals for ending the dispute about black representation and expressing her disapproval of recourse to UDI. The Queen accepted his advice. Wilson went to Salisbury on 31 October, but Smith flatly refused to comply with the Queen's wishes and suggestions, and rejected the proposals. Wilson flew back to London. Ten days later Smith announced UDI.

Wilson's action in bringing the Queen into the Rhodesian situation caused controversy. The Queen, too, was criticised for allowing herself to be involved. The accusation was that Wilson had tried to exploit the Crown in the interests of the policy of the British Labour government, and that the Queen had lent herself to this. Criticism of the Queen was made from two opposing directions: she had tried to persuade her government in Southern Rhodesia to do something it did not want to do; and she had previously allowed Ian Smith and the white minority to deny the black majority their just share in representation.

The Rhodesian situation caused controversy and aroused emotion throughout the Commonwealth, and in the predominantly black countries there was some ill feeling towards the Queen. When the Queen flew to Jamaica the following February her departure from Heathrow was postponed for an hour while her plane was searched for a bomb which a woman telephone caller had said was on board the plane. In Jamaica she found black demonstrators carrying slogans such as "Rhodesia Sold Out By Britain". In her speeches she made it clear that the Crown deplored all actions by governments which "deny the fundamental principles of human rights" and approved "measures which may be used to put an end to the illegal government of Rhodesia". There was no doubt in Jamaica about what the Queen said, but some of her listeners wondered if she really meant it. If so, why did not her government do something about it?

This doubt deepened. In Jamaica her listeners had been citizens of a country in which the blacks were politically strong. The next country she visited was the Bahamas where the blacks were weak, and were dominated by a white minority government. There was a good deal of political corruption in the Bahamas, the poorer people were exploited, and American crime syndicates were known to be making fortunes there. While the Queen was in the country, a young lawyer, Lynden Pindling, wrote a letter to her calling for a Royal Commission of Inquiry. Some of his complaints related to the sale of Crown land to entrepreneurs at minimum prices to be re-sold at vast profits. Later that year, as a result of the general election he and his supporters had precipitated, Pindling became the first black Prime Minister of the Bahamas. It was unfortunate that the Queen's visit to the Caribbean had come so soon after the announcement of UDI in Southern Rhodesia. Wilson's apparent failure to deal with Ian Smith raised doubts about the British government's will and power to give black people equal status with whites. This cast a shadow over the Queen's visit, and raised doubts about the future of Commonwealth relations in that part of the world.

In 1966 the Prince of Wales reached the age of eighteen. The question arose as to how he had best spend the next few years in preparation for the public duties which lay ahead. His education had been discussed before. An important decision had been taken in his infancy: unlike his mother, and his grandparents, he would not be educated at home but go out of the Palace to school and so far as security permitted share the life of other boys of his own age.

Consequently, when Charles was eight years old he was sent to a day school in London, Hill House Preparatory School for Boys, situated a few hundred yards from Buckingham Palace. The choice was his father's: the features of the school were no corporal punishment, scope for competitiveness and encouragement of the will to win. The Queen told newspaper editors that she hoped that as little publicity as possible would be given to Charles's time at school. Though the Queen felt strongly that he should go away from home as soon as reasonable the main influence on his schooling was his father. From the age of nine to thirteen, Prince Philip had been at Cheam, a preparatory boarding school in Surrey, where his uncle, Lord Milford Haven had been before him, and after that at Gordonstoun and the Royal Naval College. At the age of nine, Charles also went to Cheam. He seems to have enjoyed it. His teachers had reported objectively on him: though he had not shone he had acquitted himself well. Then came the question of where he should go next. The Queen, influenced by the Queen Mother, thought that he might go to Eton – it was on the doorstep, and what education she had received outside the Palace, her tutorials from its Provost, Sir Henry Marten, could be said to have come from Eton. But Charles went to Gordonstoun. It was generally supposed that he did so because his father wanted him to go there. Asked about this in an interview with the author in 1974, Prince Charles replied:

I wasn't made to follow in my father's footsteps, in any sense or in any way. His attitude was very simple: he told me what were all the pros and cons of all the possibilities and attractions and told me what he thought was best. Then he left it to me to decide. I freely subjected myself to what he thought was best because I had come to see how wise he was. I had perfect confidence in my father's judgement.

I'm glad I went to Gordonstoun. It wasn't the toughness of the place – that's all much exaggerated by report – it was the general character of the education there – Kurt Hahn's principles ... I didn't enjoy school as much as I might have, but that was only because, as I said, I'm happier at home than anywhere else; but Gordonstoun developed my will-power and self-control, helped me to discipline myself ...

Prince Charles's years at Gordonstoun passed with very little publicity. By the time Charles left it is doubtful if the man in the street could remember much about what happened to him there – with two exceptions. In June 1963, when Charles, aged fifteen, was in his second year at the school, he went on an expedition on the school yacht. While he was at Stornoway, on the island of Lewis in the Hebrides, he was given permission, with four other boys, to visit the local cinema. In the street the Prince was recognised and a crowd began to gather. To get away from them the Prince's detective, who was with Charles all the time he was at Gordonstoun, took the boys into the Crown Hotel, and then went to the cinema to get the tickets. While he was absent the bystanders began to look into the hotel through the windows. Disliking this, Charles moved into an adjacent room. This, he discovered, was the hotel bar. He had never been in a bar before, and to cover his confusion ordered "the first drink that came into my head, which happened to be cherry brandy, because I'd drunk it before when it was cold out shooting". At this moment a journalist entered the bar, with the inevitable result, stories appearing in the popular press with such headlines as "Under-age Heir to Throne Orders Drink at Bar".

The developments ranged wide: Charles, it was said, was not being brought up properly by his parents; the hotel manager received a summons from the police for selling drinks to a minor; the headmaster of Gordonstoun made statements about discipline at Gordonstoun, and some newspapers, learning that he kept a cane in his study, predicted that he might use it on the heir to the throne; antiblood sports supporters alleged that had he not gone out shooting he would not have discovered the existence of cherry brandy.

The second incident occurred two years later. The German magazine *Die Stern* printed extracts from an exercise book which Prince Charles had used at Gordonstoun in which he had expressed some mature and sophisticated observations on the evil effects of power. According to *Die Stern*, they had acquired the exercise book as a result of Charles having sold it because his parents kept him short of pocket-money. It was soon revealed that the exercise book had been stolen, illegally sold and purchased, and that the piece which had so impressed *Die Stern* was not written by Charles but was a précis he and his class had been set to write of the views of the eminent nineteenth-century historian, William Lecky. A statement from Buckingham Palace disposed of the misrepresentations circulated by *Die Stern* and other publications, adding: "The suggestion that his parents keep him so short of money that he has to find other means to raise it is also a complete invention."

After Gordonstoun what was to be the next step in Prince Charles's education? The Queen initiated discussions with a small group of advisers, including the Prime Minister, the Archbishop of Canterbury, the Chairman of the committee of university vice-chancellors, her Private Secretary, and Lord Mountbatten. "Uncle Dickie" was on the committee to represent the Defence services rather than as the boy's great-uncle and, in Charles's words, "HGF" – Honorary Grandfather. The committee held a number of meetings, eventually recommending that Charles should have a spell as a student at Trinity College, Cambridge.

Early in 1967 came the news which made a further contribution to the process by which the modernisation of the royal family was taking place: the Earl of Harewood, the Queen's first cousin, asked the Queen's permission for a divorce. Harewood, aged forty-three, son of the Queen's aunt, the Princess Royal, who had died in 1965, had been married for several years to a distinguished pianist, Marion Stein. The Queen had done her best to keep the pair together, but her efforts had failed: the Countess had finally made up her mind that the marriage should be terminated. This was not surprising: the Earl had not lived with her for some time, and did not want to go back to her – nor did she want him back. He lived with the violinist Patricia Tuckwell, by whom he had a son, and wanted to marry her.

In view of questions about royal divorce and remarriage which were to come later, the outcome of the Harewood situation was important. The Queen had no power to prevent Harewood obtaining a divorce, but under the Marriage Act of 1702 if he wished to remarry within twelve months he would need the sovereign's assent – if he waited for at least a year such assent would not be necessary. There were other considerations: moral, ecclesiastical and social. The Queen had been brought up to regard behaviour like Harewood's as immoral; her father might have given his consent to the divorce and remarriage, but only at the price of Harewood moving out of the royal family. The ecclesiastic problem arose from the Queen continuing to be the Head of a Church which did not officially recognise divorce. The social consideration moved the Queen's mind in a different direction: by 1967 public opinion was much more tolerant about divorce than it was in the Queen's childhood, and if the Queen were publicly to disapprove of the Harewood divorce and remarriage her views might look so old-fashioned as to be an embarrassment to the monarchy.

The Queen decided to put her predicament in the hands of her Prime Minister. Wilson advised her to let him put it to the Cabinet. Looking at it in relation to the Act of 1702, the Cabinet advised the Queen to give her permission for the divorce and remarriage. Constitutionally she had to take the Cabinet's advice. Acting on this advice meant that the Queen was able to bypass her responsibilities as Head of the Church of England, and avoid a situation in which the monarchy might seem to be archaic and out of touch. The only condition she imposed on agreement to divorce and remarriage was that the wedding must take place outside the United Kingdom, which duly it did.

As many critics – and supporters – of the monarchy pointed out at the time the problem posed by this royal divorce and remarriage had been resolved not on principle or by doctrine but by a clever political operation masterminded by the Prime Minister. This took authority from the monarchy, and changed the basis on which such situations should be resolved in the future. The Harewood divorce created new standards which would be relevant a few years later when Princess Margaret parted with Lord Snowdon, and, later still, when Prince Charles's marriage to Princess Diana came in question. It seemed in keeping with the spirit of permissiveness which was the feature of the sixties, and was to grow and spread. It brought the monarchy a little further out of its religio-mystic shade into the common light of permissive day.

In the same year there was a further easement in the Queen's relations with the Duke and Duchess of Windsor. A plaque to commemorate Queen Mary was to be unveiled at Marlborough House where she had lived for the last thirty years of her life. The Queen decided that the Duke should be invited to the ceremony, and she asked him to bring the Duchess. The Windsors arrived from New York. When they landed at Southampton they were met by Mountbatten, representing the Queen. There was, up to a point, a family reunion. The Duchess of Windsor curtsied to the Queen, but those present observed that she did not curtsy to the Queen Mother. After the event, the Duchess made remarks which indicated that she was conscious of the reserve with which the Queen Mother had greeted her. The Windsors were not mentioned in the Court Circular published in *The Times* the following morning, and left for Paris that afternoon. But the way had opened up for a relationship of a kind, and in the remaining five years of the Duke's life he and his wife received visits from the younger members of the royal family, and from Mountbatten.

At this time the Labour government made its first attempt to get Britain into the European Economic Community. Again President de Gaulle used the French veto to reject Britain's application, saying again that it would not be possible for the United Kingdom to be a member of the EEC so long as the connections with the countries of the Commonwealth remained in place. He also made some hostile observations on the subject of Britain's relations with Canada. The centenary celebrations of Canadian statehood were about to begin, and the Queen was scheduled to visit the Dominion and take part in them. De Gaulle took this opportunity to announce that the Canadian nation had been founded by the French, not the British, that the British had always exploited Canada, and that those parts of Canada which felt French not British, notably Quebec, should be free to govern themselves. During a visit to Canada he ended a speech in Quebec with the tactless words: "Vive le Québec libre."

The Queen's visit to Canada was now in some respects a repeat of the events of three years earlier. Out of Canada came threats that if the Queen went to Canada her life would be in danger. Demonstrators warned her to keep out of French-speaking areas. There were demands in the British parliament that she call off her visit. Some British newspapers predicted that she *would* call off her visit. The Queen behaved true to form. She went. What she had encountered in some parts of Canada three years previously had not been forgotten by her advisers. They had every reason to suppose that in those areas her reception three years later might be worse. Parts of her tour, accordingly, were revised. The Canadian government had arranged for her to make a widely advertised public visit to the mammoth Expo 67 exhibition in Montreal, which had been arranged to mark the centenary. In the event, on advice, the visit she made to the exhibition was virtually a private one, the public being admitted only after she had left. Again, her courage, charm, her obvious understanding of her complex duties, and above all the good sense with which she accepted the problems, impressed the bulk of the Canadian people. The visit was judged a great success. But some of the Canadian newspapers, including friendly and influential ones, wondered if the Queen would be asked to come back again.

Whether Britain had a place in the new Europe that was being created; how she stood with the newly independent countries of the Commonwealth; what relations in future she would have with white dominions who might go down the road South Africa had taken; how Britain was to handle problems like that of Southern Rhodesia, were now highly topical questions. At this time the Duke of Edinburgh made some forthright and considered comments on them in a private conversation with Tony Benn, then Secretary of State for Industry. These remarks were noted by Benn in his diary, parts of which have been published.

According to Benn, Prince Philip, when asked about the future of the monarchy, said that in his view its relations with the countries of the Commonwealth would change and that it would also behave differently in relation to the people of the United Kingdom. Taking Canada as an example he said that the Canadians did not really want the monarchy and were heading for "a republic or something". So far as the role of the Queen in government was concerned it should be relieved of meaningless procedures, such as meetings of the monarch with members of the Privy Council, and the role should be made more useful by audiences with other key ministers as well as the Prime Minister so that the Queen learned more in detail at first hand about what was going on. As for popular perceptions the Queen was still looked up to by some sections of the community – for instance, the people of the East End of London "still wave their little flags and are very keen on the monarchy". But he also believed that as more people became more affluent and more sophisticated they took less interest in the monarchy or at any rate had less inclination to show it.

Benn noted in his diary that Prince Philip had obviously thought a good deal about the monarchy's role in Britain, and about Britain's place in the world, and that even "if he sounded like a Tory MP" he saw many things very clearly, and certainly could not be accused of being blind to, or opposed to, the need for change, and constructive adjustment to what modern life required.

Around this time a number of developments took place which seemed to mark if not cause changes in the way the royal family appeared to the public. They followed the arrival at the Palace in 1965 as assistant press secretary of a young Australian, William Heseltine, who had earlier worked in the office of the Australian Prime Minister, Sir Robert Menzies. He had then had a spell in Buckingham Palace, but had returned to Australia to become Sir Robert's private secretary. Now Heseltine was back in Buckingham Palace again; and when Commander Colville retired in 1968, Heseltine became the Queen's press secretary. From then on, as *The Royal Encyclopaedia* noted, Heseltine "played a key role in creating greater access for the press to the royal family".

The change was soon evident to all. Colville had been uncommunicative and defensive, appearing to think that apart from giving out dates of appointments his role was to be silent and ensure silence. Heseltine, articulate and co-operative, seemed to assume that it was his duty to provide as much information as possible. He treated newspapermen as friends whom he was there to serve, and his manner was open and trusting. Coming from a country known for the easy informality and relaxed demeanour of its citizens he was remarkably unstuffy himself. Whereas most journalists had referred to his predecessor as "The Commander" they referred to Heseltine as "Bill". It was not just his attitude that changed things at the Palace; like the Prince he had clear ideas about what the image of the monarchy should be and of how the royal family should behave in its relations with the public. He had a policy, which he intended to put into effect. He was backed by Prince Philip and Mountbatten, and the Queen followed their lead.

In the autumn, a two-part series appeared in the colour supplement of the *Observer* which in many respects was a striking departure from anything of its kind ever seen before. By special arrangement with the newspaper the Queen allowed its photographer, David Montgomery, to take a number of pictures of her in relaxed situations in which she appeared not as a royal personage but as a human being. Several of these were with her husband and children, some of her on her own. Until this article appeared she could have been seen thus only by a handful of friends. One picture showed her sitting in front of an electric fire with her shoes off. What was so striking about these pictures was not so much their content as their character. How far they had been posed, to what extent they had been calculated, how revealing they were, was beside the point; what was significant about them was that they took the reader into the privacy of the Queen's life as they had never before, and this could not have been made possible without her co-operation.

On handing over to Heseltine in 1968 Colville had made a significant observation about the royal family and the media: "Royal lives have been progressively more exposed to public scrutiny and there is now a constant conflict of what may be termed in the public interest and what is private." The royal family tried to face this fact. They looked to Heseltine for guidance. *The Royal Encyclopaedia* records baldly that he was "closely involved in the production of the television film *Royal Family* (1969) and in the coverage of the investiture of Prince Charles as Prince of Wales (also 1969)".

Charles was to be invested Prince of Wales in 1969 when he had reached the age of twenty-one. In preparation for this he had left Cambridge for a few months to go to University College, Aberystwyth, where he studied Welsh history and learned to speak Welsh. Dermot Morrah, historian and the Queen's Arundel Herald, was commissioned by the Queen to write a book about him, which appeared under the title of *To be a King*. The Prince was supplied with a public relations consultant, Nigel Neilson, who headed a company called Neilson McCarthy Ltd. One of Neilson's directors was his old RAF colleague, Wing Commander David Checketts, now the Prince of Wales's equerry. Checketts had accompanied the Prince to Australia when, at the age of seventeen, he had spent several months at Timbertop, the country branch of Geelong Grammar School in Victoria, "the happiest year of my life". Checketts was extrovert, forward-looking, shrewd and gregarious. He got on well with Charles, and influenced him much more in Heseltine's direction than in Colville's.

In July 1969 came a milestone in the development of the royal family's relations with the media – the screening of the 105-minute television documentary made by the BBC entitled *Royal Family*. Two years previously Independent Television had made a series about Mountbatten called *The Life and Times of Lord Mountbatten*. The royal family were impressed, and eventually agreed to a film being made about themselves. For a year BBC cameras followed the Queen and members of the royal family. The scenes that were shot varied greatly, from the Queen talking to the Prime Minister and formally receiving the new American Ambassador to the Court of St James, to the royal family picnicking in the open air at Balmoral with Prince Philip grilling the chops. The documentary took the public behind what had hitherto been closed doors and showed them not only what they had not seen before but what it had been thought they ought not to see. The twenty-three million British viewers had heard the Queen's voice before but only on a few set public occasions such as her speech on Christmas Day, but only a handful of people had heard her talk and laugh off duty.

A week later came the investiture. In 1958, on the occasion of the British Empire and Commonwealth Games at Cardiff, in the course of congratulating the Principality on a memorable year, the Queen had said that she would like to mark her appreciation by "an act which will, I hope, give as much pleasure to all Welshmen as it does to me. I intend to create my son, Charles, Prince of Wales today. When he is grown up, I will present him to you at Caernarvon."

Preparations for the event had been announced two years in advance, some of them being greeted with hostility, some with derision, notably the information about Prince Charles spending the summer term of that year learning Welsh at Aberystwyth. In the opinion of one of Britain's leading historians, A. J. P. Taylor, this was "a sordid plot to exploit Prince Charles ... for political reasons, and what is worse, for reasons of party". The news infuriated the

Welsh nationalists. Their party, Plaid Cymru, officially dissociated itself from this "piece of English trickery", and announced that it would ignore the ceremony. The Free Welsh Army, which sympathised with the IRA, denounced it. There was so much talk about bomb threats and demonstrations that months before it took place, the government thought seriously about calling it off. Prince Charles, who behaved admirably from start to finish, was opposed to such a decision, though he spoke understandingly about resistance to his visit: "I've hardly been to Wales, and you can't expect people to be over-zealous about the fact of having a so-called English prince come amongst them and be frightfully excited about it." The Queen was ill at ease: the investiture, and the danger to which her son now seemed likely to be exposed, was the result of her promise to the people of Wales in 1958. It had seemed a good idea at the time; it did not seem the same on the morning of the great day, July 1, 1969, when it was learned that two terrorists had blown themselves up while attaching a homemade bomb to a railway bridge.

Since it was a state occasion the Earl Marshal, the Duke of Norfolk, was put in charge of the arrangements. Asked at a press conference about what would happen if it rained on the day the Duke delivered one of *his* most memorable observations: "If it rains we shall all get wet." He made it clear that the ceremony would be in keeping with all precedents: "There will be no monkeying about in the name of modernisation." Because the proceedings were to be televised, Lord Snowdon, Constable of Caernarvon Castle, the site of the investiture, was asked to design the setting and decorate the castle. Not everybody was happy about the coming of the television cameras but as the Duke of Norfolk said, "We've got to live with these things if people invent them." There was much praise for the Constable's handiwork, including some of the costumes he designed, and also criticism of it. There was a thought-provoking mix of antiquity with modernity. The dais on which the Queen would stand for her son to pay homage to her was covered by a specially designed canopy of acrylic sheets, a gift from ICI, supported by steel rods which looked like lances. Lord Snowdon wore a uniform which he created for the occasion – bottle-green zip-fronted with a belt of corded black silk and two tassels, an outfit which gained him the sobriquet "Buttons". The Earl Marshal wore the uniform which he always wore on state occasions; it had, he said, belonged to his father, though the hat was his own idea. Much money was made in

Caernarvon; householders exploited the shortage of hotel accommodation in the little town to charge extortionate prices for sleeping three people in a room. There was a roaring trade in Welsh Dragon flags made in Hong Kong. The BBC provided a six-hour programme using thirty cameras costing about two million pounds. In and around the town there were a number of bomb explosions, but no casualties other than those noted above. Reports that Prince Charles was wearing a bullet-proof vest for the occasion were indignantly denied. The ceremony came to climax when Charles knelt before his mother on the dais with his hands between hers and paid homage to her, saying: "I, Charles Prince of Wales, do become your liege man of life and limb and of earthly worship, and faith and truth I will bear unto you to live and die against all manner of folks."

The following November Prince Philip was interviewed on American television. It made a memorable contribution to the process by which the royal family and its affairs were becoming increasingly open to the public gaze, and ears. One of the subjects brought up by the interviewer was the financing of the royal family. Was it true that the royal family was spending more than the £475,000 which it received as the annual Civil List from the taxpayer? Prince Philip said that it was: the royal family was spending more than it was paid. "We go into the red next year ... We've kept the thing going on a budget which was based upon costs of eighteen years ago ..." The Prince's exposition of the royal family's financial situation was received by many people not so much as a further step in royal self-revelation as an attempt to exploit the television medium to obtain an increase in their Civil List emoluments. Discussions were in progress between the Palace and the government departments concerned about the possibility of the Civil List being upgraded: some members of the Cabinet complained that Philip's remarks in public constituted an attempt to influence the outcome of these talks and was therefore an interference in what was a political matter. The Prime Minister, however, did not complain. Harold Wilson continued to feel that it was good for the Labour Party to remain friends with the royal family and to be seen to be so by the public. He felt in particular that Prince Philip was on the government's side.

About 200 million worldwide saw the investiture. On the general issue of the effect on the royal family, and the monarchy as an institution, of voluntary exposure on television, the majority of public opinion was for it, since it was intriguing, revealing, and novel. On the other hand, thoughtful people were divided about it. Many welcomed it; it made the royals more human, more likeable, and therefore strengthened monarchy; republicans and those who wanted a more homely kind of royalty thought that letting in more light on the royals would dissipate the mystique with which it was still invested. The view of Milton Shulman, a distinguished and perceptive television critic, who had had considerable experience of working in the medium as a highly placed executive, was that in their own interest the monarchy and good monarchists should weigh the matter carefully. As though he were sending a clear message directly to Bill Heseltine, Shulman wrote in the *Evening Standard*:

Richard Cawston's film, *Royal Family*, could not have had a better critical reception if it had been the combined work of Eisenstein, Hitchcock and Fellini. But the making and showing of such a film with the Monarch's co-operation may have constitutional and historical consequences which go well beyond its current interest as a piece of TV entertainment.

What has actually happened is that an old image has been replaced by a fresh one. The emphasis on authority and remoteness which was the essence of the previous image has, ever since George VI, been giving way to a friendlier image of homeliness, industry and relaxation.

But just as it was untrue that the royal family sat down to breakfast wearing coronets as they munched their cornflakes, so it was untrue that they now behave in their private moments like a middle class family in Surbiton or Croydon.

Judging from Cawston's film, it is fortunate at this moment in time we have a royal family that fits in so splendidly with a public relations man's dream.

Yet, is it, in the long run, wise for the Queen's advisers to set as a precedent this right of the television camera to act as an image-making apparatus for the monarchy? Every institution that has so far attempted to use TV to popularise or aggrandise itself has been trivialised by it.

The expansion of television coverage in the sixties opened many doors into the privacy of the royal family. Increased exposure on television coverage inevitably led to more stories in the newspapers. All this new attention to the royal family tended to modernise and demystify the image of the monarchy. In the swinging sixties, the decade of the Beatles and the mini-skirt, such a change in the image seemed desirable if not necessary. But, as Milton Shulman warned, the effect might do the monarchy more harm than good.

9

Silver Jubilee.
Prince Charles marries
1971–81

THE YEAR 1970 MARKS the beginning of a new phase in the Queen's life, and a change in the image she presented to the public. As a result of the BBC film on the royal family she had become less perceived as royal and much more as real, the mystique of the monarch disappearing, the everyday life of wife and mother becoming more visible.

Harold Wilson was defeated in the general election of June 1970, and was succeeded by Edward Heath. The new Prime Minister's priority was to effect Britain's entry into the European Economic Community. General de Gaulle was no longer in power, but the objections to Britain being admitted to the EEC, so long as the links with the Commonwealth countries remained, continued to exist.

The prospect as the Queen saw it was not propitious. The old and tried white Dominions, such as Australia and New Zealand, dependent on their vital dairy produce trades with Britain, wanted no change in their links with the United Kingdom. That in itself would have posed problems for the Queen – as it did for the British Parliament – and these would be compounded by the growing strength of republicanism in Australia and New Zealand. Many people in these two countries might have been willing to accept a continuation of the historical relationship with Britain so long as it was to their economic interest to do so. They would not feel the same way if they had nothing to gain, and a good deal to lose, when Britain entered into a new relationship with the countries of Europe.

The Queen had also to face the problems arising out of the relationships developing between the United Kingdom and the newly independent countries of the Commonwealth. For decades British legislators, and their civil servants, had faced the inevitability of colonies becoming independent self-governing countries, and with varying degrees of enthusiasm had worked to bring it about, hoping, and in many cases expecting, if not assuming, that the newly independent countries would introduce regimes reflecting the principles and practices of the British political system. There had been those who had predicted that this would not be the case. In the early seventies it looked as though they would be proved right. Even allowing for the birth pains of the new regimes, and for their need to have time to learn from their mistakes, it was clear that the transition period would be turbulent and protracted. In short, in the early seventies, having to contend with the problems of young as well as old member countries, the Commonwealth was not in the condition which twenty-five years earlier King George VI had wished and hoped for it. Nobody was as conscious of this as his daughter.

Ghana was an outstanding example of the instability which had followed independence. Ghana had become independent in 1957, the first West African State to do so. In 1960 it adopted a republican constitution, and over the next decade there were five different regimes. What ensued in Ghana could not be claimed as a success for British tutelage. Nigeria, the most populous – one hundred million inhabitants – and the richest nation in black Africa, and to some extent, therefore, the spokesman of the continent, had become a republic in 1963. In 1966 the army had carried out a coup, suspended the constitution, dissolved the legislature, and outlawed all political parties. For three years there was bloody civil war. Uganda had become independent in 1962. Britain had been proud of Uganda's peace and prosperity, but soon the country was torn with dissension and violence. In 1966 the Prime Minister, Milton Obote, suspended the constitution, the President fled to England, and a republic was declared. British firms were treated with hostility, and when General Idi Amin ousted Obote in 1971 he announced that all foreign businesses were to be taken over. South Africa had by now intensified its apartheid policies: the MCC called off its cricket tour. Southern Rhodesia declared itself a republic outside the Commonwealth. Relations between India and Pakistan were hostile, and within Pakistan the eastern province was shortly to break away and form the new independent state of Bangladesh.

There seemed very few countries of the Commonwealth in the early seventies of which it could be said that the Queen could go there and be sure of a welcome and a safe return home. If there was to be a Commonwealth tour at this time Australia and New Zealand seemed by far the best. There was an additional reason why the Queen should visit Australia: at a time when the prospect of Britain joining the EEC looked more and more likely republican feeling in Australia was growing.

Heseltine used the Australian tour to experiment with another measure intended to bring the monarchy nearer the people. He knew that Australians felt strongly that the royals put too much distance between themselves and the people, literally and metaphorically, and that they resented this. The royals, Heseltine saw, behaved in a way increasingly at odds with the Australians' easygoing and relaxed way of life. Heseltine consequently arranged with the Queen that in Australia there would be a number of "walkabouts".

The "walkabout" consisted of the Queen, at various selected spots and with appropriate protection, walking for some distance through a crowd gathered on either side of her. The long-standing complaint had been that the crowds had had contact with the Queen only when she came on to the platform of a huge hall, when she had taken part in some ceremony or had made a short speech, and had then disappeared, probably into a reception for a relatively small group of privileged guests. Otherwise, the Queen simply passed by in a motorcade through crowds kept at a safe distance from her by policemen.

Heseltine began his "walkabout" experiment in Wellington, New Zealand. The Queen made her official ceremonial appearance, and after that she walked through the crowd. She stopped and chatted several times, and she was near enough to receive gifts and flowers. The début of the walkabout in Wellington, New Zealand, was hailed by the media commentators as a great success. The term was coined by the *Daily Mail*'s Vincent Mulchrone, but, as *The Royal Encyclopaedia* points out, he

> misused the term, which was *traditionally* applied to the wan-
> derings of the Australian Aborigines who wanted to get away
> from people and civilisation. However, Mulchrone knew that the
> word had a nice Antipodean ring, and his journalistic instinct
> proved sound: the name stuck and the act itself captured the
> imagination of media and public alike.

The new device, destined to give a distinctively popular aspect to royal programmes, was given a few more trials in New Zealand, and drew more praise. When the royal family moved to Australia the walkabout was executed with more confidence and greater expectations of results. Both were justified. The success of Heseltine's innovation was reflected in the opinion polls and in newspaper comment. The *Sydney Sunday Telegraph* said that the success of the tour "has surprised the optimists and staggered the pessimists. No more will they [the royal family] appear remote figures removed from reality ... they have been seen as warm and human ..."

While the Australian tour was in progress there was a contretemps occasioned by news that President Nixon had invited the Duke and Duchess of Windsor to the White House for a gala dinner in their honour. President Nixon and his wife were immediately advised by the British Ambassador in Washington that the Duchess should not be addressed as "Your Royal Highness" and that lady guests at the White House dinner should be told that they were not to curtsy to her. This heavy-handed advice did not go down well in Washington, and even the British took exception to it. The Ambassador's wife said afterwards: "I curtsied anyway – and I called the Duchess Your Royal Highness."

President Nixon's banquet for the Windsors went down well with the public at large. The Duke was now seventy-six, and in Britain people had the feeling that he would not live to be much older. In January that year the BBC had screened an hour-long television interview with him and the Duchess. The programme was not exciting but it was well received and more than twelve million viewers watched it. News of its success, and of the apparent popularity of the Windsors in Britain, reached the United States. It may have been a factor in the attempts made from Buckingham

Palace to limit the publicity in the United States for the glamorous Windsors banquet in the White House, for the British royal family were shortly to visit Washington at the end of a brief tour of Canada.

The visit to Washington was not an unqualified success. The blame for this was put on Princess Anne, who was now playing a much greater role in the projection of the image of the royal family. Her role was not a popular one. On this occasion she evoked censorious criticism. It could be said that she got the worst press a British royal had ever received while travelling abroad. Whereas the Queen looked well and happy, said some American newspapers, her daughter looked fatigued, bored and ill-humoured. The *Washington Daily News* was particularly hostile about her. This tabloid was no friend of Britain, but it was not irresponsible, and was read extensively. Princess Anne, it recorded, was "snobbish, pouting, bored, sullen and disdainful". Another newspaper suggested that she was not fitted to be an ambassador and should be confined to such tasks as "opening rhododendron shows in Kent". When the Princess returned home, British newspapers joined in the criticism of her behaviour in the United States. "What a spoiled brat" said one. More sympathetic comment came from those who claimed that the security measures for the visit prescribed by the President had subjected Princess Anne to restrictions and frustrations they were not accustomed to. But whatever the explanation and the mitigation, Anne had given herself an image in the United States which was to be reflected in the United Kingdom and which would embarrass the royal family for some years to come, until in the early eighties she transformed it over time by hard work for the Save the Children Fund and other causes.

One of the first matters dealt with by the new Prime Minister had been the request for an increase in the Civil List Allowance which the Queen had formally submitted to the House of Commons a month or so before the general election. Wilson was glad that it had not arrived while he was still in office. The basis of the Queen's submission was that the allowance remained at the level which had been agreed in 1952, nearly twenty years previously. The news that the Queen had asked for an increase led to an angry debate. The question of whether the Civil List allowance should be increased or not was immediately joined by the question of whether it was right for the Queen to be the one person in the country exempt from paying income tax. Complaints surfaced as never before about her immunity from taxes on her private wealth, particularly from death duties.

The Queen's request to the House of Commons came, as was the appropriate procedure, before the Civil List Select Committee. Among its members was one of the MPs for Fife, Mr Willie Hamilton, an outspoken republican. Willie Hamilton denounced the Queen's request as "the most insensitively brazen pay claim made in the last 200 years". He proposed that the Civil List be abolished, and the Queen be treated like the rest of the people in employment, and simply be paid a salary for doing her job.

The question of the Queen's income from the Civil List and from her private sources is dealt with later, but it should be recorded here that according to his biographer, the public discussion about the royal finances at this time caused Lord Mountbatten so much uneasiness on the Queen's behalf that he advised her to provide the public with information about them. He told the Queen and Prince Philip that if the huge sums being bandied about as well-informed estimates of the royal family's private wealth became accepted "the image of monarchy will be gravely damaged". He suggested an article in a serious newspaper which would provide the basis for a realistic public discussion.

As a result, on 9 June Jock Colville, now a banker, made a statement in *The Times*, which had every indication of having been authorised by the royal family. He said that the Queen was worth about £12 million. How much good his statement would have done the royal family had it been the only source of information is in itself problematical, but there came further disclosures. The Select Committee reported that, as well as incurring costs in carrying out their duties paid out of the Civil List allowance, the royal family incurred costs in discharging their duties which were borne by various government departments. For example, the royal yacht, *Britannia*, which the royal family used for various purposes, was paid for by the Navy, at a cost of about £5 million a year. The royal train was paid for by the Ministry of Transport. In short, as well as those public activities of the royal family which were paid for out of the Civil List, and their private activities, such as horse-racing and polo, paid for out of their own pocket, there were a number of other activities which were paid for neither out of the

Civil List allowance nor out of the royal family's private pocket but by the tax-payer.

From the enquiries of the House of Commons Select Committee emerged the revelation that the activities of the royal family, apart from those it financed out of its own purse, were very costly indeed, and gave rise to the question of whether in view of the contraction of the scope and influence of the royal family's public activities, especially regarding the Commonwealth, this expense was worth while. Here was the seed of the doubts and misgivings about the financing of the royal family which were to become a much more serious issue in the 1990s.

In May 1972 in the course of a visit to France intended to show the French that Britain was looking forward to becoming a member of the European Economic Community, the Queen, accompanied by Prince Philip and Prince Charles, went to see the Duke of Windsor. The Duke was dying, but defying all advice, dragged himself out of bed, and greeted them sitting in an armchair in his bedroom. After talking with the Duke, obviously at death's door, the Queen spent a few minutes with the Duchess. A week later the Duke was dead. He was to be buried in the Royal Burial Ground in the gardens of Frogmore House, a royal estate about half a mile south of Windsor Castle, in Windsor Home Park. The Duchess, brought over from Paris, on a royal flight, stayed with the Queen at Buckingham Palace. Before being taken to Frogmore the Duke's body lay in state at St George's Chapel, Windsor. Thousands filed past. The Duchess returned to Paris. It was the end of a chapter. The Duchess soon became an invalid, never left her room, seemed unable to recognise the few people allowed access to her, and for nearly ten years lived cut off from the world until her death in 1986.

Later in 1972 the Queen and Prince Philip celebrated their twenty-fifth wedding anniversary. A leader in *The Times* praised the Queen for her service to the country and to the Commonwealth, adding: "Today we can also declare that the Queen, the Duke and their children have set a standard of family life and family happiness that everyone must respect."

Britain became a member of the European Economic Community in January 1973, the Conservative government's initiative being supported by sixty-seven Labour Party MPs. The Queen had now to face the problem that whatever was said and argued the sovereignty of the Crown-in-Parliament could never be the same again: it was diminished. She had also to face the fact that the influence of the Crown could never be the same again, and that this would be perceived in Britain, in the countries of the Commonwealth, and in the world outside. More light of day had been let in on the mystique of the monarchy. Some millions of Europeans now in theory ranked with the people of Britain as fellow citizens. For them the British monarch was just another important person in the way of life which as good Europeans they would share and, it was to be hoped, prosper; but the Queen was not their Queen. Several of the countries concerned already had a royal family, and the rest did not want one. The Queen and good British monarchists therefore had to adjust to the fact that they lived in a community in which the vast majority of its members regarded the British monarchy as something between a delightful symbol of interesting times past and a dignified and authentic presentation of royalty as the media and Hollywood saw it today.

That was the problem for the Queen as sovereign of the United Kingdom. There was also the problem for her as Head of the Commonwealth. For the newer members of the Commonwealth Britain's entry into the EEC was not critical. Having become independent several years previously, they had long since been going about their business with other countries as well as with the United Kingdom and pursuing their own interests. For Britain's relations with the older, the "white", members of the Commonwealth there was a problem. Could the older members of the Commonwealth, already having difficulty in fitting into the vast new disparate Commonwealth, adjust their relationship with Britain-in-Europe, even if the republican currents flowing in their countries could be successfully contained?

The existence of these problems called for more royal visits. In 1973, therefore, the Queen began a series of tours in the countries of the "Old" Commonwealth, these expeditions following one another with unprecedented speed. The main theme of her speeches was that Britain's entry into the EEC did not in any way adversely affect the links between Britain and the countries of the Commonwealth. The message was summed up in what she said in her Christmas message broadcast a few days before Britain entered the EEC on 1 January 1973: "The new links with Europe will not replace those with the Commonwealth. They cannot alter our historical ties and personal attachments with kinsmen and friends overseas. Old friends will not be lost." She then added a sentence which provoked discussion in Britain, in the Commonwealth countries, and in the EEC: "Britain will take her Commonwealth links into Europe with her."

What did this mean? Were Britain's links with the troubled regimes in Africa to be taken into Europe? How would the EEC feel about that? Were Britain's links with, say, Australia to be taken into the EEC which had made it a condition of Britain's entry that she sever such links? How would Australia feel about having her links with the United Kingdom "taken" into the EEC? When the Queen arrived in Canada she found both welcome and hostility. The *Toronto Star* had traditionally favoured the connection with the monarchy, but in an editorial it now asked whether the time had come for Canada to have its own head of state instead of one which belonged to a foreign country. The Queen responded with thoughtful speeches emphasising the purpose of her relationship with the people of Canada was to be of service to them. Her message was supported without qualification by the Canadian Prime Minister, Pierre Trudeau, whose reply to the *Toronto Star* was in effect "The relationship with the Crown has brought much benefit to the people of Canada, and will continue to do so: why change it?" Trudeau followed up his defence of the role of the British monarch by inviting her publicly to attend personally the next Commonwealth Conference, which was to be held at Ottawa. This would be the first Commonwealth Conference which the Queen had attended outside Britain.

Trudeau's praise for the role the Commonwealth continued to play in the affairs of the world did not go down well with the French Canadians or with those Canadians who had come to the conclusion that membership of the Commonwealth was an anachronism. But it helped confirm the status of the Commonwealth in the eyes of countries who observed it from outside. When the Queen attended the Commonwealth Conference at Ottawa she was given a reassuring reception. Her charm, her dignity and her ability to get on with people, helped, but what mattered most to her cause was the perception that the Commonwealth was evidently still a going concern. This did something to mask the fact that in spite of the support of the Canadian Prime Minister the role of the Queen had come in for a good deal of criticism in Canada.

There followed a six-day visit to Australia. The Australian Labour Party was in power. The Australian Prime Minister, Gough Whitlam, had brought in a Bill, which the Australian Parliament had passed, called the Royal Styles and Titles Bill, and before it became law, the Queen had to give the royal assent. The Bill was another step in the process by which Australia was making it clear that what role the Queen now had in Australia owed nothing to the fact that she was Queen of the United Kingdom. To highlight this the new Bill provided that when the Queen was in Australia she would no longer be styled "Queen of the United Kingdom and of Her Other Realms and Territories", but would be referred to as Queen of Australia. The Queen could have signed the Bill in London, but she decided that to show her goodwill towards it she would go to Canberra to affix her signature.

By now months of speculation about whether or not Princess Anne would marry Mr Mark Phillips had culminated in the announcement of their engagement, followed by the fixing of a date for the marriage ceremony. The more that became known about the match, the more questions were asked about it. When Captain Phillips, a cavalry officer well known and respected in the eventing world, made an appearance with the Princess in a television interview, he seemed attractive, gentlemanly and good-natured, but also shy, inarticulate and somewhat ill at ease. There were reports that Prince Philip had not been happy about the engagement: he was said to deplore the fact that his prospective son-in-law had no personality, was interested only in horses and that his only income was his pay as a cavalry officer. Several newspapers pointed out that the prospective bridegroom's small income could be a problem for the taxpayer: the married couple could not exist on Captain Phillips's pay; the Princess was not entitled to spend any of the £35,000 she received from the Civil List on helping to support a husband. Would the marriage then need to be subsidised, and if so who would foot the bill?

More of this would be heard in the future. The marriage took place on 14 November 1973. About 500 million people saw the ceremony on television. Some British newspapers complained that the expense of the marriage celebrations at a time of economic recession were unjustified, especially taking into account the fact that the bridegroom was a native and a commoner. There was much more criticism when it was learned that for their honeymoon the

Princess and her husband would sail to the West Indies aboard the *Britannia*. In a television interview, Princess Anne dismissed this criticism as "none of their business" and pointed out that the royal yacht was to sail to the West Indies in any case to be ready for the Queen to use when she visited New Zealand the following February. This served only to exacerbate feelings about the cost involved in keeping members of the royal family in the style to which they had been accustomed. The country was living in a period of miners' strikes and consequent power cuts. Four weeks after the wedding the Prime Minister announced that owing to the shortage of coal a shortened working week would be introduced.

It was, therefore, in an atmosphere of gloom and apprehension about the state of the economy, and some rancour, that the Queen left Britain in January 1974 to meet her daughter and Captain Phillips in Ottawa. From there they were to make their way to Christchurch, New Zealand, where Prince Philip was waiting for them – he had gone ahead to open the Commonwealth Games – accompanied by Prince Charles, now serving on board HMS *Jupiter*. The Commonwealth Games over, the royal party proceeded to Australia. Apart from some demonstrations by Maoris protesting about the acquisition of their land by British settlers in front of the government buildings in Canberra the visit proceeded predictably until the day after the Queen opened Parliament when she was informed that her Prime Minister in Britain, Edward Heath, had called for a general election. The Queen consequently left Canberra at once to be in London to grant the dissolution of Parliament.

Since winning the general election of 1970, Edward Heath had had little success as Prime Minister. Coming to office with commitments to undo much of which the previous Labour governments had done Heath was soon forced into changes of policy which have gone down in history as the "U-turns". In 1973 he had become locked in a struggle with the coalminers, which had brought about his decision to call this election. It would be fought, he said, on the simple question: "Who governs Britain?" and which the newspapers took up as "Who runs Britain? The Government or the Miners?"

The result of the election involved the Queen in another constitutional problem. The Labour Party won 301 seats; the Conservatives won 297. Labour had a majority of four seats over the Conservatives. But seats had also been won by fourteen Liberals and nine Scottish and Welsh Nationalists. Heath took the view that if he could get the support of these parties, or even of the Liberals, he could claim to the Queen that he had enough support in the House of Commons to enable him to form a government, a coalition government, and ask her to commission him to try and do so. This, as existing Prime Minister, he was entitled to do, and he asked the Queen to use her prerogative and let him try.

The Queen could have used her prerogative to refuse. She could have told Heath that in the interests of the country she must refuse his request. She could have taken the view that Heath having called an election to give him the power to impose his will on the miners the outcome of the election had denied him that power and the miners' strike was still going on, and was crippling the country. Days if not weeks could elapse before Mr Heath, and the Queen, discovered whether he could or could not obtain enough support from the Liberals and the Nationalists. By then the country might be in chaos. However, the Queen decided that he must be allowed to try. She was criticised for doing so.

Armed with her support, Heath held talks with Jeremy Thorpe, the Liberal leader. These negotiations soon collapsed. Thorpe would agree to enter a coalition only if Heath promised to introduce a Bill for proportional representation. Heath went a long way to meeting Thorpe's terms but refused to commit to a promise of a Bill for PR. Heath informed the Queen that his quest for a majority in the House had failed, and submitted his resignation. Harold Wilson became Prime Minister for the third time.

After the opening of Parliament the Queen flew to Indonesia. She had been in Jakarta for six days when she was informed of the attempted kidnapping of Princess Anne. An armed man had waylaid the Princess and her husband on their way down the Mall to Buckingham Palace at night on their return from a charity film show. The Princess's driver, her detective, a policeman and a journalist had been wounded. Anne had almost been dragged out of her car, Mark had held on to her at risk of his life. The Queen had only a few more engagements ahead of her in Jakarta; she completed them as planned. But it became known at once that she had been shocked by the news: it was a grim confirmation that the lives of the royal family and herself were always in danger.

In 1974, at the age of twenty-five, Prince Charles had a long "Conversation" with the author which was published on two consecutive Sundays in the *Observer*. He spoke about how happy he had been at home: "I've observed my father's wisdom and judgement and appreciated it, benefited from it ... I love my home life. We happen to be a very close-knit family. I'm happier at home, with the family, than anywhere else." Of times away from home the best had been his spell in Australia. "More than any other experience, those years opened my eyes. You are judged there on how people see you, and feel about you ... Australia got me over my shyness. I was fairly shy when I was younger."

The Prince talked with knowledge and confidence, and with refreshing candour, on a variety of topics. Music: he took up the cello after he had heard Jacqueline Du Pré play at a concert. "Have you ever sung in a big choir? It's marvellous. I sang in the Bach B Minor Mass. There's nothing like it." He talked about life in the Navy, about how a member of the royal family learns the job – "You learn the way they say the monkey learns: watching its parents." He looked back on the value of learning Welsh in Aberystwyth, and spoke of his plans for the setting up of Trusts financed by industrialists to create opportunities for young people to make a start in business activities – a vision which came to life in the establishment of the Prince's Youth Business Trust. He described his conception of the future of the Commonwealth.

There were two subjects on which his comments were of special interest to his readers then, and are of even more interest now: marriage and Abdication.

Whatever your place in life, when you marry you're forming a partnership which you hope will last, say, fifty years – I certainly hope so, because, as I've told you, I've been brought up in a close-knit happy family, and family life means more to me than anything else. So I'd want to marry somebody who had interests which I understood and could share.

Then look at it from the woman's point of view. A woman not only marries a man; she marries into a way of life, into a job, into a life in which she's got a contribution to make. She's got to have some knowledge of it, some sense of it, or she wouldn't have a clue about whether she's going to like it, and if she didn't have a clue it would be risky for her, wouldn't it? If I'm deciding on whom I want to live with for fifty years – well, that's the last decision in which I would want my head to be ruled entirely by my heart. It's nothing to do with class; it's to do with compatibility.

There are as many cases of marriages turning out unsatisfactorily because a man married "above" himself as there are when he married "below". Marriage isn't an "up" or "down" issue, anyway: it's a side-by-side one.

On the subject of Abdication the Prince gave his views in answer to a question about whether monarchs should voluntarily retire when they attained a certain age, and whether, if they did not, the heir might spend many frustrating years without a real job to do. The Prince said:

> No, I certainly don't think monarchs should retire, and be pensioned off, say, at sixty, as some professions and businesses stipulate. The nature of being a monarch is different. Take Queen Victoria. In her 80s, she was more loved, more known, more revered, and a more important part of the life of her country than she had ever been before ...
>
> The other point you made: if the monarch lives long and remains on the throne, isn't the heir-apparent kept out of things? Again, I'd say not. What matters is what he *makes* of things. There's plenty I can do. Especially when I am young. Precisely because I am *not* the sovereign, and therefore not so bound by the constitution, I might be able to consider a wider range of possibilities of contributing.

The following year the thorny question of the Civil List arose again, culminating in a debate in the House of Commons about increases in remuneration for the members of the royal family. The rise in oil prices in 1973 had precipitated an unprecedented rise in inflation; in mid-1975 it had reached a record level of twenty-one per cent. The Civil List, as we have seen, had been increased only once since the Queen had come to the throne in 1952, and newspapers carried stories, which must have been based on information from Buckingham Palace, that in 1971 and 1974 the Queen had personally met a deficit out of her private means. The government spoke of an annual review of the Civil List. The debate in the House of Commons was acrimonious. Several speakers pointed out that planning what the Queen should be paid by the taxpayer was bedevilled by the degree of secrecy which existed about the extent of the Queen's private fortune and her assets. How could the government decide what the Queen should have without knowing what she already had? It could have been predicted that some time after the public debate of 1975 the day would come when the Queen's immunity from taxation would have to end, though few would have predicted that eighteen years would pass before the Queen would decide that she should pay income tax like everybody else.

The first part of 1975 was exceptionally busy for the Queen. After visiting Bermuda, Barbados and the Bahamas she went on to make her first State visit to Mexico. In April she flew from London to Jamaica to open the 1975 Commonwealth Conference, thence to Hong Kong, and on to Tokyo for her first State visit to Japan. She returned to Britain to find a mixture of despondency and hope. In June, inflation had risen to twenty-five per cent; pay awards were running at a level of more than thirty per cent. On the other hand, one of her first major engagements on her return was to open the pipeline that would bring the first North Sea oil into the United Kingdom.

Princess Margaret came back into the news in January 1976. For three years it had seemed that her marriage with Lord Snowdon had become a front behind which wife and husband went their own ways. The Princess had been seen going to the theatre and to parties with a number of different men; rarely was she seen with her husband. Now, she broke off the traditional long Christmas holiday with the royal family at Sandringham to fly to the Caribbean island of Mustique for a holiday in the sun. She was accompanied by a man much younger than she, Roddy Llewellyn. Photographs of the two together appeared in the *News of the World*. Within a few days Lord Snowdon moved out of the royal residence and made it known to the Queen that he intended to obtain a divorce. In fact for the time being he agreed merely to a legal separation. A statement was issued from Buckingham Palace: "Her Royal Highness the Princess Margaret, Countess of Snowdon, and the Earl of Snowdon, have mutually agreed to live apart. The Princess will carry out her public duties unaccompanied by Lord Snowdon. There are no plans for any divorce proceedings." By this time Lord Snowdon was in Australia taking photographs. He too issued a statement: "I am naturally desperately sad in every way that this has had to come. I would just like to say three things: first to pray for the understanding of our two children; secondly to wish Princess Margaret every happiness for her future; and thirdly to express with utmost humility the love, admiration and respect I will always have for her sister, her mother and her entire family."

The news of the royal separation coincided with the totally unexpected announcement that the Prime Minister had resigned. At the time, the suddenness of Wilson's decision caused immense speculation about what had precipitated it. Later it became known that Wilson had told the Queen when he became Prime Minister for the third time in 1974 that he would retire two years later, and that several months before he submitted his resignation he had given his personal lawyer notice of the date. The Parliamentary Labour Party elected James Callaghan to succeed him as leader of the Parliamentary Labour Party. The Queen summoned him to the Palace on 15 April, and invited him to form a new government. Some years later, Lord Callaghan, as he became, recorded in his memoirs the moments in which he became Prime Minister:

The expected telephone call soon came, and Sir Martin Charteris [the Queen's Private Secretary] was enquiring, "When would it be convenient for you to come to the Palace?"

Convenient! I am sure he enjoyed the delicate meiosis of the word ...

Audrey and I left the moment I received the summons and drove to the Palace together. There she waited in an ante-room while the Queen received me in audience and invited me to form a government. This was a necessary step to conform with the well-established convention that when the Prime Minister resigns, the Government ceases to exist.

There is no formal ceremony for the appointment of a Prime Minister. That evening I took no oath and received no official communication.

Fifteen days later, the Queen celebrated her fiftieth birthday with a grand party at Windsor. The following day there was comment on the fact that the new Prime Minister had not been present. Was there some trouble between them? It soon transpired that he had told the Queen in advance that he urgently needed all the time he could get to familiarise himself with State papers. The Queen showed her goodwill by inviting him and his wife to dinner the following week. Lord Snowdon was among the guests, his presence quashing gossip that the Queen had decided to ostracise him as a result of the separation from Princess Margaret. Notable among the guests was the new leader of the Conservative Party – the first woman to occupy that post – Margaret Thatcher.

In July the Queen made a visit to the United States, accompanied by the Foreign Secretary, Anthony Crosland. In Washington, President Ford held a grand banquet for her in the White House. The Queen went to Philadelphia, New York and Boston. She made a particularly good impression in Philadelphia with her first words in public: "I speak to you as the direct descendant of King George III." She went on to admit that Britain had learned a great lesson from the Founding Fathers of the United States: "To know the right time and the manner of yielding what it is impossible to keep." If Britain had not learned that lesson, she said, the Empire could not have been transformed into a Commonwealth. She used her American visit to further opportunities for Anglo-American business: fifty British businessmen joined fifty American businessmen on the *Britannia* for a conference on Anglo-American trade.

She then crossed the frontier into Canada, to open the 1976 Olympics in Montreal. Here she was joined by Princess Anne and her husband, and by Prince Charles and Prince Andrew. Her speeches repeated the call for good relations between the British and the French in Canada. The response of the French-Canadians was not enthusiastic; there were more signs than ever before that popular support for the connection was in decline.

The following year, 1977, was the year of the Royal Silver Jubilee. The auspices for the celebrations were not propitious. The state of the British economy in January of that year was the worst since the end of the war in 1945. More than 1.3 million were unemployed. The rate of inflation was sixteen per cent. Sterling was in danger. To protect it the government needed a huge loan from the International Monetary Fund. To get it required the promise of huge cuts in public expenditure.

Prince Philip wrote an article for the *Director* referring to the state of the economy and containing the observation: "People are slowly coming round to the feeling that we have been driven too far along one road; that we have got to come back a little and not concentrate so heavily on the unfortunate, the underprivileged, but try to create a situation whereby the enterprising can make their contribution ..." His remarks came under fire from many quarters as an intrusion into the field of politics, and therefore unconstitutional. Some of his critics said they were also irresponsible, uninformed, and damaging to the country's interests. Several Labour MPs complained bitterly. The Prime Minister evaded the question of whether the Prince had behaved unconstitutionally and merely said that he did not share the Prince's views. Prince Philip, unabashed, wrote further articles about the state of the nation.

The Queen now began an eight-week tour to include Samoa, Fiji, New Zealand, Australia and Papua New Guinea. One Australian opinion poll had indicated that fifty-eight per cent of the adult population were ready to see the end of the monarchy. This relatively steep rise in republican feeling was attributed to the clash which had occurred two years previously between the Governor-General, Sir John Kerr, and the Prime Minister of the Labour government, Mr Gough Whitlam.

The conflict between Sir John and Mr Whitlam had been precipitated by a step taken by the Leader of the Opposition, Mr Malcolm Fraser. Such was the incompetence of the Whitlam government, announced Mr Fraser, he would bring it down and force a general election. He would do this by preventing the passage of the budget appropriations bills through the Senate, a move which if successful would leave the country without any money to pay its way.

Mr Fraser's dramatic move was much criticised on two grounds: he was able to make it only because by the death of a Senator he had suddenly acquired a majority of one in the Senate; and his use of that majority broke for the first time an honoured historical convention that the Senate did not oppose money bills which had the support of the majority in the House of Representatives.

The Governor-General took the view that he could not stand by and watch the government try and govern without funds. If he did, many businesses would be denied payment of their bills and thousands of people would be deprived of their wages and put out of work. He called on Mr Whitlam to announce a general election. The Prime Minister rejected his request. He pointed out that the government had funds at its disposal for some weeks to come, and that in any case it was constitutionally wrong for the Governor-

General to dismiss an administration whose ministers had the backing of a majority in the House of Representatives. Mr Whitlam refused to go. The Governor-General, as representative of the Queen, then used her Royal Prerogative to dismiss the government.

An election consequently took place. During the campaign Mr Whitlam complained that his party had been forced out of office unjustly. Mr Fraser, on the other hand, denounced the government for the increase in inflation and in unemployment which had taken place during its time in office. Mr Fraser won impressively.

When the Queen arrived in Australia the political atmosphere was still highly charged with the aftermath of the Governor/Gough Whitlam affair. Many people thought that the Governor-General's decision to call an election which the government, though it had a parliamentary majority, looked fated to lose was a highly political exercise of his powers. Some people construed his action as a monarchist blow against republicanism: Whitlam had abolished the British national anthem and was in favour of ending the connection with the British Crown. Many people – outside as well as inside Australia – believed that the Governor-General's decision was the Queen's decision, and that the blame for it should go to her; in fact, such a decision was the responsibility not of the Queen but of her equivalent in the Australian political system, the Governor-General, to whom her prerogative powers were delegated. This was not sufficiently understood to prevent criticism of her on constitutional grounds. Much else, too, was misunderstood, and is misunderstood to this day: for instance, many people think that Sir John Kerr was a dyed-in-the-wool Australian upper-class pro-British reactionary; in fact, he was the son of a boiler-maker and had been recommended to the Queen for this post by Mr Whitlam.

The future of Prince Charles was affected. In the mid-seventies, as a result of his love for the Australians, which was reciprocated, and a feeling that this promising young man should be given a worthwhile job to do, a movement had developed in the United Kingdom and in Australia – Gough Whitlam was in favour of it – to make Charles the next Governor-General. The Kerr/Whitlam Crisis aborted this. In 1988 the matter was raised again informally. The Prince would consider it only if it had unanimous political support. It had not.

In 1977 the focus was on the Queen's Silver Jubilee. She delivered her Jubilee speech in May. Taking advantage of the Labour government's tiny overall majority of three, the Scottish and Welsh Nationalists were pressing hard for devolution. In her speech the Queen made no bones about where she stood. "Perhaps this Jubilee is a time to remind ourselves of the benefits which union has conferred at home and in our international dealings, on inhabitants of all parts of this United Kingdom." She could readily understand the aspirations of the Scots and the Welsh peoples, she said. "But I cannot forget that I was crowned Queen of the United Kingdom of Great Britain and Northern Ireland." Later in the month she made a tour of Scotland. There were very few manifestations of Scottish nationalism, certainly no more than there had been when she toured Scotland in the year of the Coronation twenty-four years previously.

By now the activities of the IRA had become a major problem for the police. The Commissioner of the Metropolitan Police Force, it was rumoured, "gulped" when he heard that after the Jubilee thanksgiving service in St Paul's the Queen proposed to do a walkabout from the Cathedral to the Guildhall some hundreds of yards away. The Queen was determined to do this. The Commissioner did his job. All was well.

The year 1977 was good for the Queen, but 1978 was bad. Princess Margaret's standing with the public was diminishing perceptibly. Roddy Llewellyn, had gone into the entertainment business as a singer, and he had recorded some songs. His personal relationship with Princess Margaret was being exploited to obtain publicity for his recordings. These were thought to be of very little merit. In February 1978, when he was on holiday with the Princess in Mustique, he was suddenly smitten by a gastric ulcer, and was flown to hospital in Barbados. The Princess accompanied him. Her concern for her friend occasioned a great deal of publicity. Later the Princess, too, fell seriously ill, the diagnosis being hepatitis brought on by alcohol. The Bishop of Truro made some comments on the Princess's relationship with Llewellyn and suggested that the time had come for her to retire from public life.

In May an announcement from Buckingham Palace revealed that the Princess and Lord Snowdon were to be divorced on the grounds that they had lived apart from each other for two years. Speculation increased that Margaret wanted to marry Roddy Llewellyn, and there were stories that the Queen had warned her sister that if a marriage took place Margaret would have to live abroad. When

Roddy Llewellyn left the country – some say after considerable pressure on him to do so – people waited to see if the Princess followed him. She did not. On the contrary she continued to carry out her engagements. Llewellyn remained abroad for several weeks, at one point making a statement that there could be no question of a marriage between him and Princess Margaret, and in due course returned to Britain. He was seen from time to time in Princess Margaret's company, but there was no further speculation about a marriage. There had been widespread sympathy and admiration for the Princess at the time it was thought she might marry Townsend: there seemed nothing of the kind twenty-five years later when there was gossip that she might marry Roddy Llewellyn. Some of the comment reflected a sense of guilt: if she had been allowed to marry Townsend her life thereafter might have been settled and serene.

The early months of 1978 produced another problem for the Queen, this one of a constitutional as well as personal nature. Her first cousin, Prince Michael of Kent, aged thirty-six, younger brother of the Duke of Kent, thought to be a confirmed bachelor, informed her that he wished to marry Marie-Christine von Reibnitz, who until recently had been married to a British banker, Mr Tom Troubridge. The former Mrs Troubridge was a divorcee, a Roman Catholic, and it was murmured, and proved to be the case later, the daughter of a former Nazi SS officer, Gunther von Reibnitz.

Marie-Christine von Reibnitz had been brought up in Australia. She had met Prince Michael through Prince William of Gloucester, killed in an air accident in 1972, and she and Prince Michael became friends. Soon they were in love. In due course the Queen gave her permission for the marriage to take place, but since as a member of the royal family Prince Michael was subject to the Act of Settlement of 1701 there would have to be conditions: Marie-Christine being a Roman Catholic, Prince Michael must give up his right of succession; he must undertake that any children of the marriage would be brought up as members of the Church of England; the marriage must take place outside the country. It took place in Vienna, conducted in German, a civil ceremony, since neither the Anglican nor Catholic Church recognised it – the Pope because if there were children they would not be brought up as Catholics, and the Church of England because it did not recognise nullity. Princess Anne attended the wedding. So did Mountbatten; as a friend of Prince Michael's father he had played a considerable role in paving the way for the marriage to take place. Members of Prince Michael of Kent's family were present: the Duke of Kent, his elder brother; and his sister, Princess Alexandra.

The Queen's visits to European countries showed that whatever Europeans thought of the United Kingdom they were immensely interested in the Queen, notwithstanding the fact that several members of the European Economic Community had royal families of their own. The State visit to Germany in 1978 was a noteworthy example of her popularity on the Continent. The Germans knew that British public opinion was on the whole hostile towards the EEC, complaining that they drew no benefit from it, and blaming it for the increase in their cost of living. This did not prevent vast crowds turning out and cheering her as though she meant something to them.

That year indeed an onlooker might have said she was better received in Germany than in Canada. The visit to Canada was the second in three years, a statistic which tells its own story. A general election was in the offing, and the Canadian Prime Minister was keeping a careful eye on the attitude of the French-Canadian voters. The government of Quebec was pressing for a considerable reduction of the powers of the Federal government in Ottawa; Mr Trudeau had introduced legislation which went some way towards that, but in the view of the Quebecois not far enough. This was no time for Trudeau to seem attached to the British connection. When the Queen arrived for a two-week visit, her main commitment being to open the Commonwealth Games in Edmonton, Mr Trudeau was not in the country to receive her – he was on holiday in Morocco. This seemed discourteous, and a rude break with the custom in the United Kingdom and in the Commonwealth that when the monarch enters or leaves the country the Prime Minister is in attendance.

The Queen returned home to find mounting concern about the country's economic situation and the attitude of the trade unions. A limit of ten per cent for wage increases had been established, but as Sir Geoffrey Howe, the Opposition spokesman on economic affairs, had said the ten per cent, beginning as a guideline, had become a norm, then a target, and finally a platform. In July the government issued a White Paper which stated that pay rises in 1978–9 should be kept within five per cent, a statement which the leader of the biggest union in the country, the Transport and General Workers, immediately denounced as unrealistic. That it would be difficult to implement this policy was clear: thousands of workers in jobs controlled by the government had already been promised increases of ten per cent or more.

The Prime Minister decided to address the annual Trades Union Congress in September. When he emphasised the five per cent ceiling there were shouts of "shame" and boos. Four weeks later the annual Labour Party Conference in Blackpool voted by a majority of two to one to denounce the five per cent ceiling. The winter of 1978–9, "the winter of discontent", brought a series of strikes for higher pay which reduced industrial output to the level of a three-day week. The road transport workers' strike, launched in support of a demand for an increase of twenty-five per cent, was a massive assault on the government's pay policy. Other workers, including many in the public services, went on strike, including ambulance staff, water and sewage workers, gravediggers and dustmen. There were piles of garbage on the streets. In Liverpool unburied bodies were stored in disused warehouses. The combination of strikes, deprivations, physical discomfort and violence on the picket lines angered and alarmed the public. In February the government's pay policy had been breached beyond repair and increases of ten per cent and above were being given. By the end of March its pay policy was no more.

In March the government came under severe pressure from another quarter. With an overall majority of only four, kept in power by the support of the Welsh and Scottish Nationalist MPs, given in return for the promise of devolution for Wales and Scotland, it had now to make the promise good. The promise was a conditional one: there would be devolution only if the people of Wales and Scotland voted in favour of it in a referendum which showed that devolution was wanted by a majority of at least forty per cent of those entitled to vote. The referendum was held on 1 March. In Wales devolution was rejected decisively. In Scotland devolution obtained a majority but it was below the forty per cent required. The Scottish MPs now claimed that forty per cent had been an unreasonable figure and that since there had been a majority in favour of devolution it must be granted. The government refused. The Scottish Nationalists announced that they would no longer support it. Margaret Thatcher, Leader of the Opposition since 1975, seized her chance, and tabled a vote of no confidence. The government was defeated – by one vote. Callaghan called a general election for 3 May. The Conservatives won with an overall majority of forty-three.

The first of Mrs Thatcher's major problems which affected the Queen was Rhodesia. UDI and economic sanctions were still in force, and for seven years Rhodesia had been harassed by guerrilla war. Armed forces of the Patriotic Front, directed by Mr Mugabe and Mr Nkomo, operated from bases in neighbouring countries, Zambia, Mozambique and Botswana, and Rhodesian army forces retaliated with frequent raids across the border. A spokesman for the Red Cross described the fighting as "the cruellest conflict in the world". The object of British and American policy was all-party settlement talks leading to elections under United Nations supervision. Before they could effect this, Mr Ian Smith, leader of the white Rhodesian Front (RF), announced that Rhodesia would hold its own elections. These took place in April 1979. The leaders of three black parties took part, including Bishop Muzorewa, head of the United African National Council (UANC), but the two leaders of the Patriotic Front, Nkomo and Mugabe, did not. As a result Bishop Muzorewa's party gained an overall majority of fifty-one, and a new state known as Zimbabwe Rhodesia, with a new constitution, came into being on 1 June. This brought little improvement in the situation. Some of the black political leaders would have nothing to do with the new government, regarding Muzorewa as a tool of Mr Smith and the whites; Mr Sithole, leader of the Zimbabwe African National Union (ZANU-Sithole) condemned the elections as "neither fair nor free".

Before Mrs Thatcher became Prime Minister she had been a supporter of Mr Smith, and had favoured the establishment of a Smith regime which gave majority rule to the blacks but which reserved important powers for the whites. She was ready to support Bishop Muzorewa, and to lift sanctions. This policy was strongly opposed by the United Nations and by most Commonwealth governments. It was generally believed that the Queen, as Head of the Commonwealth, took the side of the Commonwealth majority and the United Nations. Soon after becoming Prime Minister in May Mrs Thatcher changed her mind. She decided after all not to recognise Muzorewa, and not to lift sanctions. Nevertheless there were fears in many Commonwealth countries that she might try to impose her original views at the coming Commonwealth conference to be held at Lusaka, the capital of Zambia, in August. Friction with black Commonwealth members, if nothing worse, was expected.

The Queen, as usual, as Head of the Commonwealth, would attend and preside over the Lusaka conference. There was good reason for the government to try to prevent her from going. The guerrilla war was raging, and Lusaka was not far from the fighting – there were guerrilla bases only just outside the city, and civilian aircraft approaching the airport had been fired on. If Mrs Thatcher had advised the Queen as sovereign of the United Kingdom that she should not go the Queen would have been obliged to take her advice. But the Queen took the view that she was going to the Lusaka conference as Head of the Commonwealth; thus in that role she was not under the same obligation to take the British Prime Minister's advice. She went.

Nobody can know yet – if ever – all that happened behind the scenes in Lusaka. Mrs Thatcher had to listen to a good deal of criticism, and some very hard things were said about her. For the Queen there was nothing but praise. She had had the advantage of arriving in Africa some days in advance of the British Prime Minister, and of having had contacts with several of the Commonwealth Prime Ministers. According to accounts from members of the staff of some of the Commonwealth Prime Ministers present the Queen played a valuable role in reducing suspicions and animosities which had developed over the last few months, and in creating a more relaxed and co-operative atmosphere than had been anticipated for the opening of the conference. As usual in conversations with the Prime Ministers she talked about, and listened to, what was of concern to them in their own countries. But she dwelt also on what the conference could do to help with a solution of the problem in Rhodesia. She said that it would be helpful if the African Prime Ministers encouraged the local newspapers to create an atmosphere of discussion rather than one of recrimination, to look at possibilities of agreements rather than of dissension.

There was much speculation, and there has been much since, about the role of the Queen once the conference had got going, particularly about her influence with her old friend Kenneth Kaunda, President of the host country, who controlled these local newspapers. And there has been much praise for Mrs Thatcher's role in taking advantage of the conference openly to express reappraisal of her views about the future of Rhodesia. What effect the Queen's involvement in the situation had cannot as yet be assessed owing to the secrecy which surrounds her role in such matters, but *The Annual Register* provides as well-informed and authoritative an account of it as we are likely to get:

> The Lusaka conference opened in an atmosphere heated by some intemperate anti-Thatcher fireworks in a local government-controlled organ, but cooled by the presence of Her Majesty the Queen, whom the same newspaper declared "could easily be elected Queen of the World".

At Lusaka Mrs Thatcher agreed to a proposal for an all-party constitutional conference to take place in London the following September to secure agreement on all issued affecting Rhodesia by 15 November. The Lancaster House conference agreement was signed on 21 December. UDI ended. Sanctions were lifted. Lord Soames went out to Rhodesia as Governor and managed the country until one-man, one-vote elections as a preliminary to independence took place early the following year. In March the Governor, Lord Soames, announced the results. The Patriotic Front parties had won an overwhelming victory. He asked Mr Mugabe, whose wing of the Front, ZANU, had gained an overall majority of the seats, to form a government. At midnight on 17 April in Salisbury the Prince of Wales welcomed the new state of Zimbabwe as the forty-third member of the Commonwealth.

Mrs Thatcher, in agreeing to the decisions taken at the Lancaster House conference, and in particular to dropping Muzorewa and accepting Mugabe, had changed her mind. She had come round to the view of the Commonwealth in general, and of the Queen. There was speculation that they might differ on other issues, a subject dealt with later. But at the end of 1979 there could be no disagreement about the good work done at Lusaka. The conference, said *The Annual Register*,

> ... could be regarded as a high point in Commonwealth history. As Mr Malcolm Fraser, the Prime Minister of Australia, put it, it proved the Commonwealth had the capacity to make a major contribution in international affairs through the rest of the century.

The part the Queen had played at Lusaka was fully known to the Commonwealth Prime Ministers, and known to a lesser extent to many others. Nobody dissented from the view taken by her press secretary in a statement he made when she had got back from her seventeen-day tour of African countries which, he said,

> had proved that the Queen's role as head of the Commonwealth is no longer a hangover from colonial days. Instead there has been a spelling-out of a new perception of her role.

Soon after the Queen returned from Africa she and her family had to bear one of their most bitter personal blows – the death of Lord Mountbatten on 27 August at the hands of the IRA. Lord Mountbatten was at his holiday home in County Sligo in the Republic of Ireland. He was steering his fishing boat, *Shadow V*, out of the little harbour of Mullaghmore when, just as he had cleared the harbour wall, a bomb secreted in the deck at his feet, probably detonated from the shore, exploded and killed him. Two other members of the family and his boatman were killed, and his daughter and her husband were badly injured.

Mountbatten had been an active presence in the lives of the royal family for as long as they could remember. Most of them, though they admired his gifts and held him in affection, had mixed feelings about him. The Queen Mother viewed him with suspicion: at one time he had been the Duke of Windsor's closest friend, which made him, in her book, an enemy of her husband; the fact that later Mountbatten deserted the Duke of Windsor and sought to ingratiate himself with her husband when he became King did not diminish her suspicions about him but, rather, added to them. The Prince of Wales, as has been mentioned earlier, felt he owed a great deal to Uncle Dickie, his HGF, his Honorary Grandfather.

On the last page but one of his biography of Mountbatten, Philip Ziegler wrote as follows:

> A picture of Mountbatten without his warts would indeed be unconvincing, for, like everything else about him, his faults were on the grandest scale. His vanity, though childlike, was monstrous, his ambition unbridled. The truth, in his hands, was swiftly converted from what it was to what it should have been. He sought to rewrite history with cavalier indifference to the facts to

magnify his own achievements. There was a time when I became so enraged by what I began to feel was his determination to hoodwink me that I found it necessary to place on my desk a notice saying: REMEMBER, IN SPITE OF EVERYTHING, HE WAS A GREAT MAN.

The Queen, with her "long cool stare", would certainly have been as well aware of Uncle Dickie's virtues and weaknesses as his biographer was. But her knowledge would not have softened the blow of his abrupt departure from her life, and the life of her family.

In early November 1979 a book about British spies was published: *The Climate of Treason*, by Andrew Boyle. As a result a question was put down for the Prime Minister in the House of Commons which referred to Sir Anthony Blunt, Surveyor of the Queen's Pictures and adviser on pictures and drawings from 1945 to 1978. When she replied to this question on 20 November, Mrs Thatcher informed the House that Blunt had been questioned as a presumed spy in 1951, had admitted helping the traitors Burgess and Maclean to escape that year, and in return had been given immunity from charges. Successive Attorney-Generals had in 1973, 1974 and 1979 agreed that in view of the offer of immunity there were no grounds for criminal proceedings. Mrs Thatcher added that in 1964 the Queen's Private Secretary had been told of Blunt's 1951 confession and of his acceptance of immunity, and of the reasons for which the offer of immunity had been made.

Immediately after the Prime Minister had made her statement Buckingham Palace announced that Blunt had been stripped of his knighthood – in the Victorian Order, in the gift of the monarch. It was generally assumed that since this had not been done before it was only then that the Queen had learned that he had been a spy. It soon became clear that if in 1964 she had not known all about the Blunt situation her Private Secretary *had* certainly known. Why then had Blunt not been stripped of his knighthood until 1979? Had the Private Secretary not told her in 1964 what the government had told *him*? Had the Queen been told, but had been asked by the government for security reasons to do nothing about Blunt, at any rate for the time being? Had Blunt some kind of blackmailing hold on the government, or the Queen, or somebody in the Court? These and other questions have not yet been answered and may never be.

In 1980 Prince Charles bought a house in Gloucestershire:

Highgrove, a stately home in charming grounds, an ideal house for a married couple and a family. He was now thirty-two years old, two years older than the age by which he had been heard to say in his middle twenties that it was a good thing for a man to be married. There had been speculation that for some time members of his family had been urging him to take a wife, most strongly his father. From time to time in newspaper articles the hope was expressed that he was not going to go the way the last Prince of Wales had gone. Some said that Prince Charles did not really want to get married, and dwelt on the impression that he had created of being a natural bachelor.

On 24 February 1981, it was announced that the Prince of Wales had become engaged to Lady Diana Spencer, daughter of Earl Spencer, at one time an equerry to the Queen. The marriage, which took place in St Paul's Cathedral on 29 July 1981, was described by the Archbishop of Canterbury, Dr Robert Runcie, as the "stuff that fairy-tales are made of". It was estimated that 750 million people in all continents watched the ceremony on television. The general view of the marriage at the time was recorded in *The Annual Register*:

> The heir to the throne, himself popular with all classes, was marrying a young and beautiful English girl who had already earned universal respect and affection for her discreet and yet charming behaviour in face of all the embarrassment and publicity that afflicted her both before and after the engagement was announced ... A future King had chosen a future Queen whom everyone took to their hearts.

Many people remarked that what was known about Lady Diana and her background, aged only twenty when she married, thirteen years younger than her husband, was not very consistent with what the Prince had said about the qualifications of a potential Princess of Wales when he had spoken on the subject a few years previously. But the Prince's choice of a bride was so popular that the inconsistency would have occurred to few people at the time. Those who noticed it might have thought that to mention it would be censorious, and that in any case a man has a right to change his mind. In the next few years the Prince may well have come to the conclusion that his chances of finding the kind of partner he had described were even slimmer than he had suggested they might be in 1974, and that if he waited for the ideal one to come along he might remain a bachelor indefinitely. That would please nobody. Better, in the circumstances, to marry a young lady from outside a royal family who, with the moulding of experience, would soon adopt to royal life.

For those who were unable to witness it for themselves the enthusiastic admiration for the new Princess at the time of the wedding would be difficult to describe. Her beauty, warmth and simplicity gave her an immense appeal. Her comparatively un-royal background and the relatively un-royal way in which she behaved was another prodigious asset. What captured hearts above all was the immediate egalitarian ease of her relationship with everybody she met. For the time being the general view was that to have brought the Princess of Wales into the royal family was the best thing that had happened to the monarchy for many years past, and at a time when the institution needed more popular support. Her arrival on the scene created a situation in which for the larger part of the decade the stock of the monarchy rose to a very high level – as one member of the household put it "royal activities were demand led". And the early years of the marriage added to the reputation of the Prince of Wales.

10

New problems
1982–91

THE "FAIRY-TALE" MARRIAGE of the heir to the throne to a young woman working at a kindergarten cast a benign and cheerful light upon the opening of the 1980s, but as the decade advanced it presented the Queen with many and various problems. In hindsight these made a fateful prelude to the traumas which were to come in the 1990s.

For the Queen, personally, one of the highlights of the early eighties was the change in Princess Anne's image. This was reflected in a lengthy "Conversation" printed in the *Observer* over two successive Sundays. Until this interview appeared the Princess had been perceived as a not very intelligent or thoughtful woman whose only interest was in riding horses, and who swore at cameramen who photographed her when she fell off. In the interview the Princess came over as reasonable, self-critical, articulate and frank, and, above all, with a great concern for the under-privileged. There was no clearer evidence of the change in her image than the number of excerpts from the interview which appeared in other newspapers.

One of the most-quoted parts of the "Conversation" was a passage in which the Princess discussed her previous "image":

Q. Do you recognise yourself as you appear in the national press?

A. Could I ask *you* a question? You've never met me before but I dare say you've read about me in the newspapers. Am I like what you expected?

Q. No, very different. Very different.

A. Tell me what you expected to find, and tell me what you actually *did* find.

The interviewer complied. The Princess was very amused. She gave her views on how it was that people had got her wrong. She went on to discuss her various interests, her curiosity about how other people lived, what she liked about being a member of the royal family and what she did not. When she was asked what she would like to do if she could choose another way of life she answered:

> perhaps the thing I might do best is be a long-distance lorry driver. I think I could manage that quite well. I have a HGV licence and I like driving heavy goods vehicles. I like driving, and especially big vehicles. It's a tough life if you are doing it for a living, and regulations being what they are now, it's in many ways tougher than it was. I'm sure it's a challenging kind of life. And it's an independent kind of life too; that's one of its main advantages.

The Princess went on to deal with a number of the misconceptions which she felt people had about her, in particular that all she cared about was riding horses. She talked about her public duties and the charities she worked for, especially those for children, and outstandingly the Save the Children Fund. In the next few days the excerpts from the interview which were reproduced in the tabloid press gave more space to her likes and dislikes than to her concern for under-privileged children – "Anne would like to be a lorry driver" – but nevertheless the excerpts revealed to her readers that in spite of what they might have believed previously she was in fact a sensible, thoughtful, sympathetic and articulate individual. Many readers of the interview and excerpts wondered if the interview had somehow been contrived, "fixed", to make her seem different from what in fact she was. Fortunately for the interviewer, the Princess was soon asked to appear on a live BBC radio programme, in which she was asked questions on many of the serious problems which she had dealt with in the "Conversation", such matters as the upbringing of children and the problems of married life. She immediately showed that the image of her conveyed by the interview in the *Observer* was a true one, and that much of what had been written about her previously had been unjustified.

It was all the more regrettable, therefore, that in the early 1980s responsible newspaper reporting of Princess Anne's good work for public causes in the United Kingdom and overseas was to some extent submerged in the flood of reportage from the mass-circulation newspapers about the Princess of Wales. At a time when few newspapers were recording Anne's visits to suffering children in Africa, visits made in considerable discomfort and at not inconsiderable risk, much more space was lavished on the dresses Diana would wear to Royal Ascot. The arrival on the scene of Princess Diana increased press coverage to unprecedented levels. She was seen not so much as a new royal, but as a new film star. Press attention intensified when it became known she was pregnant, and soon reached embarrassing proportions.

This was yet another instance of the process which had begun with the televising of the Coronation. Any additional exposure of the royals to the popular gaze created an immediate demand for more of the same. By now the royals had become celebrities. They had been received into a category in which newspapers wrote about them not for what they did but for what they were. The media created an appetite for news about the members of the royal family and then went on to satisfy it. They were helped to some extent by well-intentioned royal well-wishers who thought it was good for the future of the monarchy to make the monarchy more popular, and therefore were ready to acquiesce in, if not contribute to, the process by which the members of the royal family were being perceived more and more as film stars.

Wise people in the early eighties might have predicted the shape of things to come in the early nineties. Some wise people did, including some who worked in Buckingham Palace. Towards the end of 1981 the Queen, worried by the way things were going, conferred with her press secretary, Michael Shea, and with his predecessor, Sir William Heseltine, now promoted to Queen's Private Secretary. Although Sir William had much opened up the activities of the Queen to the media, not all of his colleagues at the Palace had approved of his innovations and initiatives. Some of them had entertained doubts about the wisdom of elevating a press secretary to a post whose incumbent had been historically charged with protecting the Queen's privacy and preserving her mystery rather than promoting her publicity and projecting her personality. It could have been said at this stage that some of Sir William Heseltine's chickens were coming home to roost.

Shortly before Christmas 1981, the Queen's discussions with her advisers led to Buckingham Palace inviting a number of editors in the national media, representing television as well as newspapers, to meet the Queen for a talk and a drink. Before the Queen joined them, Michael Shea outlined the reason for the meeting: that the Queen was concerned about the decline in the privacy of herself and other members of the royal family as a result of the unprecedented attention being paid to them by the national press, and in particular the pressures being created by newspaper reporters and photographers on the Princess. If pressures as a result of attentions from the press continued her pregnancy might be endangered. In his talk with the assembled editors, Shea referred to a recent incident when the Princess, staying at Highgrove, walked into the village to buy sweets and was followed closely by a crowd of photographers. She had been very upset. Shea asked the newspaper editors to consider how they could control such invasions of the Princess's privacy.

The newspaper editors were then asked to join the Queen. Ten years later one of them, Mr Barry Askew, then editor of the *News of the World*, wrote an account of the meeting in the *Guardian*:

> We started off in small groups with the Queen going around from little group to little group ... She came to my group and there were two or three of us around but everybody was in earshot. I knew one or two things about Diana, going out to the sweet shops to buy wine gums and the like. This struck me as a strange thing to do for someone who wanted privacy. So I asked why she did not send a servant to the sweet shop for her. The Queen obviously felt it was meant as an offence to her and she replied: "That was a pompous remark, Mr Agnew." I was duly lambasted in all the papers the next day. I think I was just known as "the man who insulted the Queen".

More than ever in the early eighties the Queen was being asked to make trips abroad, the emphasis now being less on promoting good relations with Commonwealth countries and more on fostering trade relations with foreign customers. The latter objective appealed more to the new Prime Minister than the former, and Mrs Thatcher frequently paid tribute publicly to the Queen as Britain's leading salesperson. The Queen's ventures in serving Mammon rather than mothering the Commonwealth placed her in some awkward situations. There had been much publicity for her visit to Morocco in October 1980, when her host, King Hassan, preferred to play a game of golf rather than attend the lunch given to celebrate her arrival. Subsequently the King did not turn up at a State banquet given for the Queen, kept her waiting for an hour at tea-time in the course of a tour outside the capital, and arrived an hour late for the dinner she had organised for him on the *Britannia*. The Queen's distaste at being so treated was reported without inhibition by the newspapermen travelling with her, but she succeeded in concealing her feelings from the King, which was as well, since she was in Morocco mainly to further the prospects of business with British firms and to prevent British interests in the country being squeezed out by the expansion of American influence.

The Queen's visit to Canada in April the following year was a sad and portentous one in that its purpose was to sever Canada's last legal tie with the United Kingdom. The process had begun in 1980 with movement towards the "patriating of the Constitution", culminating in January 1982 when the new Constitution Act, approved by the British Parliament, provided that henceforth the Constitution was amendable only in Canada. The Queen gave the royal assent in March. In Ottawa the following month, as Queen of Canada, she proclaimed the Act on Parliament Hill. Canada, though remaining within the Commonwealth, with the Queen as titular Head of State, was now an independent country. "The Constitution of Canada has come home," said Mr Trudeau. Thus came to an end the relationship between Britain and Canada which had begun 115 years previously when Queen Victoria had approved the British North America Act of 1867. Of Canada's ten premiers only the Prime Minister of Quebec refused to attend the ceremony, claiming that the new Constitution did not recognise Quebec's historic position in the federation.

By this time the Falklands War had broken out. Massive Argentine forces had invaded the islands on 2 April, and had occupied the capital, Port Stanley. The same day, Mrs Thatcher announced that a large naval task force was being assembled to sail for the Falklands as soon as possible. It put to sea on 5 April. It included HMS *Invincible*, aboard which was the twenty-two-year-old Prince Andrew, now a helicopter pilot. In late May a report reached London that HMS *Coventry* had been sunk and that HMS *Invincible* had been hit. The first part of the report was true; the second part was not, though some weeks passed before the Queen knew for certain that her son was safe.

In 1983 Prince Philip gave an interview to the author for the *Observer*. He did so as the patron of the Albert Exhibition at the Royal College of Art, held to commemorate the life and work of Queen Victoria's consort. Prince Philip said that although he admired Prince Albert, he had some criticisms of his performance as a parent:

. I think he had the weaknesses of an intellectual. He sometimes forgot to take human nature into account ... For example, he tended to forget that the Prince of Wales was not just the Prince of Wales but also his son. If your children are public persons as well as your own children you *have* to look at them in two contexts ... It's a real problem.

Asked about the differences between being a consort in Albert's day and being a consort in the late twentieth century, Prince Philip said that many of these differences were the result of changes in the relationship between the monarchy and the people:

The main problem is that in this democratic age, when members of the royal family are much more exposed than they used to be, people expect us to be all things to all men and to all kinds at all times. The effect on our children is that instead of living in a kind of cocoon of a society composed of people brought up like them, an equal society of their own contemporaries, of their own kind, as in Albert's day, they now grow up and live in an equal society which includes the whole nation. This has its problems: at one moment they're expected to be out in front or up there on high, somehow or other, and the next moment they're supposed to be having a drink in a pub ... Some, at any rate, of what people see of us gives rise to misinterpretation.

A simple example: Buckingham Palace. *The* Palace. Here we

live in this enormous house. The fact is that we didn't choose this house, we didn't build this house, we simply occupy it like a tortoise occupies a shell. We go to State occasions all dressed up but we wouldn't dress up like that if the occasion were *not* a State occasion – the State occasions are part of the living theatre of the monarchy ... live theatre in which everybody's involved, in which all those who stand and watch participate – they're part of the living theatre too.

Asked about the monarchy's readiness for change, Prince Philip said:

Of course the monarch, the consort, the members of the family adapt their behaviour to change; and if you see there's no point in going on doing something you used to do, you drop it. We've dropped a lot of things. The courts, for instance. We don't hold courts any more. We don't have débutante presentations any more – that's another thing that's somehow lost its point. There are a whole number of things we've given up – and we've introduced some new things as well – some of them to replace more usefully things we dropped, more in keeping with the world we live in.

Prince Philip spoke about the great increase in the number of visits members of the royal family now made abroad as a result of the increase in the ease of travel:

The late King only went abroad twice – to Canada and South Africa. Look what happens with us – we're abroad somewhere in the Commonwealth every year, and we go to other countries as well. The ease of travel means you are asked to do more things. People expect you to find time for more things ... Nowadays the Australians say, "We want you to come out and open a village hall", the Canadians say, "We've got a conference opening next week, will you come and address it?" Thirty years ago they wouldn't have dreamed of asking – they would have known it wasn't on logistically.

Prince Philip was giving his views at a time when royal tours abroad had reached an unprecedented level. The year before, Princess Anne had begun a massive series of visits on behalf of the Save the Children Fund. She travelled to its operating centres in Swaziland, Zimbabwe, Malawi, Kenya, Somalia and North Yemen, and in early December visited refugee camps in Lebanon. It was hard going in these areas, dangerous in some of them, particularly Lebanon. Next came Pakistan and North Africa. The newspapers were now taking Anne very seriously.

The Queen and Prince Philip seemed to be travelling abroad more than ever. Early in 1983 they were away for a month, visiting Jamaica, the Cayman Islands, Mexico and the west coast of America. In May they went to Sweden. In November they were in Kenya and Bangladesh, thence to India for the Commonwealth Conference. More and more they could be seen to be supporting the government's drive to increase British exports: Mexico, for example, where there was a huge British investment in steel production. And there was commercial thinking behind the Queen's visit to the Reagans in California and their trip to Hollywood, where a star-spangled banquet was given for them by the President.

In the mid-eighties, however, though the Queen was busier than ever, press publicity for her was not what it had been in the past. When she became Queen, there were only her mother, her sister, her husband and herself. Now there were at least twenty royals. The Prince of Wales, Princess Anne and Prince Andrew loomed large on the scene. The Princess of Wales was already being given more publicity than any of them, the Queen included. What could be written, and was written, about these other members of the royal family was generally much more readable. There were, however, exceptions.

In the early morning of 9 July 1982, a young unemployed labourer, Michael Fagan, scaled the wall of Buckingham Palace, climbed into the Palace through an open window, and, after wandering down the corridors for some time, entered the Queen's bedroom. The Queen woke up. Fagan seated himself on her bed and talked with her until, having behaved with courage and calm, the Queen was at last able to summon a chambermaid and then extricate herself from the situation. The incident received vast attention from the newspapers, different aspects of it causing a great deal of comment. There was much praise for the Queen's self-control; she had held in conversation a man who had he been a terrorist could have murdered her and made off. There was much comment on the light the extraordinary incident had thrown on the Palace's security system. The intruder had scaled the wall, entered the Palace, had gained access to the Queen's bedroom, and had spent several minutes there. When the Queen pressed her alarm bell, and later dialled on the internal telephone system, there had been no response. The Queen was removed to safety not by the Palace police but by a footman who happened to arrive on the scene. It was a bizarre story. Subsequently, the Prime Minister apologised to the Queen for the shortcomings of the Palace security system. Scotland Yard conducted an official inquiry. Three policemen were disciplined.

There was also a good deal of comment on the revelation that the Queen slept alone: where, some tabloids asked, was Prince Philip?

Newspapers were still discussing the Fagan episode when two weeks later they reported the resignation of the Queen's personal bodyguard, police commander Michael Trestrail. The *Sun* had published a story claiming that Trestrail had had a homosexual relationship with a young male prostitute. Trestrail was highly regarded at the Palace, but he had to go. There followed some speculation about the number of homosexuals employed at the Palace and about how and why they obtained their jobs. A number of articles about life at Buckingham Palace, most of them written, or informed, by Palace servants, now appeared in the tabloids. Stephen Barry, valet to the Prince of Wales, and a homosexual, wrote a book about his life in the service of the Prince. This was not published in Britain, but several stories appeared in newspapers about Prince Andrew and his girlfriends. One of these, Miss Koo Stark, who was reported to have starred in a soft pornographic film, became a household name. Twenty-year-old photographs of the Queen in bed nursing her new baby, Prince Edward, born in 1964, were reproduced in the *Sun*. These had been taken by Prince Philip and had somehow left the Palace. The Queen's lawyers became unprecedentedly busy. The disloyal behaviour of her servants and its exploitation by the tabloids created a great deal of sympathy for her; but more and more people began to wonder if she and some of the people around her were in some degree to blame for the undesirable publicity to which she and other members of the royal family were being increasingly subjected.

The year 1986 had looked like being a happy one for the Queen: on 23 July, her second son, Prince Andrew, was to marry Miss Sarah Ferguson, daughter of the Prince of Wales's polo manager, Major Ronald Ferguson. But before that happy event took place there were unhappy ones. In January, accompanied by Prince Philip, the Queen visited Nepal, followed by New Zealand and Australia. New Zealand has always been regarded as much more monarchist than Australia, but on the occasion of this visit the Queen encountered protests by the aborigine Maori people against the annexation of their lands by British settlers. There were some demonstrations. At one of them a Maori exposed his buttocks in the direction of the Queen. She may have been unaware of the incident, but it was widely reported. In Australia demonstrations against the Queen were more numerous and more significant. At one point eggs were thrown at her, one of them staining her coat. Again, newspapers made a great deal of this.

The marriage between Andrew and Sarah Ferguson took place in July, in Westminster Abbey with, it was estimated, around the world 500 million people watching the ceremony on television. The attitude of the public to the marriage was mixed. Many people felt that it was celebrated on a scale, and at an expense, which the rank and importance of the two young people did not merit, and that this showed a lack of judgement, and of sensitivity, on the part of the Queen. Prince Andrew had his critics; in spite of his manly career in the Navy, and brave performance in the Falklands War, his critics thought him a playboy. "Fergie", as she was soon dubbed by the tabloids, had many more critics than had her husband; for some years she had lived with Mr Paddy McNally, twenty-two years older than herself, a widower with two young sons, who had spent much of his time skiing in Switzerland, having made himself rich through the motor-racing industry. Sarah Ferguson had gained a reputation as a good-time, jet-setting feckless girl with unpolished manners and a lack of taste in clothes. But many people liked what they knew about her. She was not stuffy; she was spontaneous; she was warm-hearted; she was outgoing; she liked doing what ordinary people liked doing; she was *different*; and there were many stories to the effect that in early days the Queen welcomed her as a breath of fresh air in the Palace. She was at that time welcome for another reason: it was clear that Prince Andrew thought the world of her, and that the marriage would change his public image: no longer the rumbustious playboy but the happily married family man with a sound career ahead of him in the Navy.

The Queen's image in the mid-eighties was affected by speculation about her relationship with her Prime Minister. Margaret Thatcher had become Britain's first woman Prime Minister in 1979. Her first three years were not successful, but after the Falklands War her stock had soared, and after her sweeping victory in the general election of 1983 her reputation rose to heights not reached by any Prime Minister since the war. From now on there was speculation that the Queen and Mrs Thatcher "didn't get on", that the Queen was neither so politically nor personally close to her Prime Minister as she had been with Mrs Thatcher's six predecessors. It was said that personal feelings were involved. The Queen, it was reported, had come to resent the fact that the second most central role in the affairs of Britain and the Commonwealth was now occupied by a member of her own sex, a woman very conscious of her own femininity, and intending to exploit it. There was much comment that this was a woman who behaved, talked, made speeches, dressed and generally comported herself as though she, too, was a Queen. It was also said that the Queen's attitude to her first woman Prime Minister had become influenced by political considerations.

The Queen had registered the fact that Mrs Thatcher had resolved to end government by consensus politics which, irrespective of whether Labour or Conservatives were in power, had meant a degree of agreement about fundamental domestic policies such as the maintenance of the Welfare State. Mrs Thatcher's commitment to de-nationalisation, privatisation, restoration of free enterprise, and dismantling of much of the provisions of the Welfare State were much criticised, including by many Conservatives, as "divisive". Many predicted that the attempt to carry out these policies would increase unemployment to levels not experienced since the 1930s. Applied "Thatcherism" would provoke strikes and industrial protest on an unprecedented scale, and threaten the stability of the country as never since the general strike of 1926.

How much of this was conveyed to the Queen, and how much of it she perceived for herself, is not known. But she would certainly have been aware that several of her former Prime Ministers, Conservatives as well as Labour, were profoundly apprehensive about the possible consequences of "Thatcherism". Edward Heath, she knew, a former Conservative Prime Minister, had from the beginning of Mrs Thatcher's period in office denounced her policies as a threat to the fabric of British society. Monarchs anywhere any time become nervous when they hear from good sources that the Prime Minister in office is committed to carrying out policies which might jeopardise the stability of the realm. Speculation that the Queen had doubts about Margaret Thatcher and "Thatcherism" did not diminish.

In October 1983 the Queen and her Prime Minister were set a problem when President Reagan sent American armed forces to occupy Grenada, a member of the Commonwealth, threatened with a political crisis precipitated by a coup by a left-wing military group which had murdered the Prime Minister and taken over the government of the island. To protect lives, including 1,000 Americans on the island, to preserve democratic institutions and to restore law and order the President ordered the occupation of the island, claiming as justification the treaty of mutual support signed by eastern Caribbean nations, including Grenada, in 1981. Britain had been asked to co-operate with the United States in this initiative. Mrs Thatcher had not only refused to do so, but had telephoned Mr Reagan in an attempt to persuade him to call his invasion off. In the debate on the subject in the Commons, many Conservatives ranged themselves with Labour MPs, and denounced what many of them called the Americans' act of aggression.

The Queen was put in a difficult position. The Americans, uninvited, had invaded a country of which she was the Head. She had to accept the fact that her Prime Minister in Britain had failed to prevent them from doing so, but it was harder for her to accept the speed with which her Prime Minister had accepted the *fait accompli*. Fortunately it took the Americans only two days to restore the situation in Grenada, and their troops began to leave at once. Resentment against America among members of the Commonwealth rapidly subsided, which was fortunate for Queen and Prime Minister since the Commonwealth Conference was to open in Delhi four weeks later. Though Grenada came up at the Conference, and some critical things were said about the Americans, the emphasis was on Caribbean co-operation for the future.

Nevertheless it was becoming more and more clear that the perspectives of the monarch and the Prime Minister on Commonwealth affairs were not the same. They saw things differently, partly as persons, and partly because of the difference in their roles. Mrs Thatcher was not uninterested in the members of the Commonwealth but she was interested in them mainly on account of trade. She did not think that the Commonwealth had any power in the world, and she would rather have been on bad terms with the Commonwealth than with the United States whose influence in the world was second to none. She was well aware that Commonwealth attitudes, especially those of the black countries, could be an embarrassment to Britain in her relations with other members of the Commonwealth, for example South Africa. She was the Prime Minister of the United Kingdom, not of Ghana or Zimbabwe.

The Queen saw things differently. She was the Queen or Head of State of most of the fifty countries of the Commonwealth. She was the link which held them all together. The Commonwealth for her was still, if not a power, a great influence in the world and she was its leader. It was a great platform for her from which to speak. The existence of the Commonwealth gave the monarchy a standing and a meaning which transcended what the throne of the United Kingdom alone could give. And to guide, maintain and enhance the Commonwealth, the new Commonwealth, was a sacred trust and duty which as a girl she had inherited from her father and which she had promised him to carry out. In many ways for Mrs Thatcher the Commonwealth was a liability, whereas for the Queen it was a way of life.

This could be seen at the Commonwealth Conference at Nassau in October 1985 when the issue of whether or not to impose sanctions on South Africa came to a head. The majority of those present, increasingly disturbed by the pressures of apartheid on the black population, were strongly in favour of sanctions; Mrs Thatcher was strongly against them. Experience, she said, had shown that such sanctions did not work. What results they produced did harm not good. Sanctions did not reduce opposition: they hardened it. They would hurt the very people they were supposed to help. They would create unemployment in South Africa, and in Commonwealth countries doing trade with South Africa. Failing to persuade Mrs Thatcher to give way, several Commonwealth Prime Ministers tried personally to get the Queen to change Mrs Thatcher's mind. They knew that if Britain, whose trade was immensely important to South Africa, did not support sanctions the programme simply would not work. It was constitutionally in order for the Queen to pass on to Mrs Thatcher any information about the issue which happened to come her way. Mrs Thatcher stuck to her guns.

More difficulty arose between Britain and Commonwealth countries in the spring of 1986, again precipitated by Mrs Thatcher's readiness to co-operate with President Reagan. Missiles were being fired from sites in Libya at United States jet aircraft flying above international waters in the Mediterranean. President Reagan decided to mount an aerial attack on Libyan targets and asked several of his Nato allies for permission to use US airfields in their countries to enable him to do so. Britain alone complied with his request, and on 15 April, with it is said, Mrs Thatcher's express permission, American F111 jets launched attacks on Libya from British bases. A debate took place in the House of Commons the following day. The vote gave the government a predictable majority, but two former Prime Ministers, the Conservative Mr Heath, and the Labour Mr Callaghan, assured the House that had not Mrs Thatcher been in power they would have refused to let the Americans use British bases for this purpose. The Opposition charged her with "collusion". It was immediately clear that public opinion in Britain was strongly opposed to the decision to let the Americans use British bases, particularly since the Americans seemed unable to explain or justify the object of the attacks. The French Prime Minister condemned American bombing of Libya as "totally and utterly unproductive". Opinion in Europe was that the Libyan bombing was one of the most aimless though dangerous actions that President Reagan had embarked upon in his eight years of office, and that Mrs Thatcher had aided and abetted him. Much damage was done to Britain's tourist trade by the decision of many Americans to cancel visits to Britain for fear of terrorist retaliation – travel agents reported that forty per cent of business from America had been cancelled. Criticism of Mrs Thatcher was rampant, since it was put about that she had personally agreed to the use of British airfields for the bombing in order to ingratiate herself with the President. It was Grenada all over again. There was widespread speculation that the Queen was privately critical of her Prime Minister's decision to allow British airfields to be used for dubious and dangerous American purposes, which, though not the Commonwealth's business, would antagonise the majority of the Commonwealth's members.

In July that year the Commonwealth Games were to be held in

Edinburgh and opened by the Queen. On the eve of the ceremony thirty-one Commonwealth countries announced that they would boycott the Games as a protest against Mrs Thatcher's continued stand against South African sanctions. On 20 July, three days before the wedding of Prince Andrew and Sarah Ferguson, the *Sunday Times* published two articles presented as news, not comment, reporting differences of opinion on various major issues between the Queen and her Prime Minister. If these reports were true the Prime Minister would find herself in some constitutional and some political difficulty. And so would the Queen: as monarch of the United Kingdom she was being asked to approve policies which in her other role as Head of the Commonwealth she found unacceptable. The first few words of the story in the *Sunday Times* were as follows:

> Sources close to the Queen let it be known to the *Sunday Times* yesterday that she is dismayed by many of Mrs Thatcher's policies. This dismay goes well beyond the current crisis in the Commonwealth over South Africa. In an unprecedented disclosure of the monarch's views, it was said that the Queen considers the Prime Minister's approach to be uncaring, confrontational and divisive.

The *Sunday Times* then provided several examples of what it claimed the Queen was worried about, including Mrs Thatcher's heavy-handed treatment of the coalminers during the 1985 strike, and allowing the bombing of Libya from British airfields in early 1986. But the report put most emphasis on the Queen's fears for the future of the Commonwealth.

Downing Street immediately denied that any of the "information" on which the story had been based had come from the Prime Minister's office. Had then the *Sunday Times* report, claiming that its information had come directly from Buckingham Palace, been *inspired* by the Palace? Did it accurately reflect the Queen's views? Had it been issued without objection by her? Might it, indeed, have been put out at her wish?

After a week of confusion, caused partly by inaccurate or over-condensed versions appearing in other newspapers, the truth of the matter emerged. A *Sunday Times* writer, not one of the newspaper's political or diplomatic reporters, had told the Queen's press office that he was going to write a feature dealing among other things with how the Queen felt about some of the difficult problems of the day, Commonwealth and domestic, and asked for guidance. Predictably, he had been told that obviously when problems arose at home and abroad which required measures entailing hardship or suffering for her peoples the Queen would be unhappy. The Buckingham Palace source had said nothing about differences of view between the Queen and the Prime Minister. Somehow, an article which had been put to the Palace press office as a feature about the Queen's feelings on problems of the day appeared in the paper as a news story about the Queen's misgivings about her Prime Minister's policies.

Some newspapers made comments suggesting that they believed that the story as printed in the *Sunday Times* had indeed come from the Palace, and did in fact reflect the Queen's views. They consequently criticised her: if the Queen had misgivings about her Prime Minister's policies she should have kept them to herself. To behave otherwise was to behave unconstitutionally, and seriously so. History was then made by a letter published in *The Times* written by the Queen's Private Secretary, Sir William Heseltine. Sir William made it clear that it would be constitutionally wrong for the Queen *not* to express her views on affairs of State to her Prime Minister, either in her weekly confidential audiences with her Prime Minister, or, in confidence, at any other time:

In the debate about the supposed revelations of the Queen's opinions about government policies, I take three points to be axiomatic:

1) The sovereign has the right – indeed a duty – to counsel, encourage and warn her government. She is thus entitled to have opinions on government policy and express them to her chief ministers.

2) Whatever personal opinions the sovereign may hold or may have expressed to her government, she is bound to accept and act on the advice of her ministers.

3) The sovereign is obliged to treat her communications with the Prime Minister as entirely confidential between the two of them. This was central to the statement issued by the Buckingham Palace press office on July 19, as soon as the original *Sunday Times* articles appeared.

Sir William added that the Queen had behaved according to these principles for the thirty-four years of her reign, and that the suggestion that she might have now suddenly departed from them was "preposterous". In short, the Queen had behaved entirely as she should have. She was not there just to listen to her Prime Minister, and say "Yes, Prime Minister." She had a duty to respond to what she was told, and she had done that duty, and intended to go on doing it.

Sir William also said there was no secret that the Queen's press secretary had talked to the journalist who had prepared the article for the *Sunday Times*; but the Queen's press secretary had "said nothing which could reasonably bear the interpretation put upon it by the front page article of July 20". Sir William said that the statement in the article that the sources for its information came from within the Palace and were close to the Queen "constitutes a totally unjustified slur on the impartiality and discretion of senior members of the Royal household".

Looking back on these stories about conflict and tension, personal and political, between the Queen and Mrs Thatcher it is clear that they were, whatever the explanation, and with whatever motive they were written, essentially misleading and had no basis in fact. All the evidence indicates clearly that Mrs Thatcher, born and bred a monarchist, had, and has, the greatest regard for the Queen as a human being, and the Queen had, and has, a great respect for Mrs Thatcher. The two women have much in common: they are virtuous, moral, dedicated, hard-working, conscientious, proud of knowing their jobs and of doing them efficiently, and they have seen and appreciated these qualities in each other. Yet, though highminded and virtuous, they are, and have been, very tolerant of shortcomings in others, not least in their friends and their family, and they have recognised that too in each other. They have both been aware that their children might have suffered from being the children of busy duty-bound responsible public figures. They are both deeply grateful to their husbands. They share the same unspectacular values of a middle-class housewife and mother. Both are honest outspoken women who do not feign but speak their minds. Neither of them is intellectual, introspective or philosophical; both are direct, matter-of-fact, down-to-earth, practical and perceptive. Neither of them is vain, narcissistic or pretentious. Both like to get their way, and are not ashamed of that.

What differences of view they may have on Foreign and Commonwealth affairs comes from differences in perspective. They observe the same things, but they see them from different standpoints. Mrs Thatcher is the Prime Minister of the United Kingdom, and her duty is to the United Kingdom. The Queen is the Queen of the United Kingdom, but she is also the Queen of several other countries, and as well as her duties to the United Kingdom she has duties to the countries of the Commonwealth. As Prime Minister of Britain, Mrs Thatcher may feel that on an issue, such as sanctions against South Africa, in the interests of the United Kingdom she should side with South Africa. As Head of several countries of the Commonwealth who are resolved to apply sanctions to South Africa the Queen must respect, and, possibly, support their view. Mrs Thatcher may frequently have thought that being a member of the Commonwealth is an embarrassment, and wished she were not in it. The Queen may frequently reflect that to be Head of State for so many Commonwealth countries is one of the most important and valuable of her roles. There may be times when as Head of the Commonwealth she might wish that the policy of the United Kingdom were different.

A passage in Mrs Thatcher's memoirs is of particular interest in this context. It begins with a reference to her weekly audiences as Prime Minister with the Queen:

Anyone who imagines that they are a mere formality or confined to social niceties is quite wrong; they are quietly businesslike and Her Majesty brings to bear a formidable grasp of current issues and breadth of experience. And, although the press could not resist the temptation to suggest disputes between the Palace and Downing Street, especially on Commonwealth Affairs, I have always found the Queen's attitude towards the work of the government absolutely correct.

Of course, under the circumstances, stories of clashes between "two powerful women" were just too good not to make up. In general, more nonsense was written about the so-called "feminine factor" during my time in office than about almost anything else.

At this time, the tabloid newspapers, never much interested in stories about differences between the Queen and her Prime Minister, unless they were about how they dressed, were giving an unprecedented amount of attention to the royal family. There were several reasons for this. The most obvious one was that the children having grown up there were now many more royals to write about. But there were other reasons. The young royals were in tabloid news-paper terms good topics to write about. Their behaviour, some of it very different from what had been expected of them, made good stories. Newspapers in general and the tabloids in particular were going through a very competitive phase – and stories about how the royals behaved, and misbehaved, sold newspapers. The "royal soap opera" was good copy. The tabloids went to new lengths to get information, from paying Palace servants for letters to using long-range camera lenses. But it was also a feature of these times that some members of the royal family made themselves available to the media in a way and to a degree which had never been seen before.

An outstanding example of the royal family volunteering to let the public through the barriers of their privacy was the television programme in which Sir Alastair Burnet was invited into Kensington Palace to talk to the Prince and Princess of Wales with their two children. Millions watched the programme. Many people praised the royal couple for their informality and charm, but many thought that by exposing themselves and their children to the cameras in their home the Prince and Princess had not acted in the best interests of the monarchy, a view generally supposed to have been shared by the Queen and Prince Philip. The following year, another television programme in which the royals took part was screened. *It's a Royal Knockout* was organised to raise money for charity by Prince Edward, who having abandoned his career in the Royal Marines, was shortly to take a job in show business with Andrew Lloyd Webber. The programme caused much controversy. Many people thought that the behaviour of some of the young royals who appeared in it was inappropriate, and that the Duchess of York's was particularly undignified. But their main complaint was that members of the royal family should not have been allowed to take part in such a programme. Who was it at Buckingham Palace who advised on matters of this kind? Indeed did anybody in the Palace advise on matters of this kind? If so, did the Queen and the members of her family take any notice? They did. But the programme was the idea of an "outside" public relations consultant, and he was allowed to proceed with it.

By this time, 1987, a situation had developed in which while members of the royal family complained more and more about the behaviour of the press, the newspapers complained more and more about the behaviour of the royal family. Princess Anne voiced her complaints at a dinner in London attended by a number of press proprietors, speaking of "the unadulterated trivia, rubbish and gratuitous trouble-making that appeared in all sections of the so-called media ..." It was wrong, in her view, to say that the average reader or viewer did not believe what they read or saw. "They do. And the sheer volume of repeated stories, half truths and lies has its effects on the subject concerned." Joe Haines, one-time press secretary to Harold Wilson when Prime Minister, now working for the *Mirror*, wrote a piece to the effect that the royals were now a soap opera, and partly were themselves to blame, but urging in the interests of everybody that the newspapers should "start backing off". Michael Shea, the Queen's press secretary, now about to resign after nearly a decade in her service, said of the tabloid coverage: "Page after page of it is fairystory writing ..." The editor of the *Sunday Times* called on the Queen to use her position to promote better behaviour among the royals. They should be made to stop behaving like characters in a soap opera. "They need to be reminded that the public's appetite for soap operas eventually wanes ... they are replaced in the schedules with something else. Those who do not wish the monarch to go the same way sometime early in the next century must realise that casting the royal family as soap opera contains the seeds of its own destruction."

As well as comments about the behaviour of the royal family, and about the attention it evoked from the tabloid press, there was the question of invasion of privacy. In 1987 the *Sun* obtained a private letter written by Prince Philip to the Commandant General of Royal Marines about Prince Edward's wish to give up his career within the service. The *Sun* published the letter. In this case the Queen took the rare course of taking legal action, and initiated proceedings against the *Sun* for breach of copyright. By way of settlement the *Sun* donated £25,000 to charity. When the Duchess of York became pregnant newspaper photographers followed her everywhere. When she came out of hospital carrying the baby in her arms she found several television crews waiting for her at the front door. A photograph of the Queen with the new baby was somehow acquired, and reproduced in the *Sun*, without authorisation. The Queen's lawyers acted again, and again the *Sun* apologised and made a donation to charity. Soon afterwards the *Sun* received a package of letters written to Princess Anne, which it forwarded to Scotland Yard, contenting itself with telling its readers that it had done so, and that the letters were very personal. Later it became known that they had been written by Commander Timothy Laurence, an equerry to the Queen, and today Princess Anne's second husband.

The Queen's problems as a result of her two separate and sometimes conflicting roles as Head of State for the United Kingdom on the one hand and Head of the Commonwealth on the other continued to mount. In October 1987 the Queen went to Vancouver for the twenty-eighth Commonwealth heads of government meeting, at which a review of the effectiveness of existing sanctions against South Africa was to be discussed. The great majority present were in favour of stiffening them: Mrs Thatcher was still opposed to them, insisting that the history of sanctions clearly showed that they had been neither effective nor politic. The British delegation, in fact, found themselves isolated, seen as unilaterally pursuing a policy of appeasement towards South Africa.

Mrs Thatcher was in high spirits, and at the peak of her power and self-confidence. She had just won her third consecutive general election, and had been longer in office without a break than any British Prime Minister since 1827. She was not in the frame of mind to accept criticism of policies she believed in, and substitute them for policies she thought unrealistic and dangerous. The opinion of the majority was that Britain now no longer expressed the aspirations of the Commonwealth. Much was said about this to the Queen, and she had to use all her charm, good humour, and tactical knowledge, to minimise friction.

She also became involved in a political problem. Just before the Conference opened there was a coup in Fiji, hitherto an independent constitutional monarchy within the Commonwealth, the new government declaring Fiji a republic. The Governor-General, powerless to prevent this, submitted his resignation to the Queen. Through her press secretary the Queen made it known that she was "sad to think that the ending of Fijian allegiance to the Crown should have been brought about without the people of Fiji being given an opportunity to express their opinion on the proposal". Some British newspapers thought this statement meant that the Queen was involving herself in Fijian politics, and deplored it. The controversy was short-lived. Fiji decided to leave the Commonwealth.

From Vancouver the Queen crossed to Ottawa and Quebec. The Prime Minister of Canada, now Brian Mulroney, strongly in favour of tougher sanctions for South Africa, was naturally still concerned about Mrs Thatcher's resistance to them. Newspapers reported the failure of former Prime Minister Trudeau to attend a dinner in honour of the Queen. When the Queen went to Quebec she was booed again, so it was decided that the walkabout which had been arranged should be called off.

The Queen returned to London in late October 1987 to find that there was now a disturbing degree of concern about reports and rumours about the conduct of the younger members of the royal family in general and in particular about the state of the marriage of Prince Charles and Princess Diana. Speculation and reportage had begun on a significant scale in September 1985, on the eve of a visit by Prince Charles and Princess Diana to Australia, after which they would visit the United States. On 27 September the *Daily Mail* devoted the whole of its front page to a news story of which the headlines were:

What America is being told on eve of the royal visit.
AMAZING
ATTACK ON
CHARLES AND DIANA

The opening paragraphs were as follows:

AMERICA'S top society magazine has launched an astonishing attack on the Prince and Princess of Wales to coincide with their forthcoming visit to the United States.

In a sensational and detailed review of the Royal couple's private life, Diana is presented as a restless and demanding woman.

The article asks whether she has become a real-life example of the Alexis character in TV's *Dynasty*. And it labels Prince Charles a wimp.

It is published as a lengthy cover story in the glossy and prestigious *Vanity Fair* and is written by the magazine's editor, Tina Brown, an Englishwoman married to a former editor of *The Times* of London.

Ms Brown says that Charles and Diana are suffering from an

"increasing loss of reality" and are becoming alienated from each other by changes in their separate personalities.

Princess Diana's personality is getting stronger and stronger, she says, while the Prince becomes more and more reclusive and under the influence of a "motley crew of mystics, spiritualists and self-sufficiency freaks."

The article went on to make many other statements, some of which have turned out to be well-founded. The gist of it has been amplified and documented in many books which have appeared in the last two years.

From the appearance of the *Vanity Fair* article in 1985 more and more gossip appeared in the British media about the state of the heir to the throne's marriage and about the personalities of the two people involved. Much of what was reported was dismissed as the invention of ingenious tabloid reporters, and some of it probably was. In 1987, two years later, the public in general showed no sign of believing that the marriage of the heir to the throne was on the rocks. But now there were more and more indications that this might indeed be so: according to the tabloids the royal pair were hardly ever together: for formal occasions, yes; otherwise, no.

In 1988 the imminence of Prince Charles's fortieth birthday inspired a great deal of comment about his past, present and future, about what he had achieved and about what might lie before him. There was much favourable comment on his activities, particularly the Prince's Youth Business Trust, for which he had organised the moral and financial support of leading British businessmen. The PYBT provided funds, training, marketing opportunities and expert advice to young people, often from disadvantaged backgrounds, who wished to set up or develop their own businesses but had not the means to do so. Comment on some of his other activities was not so favourable. It was said that he was becoming more introspective and something of an eccentric. Small amounts of fact about him were mixed with large amounts of fiction to produce bizarre stories in the tabloids to the effect that he talked to his plants in his garden, favoured alternative medicine, practised meditation and was interested in spiritualism. Fact was often converted into fantasy: it was true that he was interested in parapsychology, but it was not true that he became so much interested in spiritualism that he had provided himself with a ouija board and had tried to get in touch with his deceased uncle, Lord Mountbatten. His readiness to help pioneer new ideas and to express unconventional views delighted some people but dismayed others – his views on architecture, for example. His outspoken defence of traditional views also gratified some and irritated others, such as his views on the importance of teaching English literature in general and Shakespeare in particular in schools. Some people criticised him for being old-fashioned, others for being iconoclastic. The Prince wanted to use his unique position to stimulate public discussion, but when he did so he was frequently criticised for not knowing what he was talking about, and when he occasionally made a joke which did not bring the house down or bordered on the ribald he was castigated for having no taste and being immature. Meanwhile there was a significant increase in the number of newspaper reports that the Prince was spending more and more time apart from his wife, and that his wife was spending more time with her own friends, including young men.

In August 1989 it was announced that Princess Anne would separate from Mark Phillips. For some years, the marriage had existed only in appearance, and seemed to have come to an end in reality long before Princess Anne formed a relationship with Commander Laurence. By the time the separation was announced a young New Zealand woman, Miss Heather Tonkin, had claimed in the *Daily Express* that Mark Phillips was the father of her daughter born four years previously. The separation agreement between the Princess and Captain Phillips was very explicit: he surrendered all claims and rights he might have to children, property and royal connection. It was as if he agreed to cease to exist.

The year also brought unhappy publicity to a very liked and respected member of the royal family, Princess Alexandra, the Queen's first cousin, daughter of the late Duke of Kent, and married to Angus Ogilvy, brother of the Lord Chamberlain, the Earl of Airlie. The Ogilvys' only child, Marina, who lived unmarried with a photographer, told the newspaper *Today* that she was going to have a baby. It transpired that Marina was estranged from the Ogilvys, and that they were embarrassed by their daughter's disclosures, for which Marina had received a substantial payment from *Today*. The only agreeable feature of the story was that Marina, though living in straitened circumstances, was not unhappy with her companion, and looked forward to having his child. However, what was not so agreeable was her claim that the distance between her parents and herself was of their creating, not of hers.

The year 1990 was eventful and difficult. When it began the Queen's government was in considerable trouble, and when it ended the Queen had a new Prime Minister. There was dissatisfaction with the government on various counts, but the main cause was the poll tax, which had become law in January. Figures soon revealed that many more families would have to pay more tax under the new law than the government had bargained for, and that the average tax paid per head would be substantially higher than that predicted by the government. Demonstrations up and down the country began at the end of February. Mrs Thatcher was singled out for obloquy: she had made no secret of her enthusiasm for it. She had introduced the idea to the government. She had said many times that it was the "flagship" of government policy. Many members of her own party fumed about it. The word "divisive", the word the monarch least wants to hear about government policy, was repeatedly used about "Mrs Thatcher's tax" and even more about her stubborn support of it. A "Mrs Thatcher must go" movement was seen to be growing behind the not too well closed doors of the Conservative Party. On 31 March a vast anti-poll tax rally in and around Trafalgar Square, estimated by some to involve 200,000 people, became difficult to handle. There were more than 300 arrests and many injuries. The government rapidly announced measures to alleviate the effects of the new tax. But there was more and more criticism of the government, and more and more calls for Mrs Thatcher to resign and make way for somebody else.

Public opinion was also disturbed by moves which would take Britain further into the European Community and reduce British national sovereignty. The European Court of Justice issued a ruling which laid down that in any case where there arose a conflict or incompatibility between a law enacted by the European Community and a law existing by a British Act of Parliament the former was to be deemed superior. This gave rise to controversy. "What exactly is the state of our sovereignty?" demanded one Conservative MP in the House of Commons. Lord Denning, a former Master of the Rolls, protested that the European Court's judicial thinking was "entirely contrary to the English system of Justice". This was followed by more news of moves in Brussels to hasten the introduction of a single currency. The Chancellor of the Exchequer,

John Major, in an attempt to offer an alternative to the difficulties a single currency would create for national sovereignty, suggested that in the short term the new European currency and national currencies could co-exist. This was not well received outside the United Kingdom. Meanwhile Britain's economic situation was bad, and getting worse. Something had to be done urgently to prevent further decline in the value of the pound. On 5 October the Chancellor of the Exchequer took most people by surprise when he announced that Britain would enter the European Exchange Rate Mechanism (ERM) in three days' time. It was a highly controversial decision. In the view of *The Times*, which had favoured, and continued to support, entry into the ERM in principle, to take that step at that time was to subject economics to politics, and that British industry would consequently have to pay a heavy price. A former Chancellor, Nigel Lawson, said that to have a beneficial effect the step should have been taken five years earlier. From now on the Europeans began to step up the pace towards economic and monetary union and to aim for a single currency by the end of the decade. More and more concern developed in Britain about the prospects for British sovereignty.

In November the annual election for the leadership of the Conservative Party took place. It was normally a formality, but this time Michael Heseltine decided to oppose Mrs Thatcher. On the first ballot Mrs Thatcher failed by only four votes to be re-elected. Advised by most members of the Cabinet that on the second ballot she would be defeated she decided to withdraw from the contest and resign. She was succeeded by John Major, regarded as her protégé. Since he had been elected Mrs Thatcher's successor as Leader of the Conservative Party, which held a majority in the House of Commons, the Queen had no problem in asking him to form a government.

One of the new Prime Minister's first tasks was to attend the European summit in Rome in December. He urged that the next range of economic and monetary changes in the EC should be slow and careful, and deplored a rapid move which might regretted. On the whole he got as much of what he wanted as he could reasonably have expected.

The Queen could not have concluded that 1990 had been a good year for her country, but she might have taken the view that it could have been worse for the royal family. She might have derived some encouragement from a section on the subject published in a book entitled *We British* written by Robert Worcester and Eric Jacobs, the former the chairman of MORI opinion polls, arguably Britain's most expert pollster, the latter for many years a distinguished commentator on political and industrial affairs. The book is a scientific study of British *attitudes* – to, for example, politics, the media, religion and work – and its method was the use of sophisticated questionnaires specially designed for the purpose of the book administered by about one hundred MORI interviewers. The part of the book which might have particularly interested the Queen follows in full:

The Royal Family

In spite of the heavy exposure of their faults and foibles on television and in the newspapers the royal family still stands high in public favour. Only doctors and the armed forces are seen to be performing their social roles better.

Approval rates, though, vary widely. Woman rate the royals significantly higher than men, + 53 on our scale against men's + 43. Old people are much more satisfied than younger. The over 55s give + 60; the 35 to 54-year-olds manage + 55, while the 15–34 age group could only muster + 33. Single people, mainly younger, are less enthusiastic for royalty. On our scale they give only + 31 approval while married people give + 50 and the older group, including widows and divorcees, + 66.

Differences, though not major ones, are also visible in class support. ABC1s are + 52 satisfied while DEs rate the royals at + 48. The royal family is especially popular in the Midlands. There it scores + 58 on the scale while it can raise only + 47 in the South and + 43 in the North.

When it comes to politics, SLD supporters turned out to be the most eager royalists. They rate the royals at + 66 on the scale. Tory supporters come next at + 58, the "don't knows" at 57, SDP + 53 and Labour supporters a relatively meagre + 38.

In view of what some of the newspapers had been saying about the effect on public opinion of members of the royal family appearing in television programmes in recent years the last two paragraphs of the Worcester/Jacobs report are particularly interesting:

But if the royal family thinks it can improve its standing among the young, the single, and Labour supporters by shedding its image as the cast of some vast, unending television soap opera it should think again. Heavy TV viewers are among its most loyal fans. The more television they watch, the more people approve of the royals. Those who watch most give the royal family a + 53 rating on our satisfaction scale. Medium viewers give it + 49, and light viewers only + 44.

Whatever else we may say about the royal family we have to agree on one thing. It plays well on the box.

In the first month of 1991 the Gulf War broke out. Unlike, for example, the Suez War, Britain's involvement raised no specific problems for the Queen. Though a former Prime Minister, Edward Heath, and a former Chancellor of the Exchequer who had also been Minister for Defence, Denis Healey, opposed the war the bulk of the country seemed to support resistance to Iraq's aggression against Kuwait. Within the European Community there was a division of opinion; some were in favour of using force, some were not. The conflict of views within the Community gave new ground to those who were opposed to closer union especially in foreign policy. There was increased apprehension at what would happen at the Maastricht summit at the end of the year when members of the Community would be called upon to agree to further steps towards not only economic and financial integration but towards a common defence policy. To the dismay of the British government a meeting of European foreign ministers in Luxembourg in June registered almost unanimous support for a single currency, common foreign and defence policies, and a "federal" goal. Britain's Foreign Secretary promptly refused to endorse the programme, and the British government came in for considerable public censure by M. Delors, the President of the European Commission, for dragging its feet at the expense of the other countries of the Community. From the back benches, Mrs Thatcher, now Lady Thatcher, uninhibitedly denounced the attempt to advance towards a "federal" Europe and in particular the moves towards a single currency.

In December 1991 the members of the European Community met at Maastricht to draw up a new European Union treaty, which would take them forward towards a united Europe. There was another conflict between Britain and the other members. This time the British won. The delegation returned to London feeling very pleased with themselves, and the Prime Minister publicly claimed that he had won "game, set and match". In particular, he had secured Britain's right to remain outside the single European currency which the other countries wanted to see in being by 1999 at the latest, and to deny the Community new powers over British social and industrial policy. These rights were achieved at the expense of antagonising several European governments to a degree unprecedented: the well-informed and authoritative German newspaper, *Die Zeit*, spoke for many of them when it accused Britain of showing itself to be an unconstructive troublemaker, and described John Major as "Margaret Thatcher in friendly packaging". From hostility in Maastricht the Prime Minister returned home to hostility in his own country. What he had *agreed* to at Maastricht was bitterly attacked not only by the Labour Opposition but by many members of his own party.

At the year's end, therefore, the Queen must have looked at the state of her country, and its relationship with the European Community with anxiety. But developments within the Commonwealth, coming to fruit at the Conference of 1991, held in October at Harare in Zimbabwe, no doubt cheered her a great deal, particularly since behind the scenes she had contributed to them. Britain's standing within the Commonwealth beginning to improve, the Queen's problems, therefore, began to diminish. In Harare, the British government again called for an early end to economic sanctions against South Africa, and again Mr Major's was a lone voice. But the atmosphere had changed. The movement away from apartheid which had begun in 1989 was being seen to be real and irreversible. In February 1990 President de Klerk, opening the South African Parliament, had lifted the ban on the African National Congress and the Pan African Congress, had announced the immediate release of Nelson Mandela from prison and had promised that discussions with him about the future of South Africa would soon begin. President de Klerk, now welcome in world capitals, had set off on a nine-nation tour of Europe, to urge that sanctions against South Africa be lifted. Nobody thought that South Africa's problem with the rest of the Commonwealth would now disappear, or soon come to a solution, but progress was obvious. Things had changed, and looked like changing more.

The 1991 Commonwealth Conference, therefore, registered a

change in what Commonwealth conferences were about: South Africa was no longer the main topic of discussion; the South Africa problem no longer divided the Commonwealth into Britain versus the rest. Many members of the Commonwealth were ready to stop denigrating South Africa and to "give de Klerk a chance". Many of them were aware that the authority of the Commonwealth in the rest of the world had declined because its members seemed to talk about only one subject: South Africa. For whatever the reasons the atmosphere within and the image without of the 1991 Commonwealth Conference was significantly different from what had been the case in the last few years. This was most simply and clearly registered when the Conference agreed that sanctions should gradually be reduced. Mrs Thatcher, had she been at the Conference as Prime Minister, might have felt vindicated. As it was, her successor, John Major, continued to oppose economic sanctions, but by welcoming the decision to reduce them, and by being emollient where Mrs Thatcher was abrasive, he was able to create the impression that the longstanding rift between the Commonwealth countries and Britain on the fundamental question of South Africa no longer existed. He spoke as though Britain believed in the Commonwealth, and in the value of the reciprocal relationship. This was in contrast to the impression which Mrs Thatcher had given in recent years. By the end of the Commonwealth Conference of 1991, to some degree aided by developments during the previous two years, the Queen could see that the countries of the association of which she was the Head, and for which in the eyes of the world she was responsible, were on better terms with each other and were doing more good work together than had been the case for many, many years. As the year 1991 drew to a close very few people foresaw the *annus horribilis* for the Queen which lay ahead.

I I

Annus Horribilis – as monarch
1991–2

SOME PEOPLE EXPERIENCE problems, unhappiness and suffering in their earlier years, to find that in their later years, possibly because of what they have gone through earlier, life is calmer and less challenging for them. Other people find the reverse. Elizabeth II is one of them. Of her forty years on the throne as Queen, monarch and mother, the 1980s have been the most difficult, and the beginning of the 1990s the worst.

By 1992 the recession in the United Kingdom had become the most severe since the 1930s. Unemployment was steadily rising towards three million. Firms were going out of business at an alarming rate, the figure for bankruptcies had broken the record, and an unprecedented number of mortgaged homes were being repossessed. There was an atmosphere of gloom and despondency. As we have seen in the earlier parts of this book, the monarchy has been particularly vulnerable to criticism in times of economic hardship, as have all people who seem to be doing well when many other people are doing badly. Appearances, behaviour and remarks which would hardly have been noticed a year or two earlier when times were good come in for criticism when times get bad. At the beginning of 1992, therefore, it might have been foreseen that anything the members of the royal family did or said would be liable to more scrutiny and censure than for a long time previously.

Notwithstanding the overcast skies at the beginning of 1992, wellwishers of the Queen and the monarchy might justifiably have predicted happy times for the next two years ahead. Going into 1992, the Queen, though she knew of problems within the royal family which had not yet become public, could have been cautiously optimistic. She was entering the fortieth year of her reign. Judging by the success of the Silver Jubilee in 1977, she could expect a happy anniversary in 1992. She knew though that the public were more, not less, disgruntled by their knowledge that she did not pay income tax like the rest of her subjects, that what had been described by some newspapers as the "antics" of the Duchess of York were giving offence, that there were rumours that the Prince of Wales's marriage was in trouble. But there was no indication that there was a major crisis ahead.

The Christmas broadcast of 1991 in which she looked forward to the coming year had given rise to some speculation. In it she made a statement which in the circumstances was generally interpreted to mean that so long as she lived she would remain on the throne and that she had no intention of abdicating to allow Prince Charles to become king: "With your prayers and your help, and the love and support of my family, I shall try and help you in the years to come." The interpretation was wrong. The Queen had made similar statements in 1947 in South Africa, at her Coronation, and at other times since. They were reaffirmations of longstanding vows. A less general interpretation was that assuming that Charles felt frustrated in his role as Prince of Wales, and that many influential people sympathised with him on this account, he and his friends would now understand that any shortcut to the throne was out of the question. Consequently, the Queen's words received a mixed reception. Some people felt that it would be a good thing for all concerned if the Queen *did* step down: Queen Victoria reigned so long that Edward VII was sixty when he became king. The Queen's statement stimulated more speculation that, deprived of a proper job, Charles was frustrated, and that this accounted for his eccentric interests, out-of-the-way ideas, and his tendency to make public statements which bordered on the political. There was comment after the Queen's speech that Charles would be deeply disappointed that abdication had been so categorically ruled out.

The speculation too was groundless. Charles, as he had said in an interview in 1974, was totally opposed to the idea of the Queen abdicating. That the Queen shared his views would not have come as a surprise to him. Nobody knew better than he did that the moment he became King he would have to start to live a life considerably less varied and interesting, with far less opportunity for leadership and initiative, than he was enjoying as the Prince of Wales.

The year opened with great publicity for the forthcoming fortieth anniversary of the Queen's accession. Many of the flood of newspaper and magazine articles looked forward to the forthcoming BBC television documentary, *Elizabeth R*, produced and directed by Edward Mirzoeff with an accompanying book by Sir Antony Jay.

Jay, a very distinguished broadcaster, whose work in the medium had included the creation of the popular television series *Yes, Minister*, had been involved in the first, and celebrated, documentary, *Royal Family*, in 1969. Edward Mirzoeff had a long and successful record in directing "fly-on-the-wall" documentaries. Between October 1990 and November 1991, Mirzoeff and his crew were allowed unprecedented access to the Queen. Eighty days of filming bore fruit in a documentary lasting 110 minutes and costing approximately £250,000. The director assured the public that the Queen did not have any veto on the final outcome.

The purpose of the film was to show what the Queen, as constitutional monarch in the late twentieth century, actually *does*. So much media focus in the 1970s and 1980s had been on what the royal family, particularly the younger ones, do. *Elizabeth R* focused much more on the concept of the monarchy and what the *monarch* does. From the royal family's point of view there were obviously other motives, as there had been in 1969. The main one was to project a favourable public image. It was an opportunity for the Queen to have direct access to the public without having to go through the filter of the increasingly hostile press. The Queen communicates directly with the public, as in her very formal Christmas Message, on only rare occasions: at other times even her major speeches come through the newspapers after having been edited, and television reporting reduces them to sound-bites.

As in 1969, in 1992 also, the royal family was unhappy about its standing in the public perception. But there was a difference. In 1969, the royal family had been perceived as remote, formal and out of touch with the modern world. The film made then demystified them, made them seem more contemporary, presented them to the viewers as "real" and "human". The problem for the royal family in 1992, it could be said, was too much de-mystification. The members of the royal family had become all too "real", their every movement scrutinised and sometimes censored by the press. In 1969 the royal family had benefited greatly from the film, and from the televising of the investiture of the Prince of Wales ten days later. They had continued to make good use of television in the seventies and early eighties, through such events as royal weddings and the Silver Jubilee. But in so doing they changed from being masters of the situation, controlling access, to servants of it. What Milton Shulman had warned them about had come to pass.

The 1992 documentary, a magnificent television programme, concentrated on the constitutional aspects of the monarch's role. But it brought out attractive aspects of the Queen's personality which had not been so evident to the general public before – her sense of humour, her *joie de vivre*. It was the most watched programme of the week. The book of the film was a bestseller.

The film showed in depth the role of the Queen as Head of State. It revealed some of the intricate arrangements made before and during a State visit (particularly for the banquet, held in his honour, in St George's Hall, Windsor) using as an example that of President Lech Walesa of Poland. The Queen came over well, reinforcing the view that "she does a good job". There was, however, no massive upward swing in her popularity, as there had been in 1969, possibly because by now the royal family had become too familiar to the public for a television programme to change perceptions significantly.

The 1969 de-mystification process had been taken one step further. Not everybody assumed that the process had been entirely to the Queen's advantage. John Grigg, who as Lord Altrincham had expressed some criticism of the Queen's image thirty-five years before, was invited to give his views about the image of the Queen as seen in 1992. In writing about the film he said that some of the

Queen's casual remarks revealed an attitude that one could not wholly admire. One such was when she was waiting for President Lech Walesa and his wife to come down from their rooms for the banquet at Windsor, during their state visit. She seemed to think it very funny that a man who, until recently, lived in a small worker's flat at Gdansk, should be dumbfounded by the size of Windsor, and that he should have only two words of English. Later, she rebuked a member of her family for "showing off" when he tried to speak to the President in Polish. A similar effort would not have come amiss, even if it had amounted to no more than two words.

Many people thought Grigg's remarks were somewhat heavy-handed, and that her lighthearted "rebuke" simply showed her lively sense of humour. However, in an essay which he wrote comparing the image of the Queen in 1992 to the image he had written about thirty-five years earlier John Grigg noted improvements. First he explained why he had thought it useful to write the original article:

> In the early years of the present Queen's reign there was a distinct danger that complacency might be setting in. After the Second World War the monarchy reverted to its pre-war routines almost as though nothing had happened, and virtually no changes were introduced by the Queen when she succeeded her father in 1952. At the same time public attitudes towards the monarchy were marked by a degree of blandness and servility quite alien to the British tradition. There was much fatuous talk of a new Eliza-bethan age, though the age was, in fact, as unlike that of the first Elizabeth as the young Queen herself was unlike her illustrious predecessor. Britain seemed to be compensating for loss of power in the world by relapsing into a state of collective make-believe, in which the hieratic aspects of the monarchy were grossly exaggerated and the healthy habit of criticising office-holders was ceasing to apply to the monarch. Something akin to Japanese Shintoism was in the air.
>
> After five years of this I felt moved to write an article on "The Monarchy Today". It never occurred to me that the article would be widely noticed ... In fact the article created a sensation. It was taken up by the media in every part of the world and I found myself at the heart of an almighty row.

Looking back in 1992 on the thirty-five years which had gone by since he had written his much-cited article John Grigg concluded that there had been some valuable changes, but not many. The

Queen had sent her children to school outside the Palace, though these were schools in the private sector, not state schools, and she had arranged for two of her sons to spend some time at universities. All four children had had far more opportunity to mix with other people than their mother did. But there were still many important changes to be made. While people from the white Commonwealth countries had served as assistants to the Queen's press secretary, "There have never been any black, brown or yellow faces in senior positions around the Queen as part of her permanent official entourage ... the Household is still very much what it was at the beginning of the reign, at any rate at the top level." Grigg praised the Queen for her behaviour in public, "much less inhibited as the years have passed ... her speeches have definitely improved, containing more human touches; and to the extent that they have remained admonitory in tone, her ever-growing maturity has made this far more acceptable."

In 1992 Grigg praised the way in which over the years the Queen had carried out her constitutional duties, especially her relations with the Commonwealth. He praised her personal conduct. The Queen's reputation had been an example to all. "Through all the bewildering and often silly changes of fashion during her reign, she had dared to be true to herself and to stick to her own ways. This virtue has as its defects a serious lack of imagination and a marked reluctance to make even desirable changes. But splendid virtue it undoubtedly is, and we are very lucky that the Queen possesses it."

The Prime Minister called a general election for 9 April. As the election campaign drew to a close, most newspapers predicted it would result in a hung Parliament with no party having an overall majority in the House of Commons. The events immediately after the general election of February 1974, mentioned earlier, were recalled, and there was speculation that the Queen might again find herself in a constitutional position which could embarrass her. In an article in *The Times* on 8 April, the day before the election, Lord St John of Fawsley, formerly Norman St John-Stevas, at one time a Conservative Cabinet Minister, an avowed monarchist, and regarded as a constitutional authority, stated what he said was the guiding principle in such circumstances: "She [the Queen] must send for the man (or woman) who is likely to command the confidence of the House of Commons." Commenting on Heath's decision to stay on over the weekend, Lord St John of Fawsley said "he was well within his rights to make the attempt [to form a Government]."

The problem did not arise; the Conservatives were returned with a clear majority, although greatly reduced, and it was obvious that their leader, John Major, would be asked to form a government. But many people pointed out that the issue might recur, and that if proportional representation had been adopted by the time it did so, the situation would be much more complex.

Events in Australia brought up again, but more sharply than before, the Queen's role in the Dominion. In December 1991 the Prime Minister, Bob Hawke, was ousted from the leadership of the Labour Party, and replaced by Paul Keating. The new Prime Minister made no secret of his intention to make Australia a republic as soon as possible. Later in the year, he and Mrs Keating were given great publicity in the British press on account of his behaviour during a State visit by the Queen. Mr Keating was photographed "putting his arm around the Queen's waist" to guide her during a reception. In fact he had put his hand on the Queen's back for a moment to draw her attention to the presence of Gough Whitlam. It was reported that when she was first introduced to the Queen Mrs Keating did not curtsy. This was the case. Annita Keating is Dutch, and for twenty-five years now the Dutch have been asked *not* to bow or curtsy to their monarch.

Taking the Australian story up to date, in early 1993 Mr Keating called a general election, promising in his party manifesto that if re-elected he would hold a referendum on whether or not Australia should become a republic in 2001. He won the election convincingly. The monarchy issue did not figure as much in the campaign as did, for example, the state of the economy, unemployment and taxation, but it was soon to become clear that Mr Keating's promise had caught the ear of the Australian people. Leaders of the conservative Liberal–National Coalition, successors to Sir Robert Menzies, who as Prime Minister of Australia in the 1950s had been a fervent royalist, now also spoke up for a republic. It seemed as though Australia is set to replace the Queen as Head of State in 2001.

In the discussion in the British media which followed these developments the question was frequently asked: is it surprising that Australia wants to sever her ties with the United Kingdom? Commentators pointed out that fewer and fewer people in Australia claimed British heritage, that Mr Keating was of Irish Catholic descent, that the major immigrant movements to Australia during the last few decades had come from Continental Europe and Asia. These people, the "New Australians", had no link with the UK and saw little reason for having a British Head of State, a foreigner, as opposed to an Australian, a fellow citizen. When Britain joined the European Community in 1973, the importance of its trading relationship with Australia began to decline. It was natural, many commentators said, that Mr Keating now insisted that Australia must be prepared to take its place in the Asian Pacific community of nations, and that an Australian Head of State would be more relevant to such an alignment than a Head of State who lived on the other side of the world. Some of the commentators struck a pessimistic note: where Australia led, it could be expected that in time, New Zealand, Canada and others would follow. On the international scene, the Queen and her successors could only be expected to play a diminishing role. This should not be unexpected at a time when Britain was shedding the last vestiges of its Empire days. It raised the question: what effect would this process have on how the people of Britain felt about the monarchy?

Given the flow of ideas about the Queen and the Commonwealth and Europe, it was not surprising that the Queen's first major speech on Europe would lead to problems. On 18 May, she travelled to Strasbourg to deliver a speech to the European Parliament. She was the last Community Head of State to do so. The invitation had been extended in 1988, but it was not until John Major took over from Margaret Thatcher that it was finally accepted. The speech itself was, as *The Times* editorial put it, "uncontroversial to the point of banality". It concentrated on "Europe's diverse family" and the role the Community had played in keeping the peace in Europe since the Second World War. Quotations from Lord Salisbury, Churchill and the Community's father, Jean Monnet, were included, Monnet's in the original French. Once again there was praise for the Queen's excellent French accent.

But the speech, in spite of being, according to *The Times*, uncontroversial, caused considerable controversy. Much of this came from the fact that in advance of it being delivered a summary of its contents had leaked to the Lobby correspondents at Westminster and the summary turned out to be inaccurate. The document that was leaked was slightly misleading in that it implied that the Queen would play down the significance of the existence of different European Parliamentary traditions, including that of the United Kingdom, and highlight the cause of European reconciliation. News of this outraged the Europhobics in the Conservative Party. Mr Major felt compelled to make a statement in Parliament that "sovereignty was not up for grabs". The public discussion that followed again underlined the problems facing the Queen and her successors: they must find a role for themselves in Europe, but the task would be beset with enormous political sensitivities. The transformation from Head of Empire to Head of Commonwealth was relatively simple and logical, and could be seen to be the result of practical pressures. This one, the commentators agreed, would not be so straightforward.

In January, the *Sunday Telegraph* announced that the Prince of Wales was ready to adopt a new role, that of "Prince of Europe". He was reported to believe that the future of Britain was inextricably bound up with that of its partners in the EC and with the new democracies of the former Eastern bloc. He was reported to be cultivating contacts with European statesmen and industrialists and to be receiving regular briefings from the Foreign Secretary. He was also said to be involved in arranging trips to the Continent for British businessmen to find out what they could learn from continental practices. The *Sunday Telegraph*'s report was dismissed by some right-wing commentators, deplored by others as another example of the Prince's eccentric views, and ignored by most readers. Very little reportage of the Prince's views on Europe followed.

During the year, the Queen Mother, usually the most uncontroversial of the royal family, became involved in a diplomatic contretemps. She had agreed to unveil a statue, in London, of Sir Arthur "Bomber" Harris, the wartime chief of RAF Bomber Command. Harris, a much respected wartime figure, had become the subject of controversy in recent years for his carpet bombing of civilian targets, most notably, for the devastating raid on Dresden at the end of the war which had almost razed the city to the ground. Many people, especially the young and post-war generations, thought that it was inappropriate that the royal family should be involved in a tribute to the man responsible for such bombing. Additionally, the honouring of Harris was seen by many as an insult to Germany, now considered to be one of Britain's closest allies.

The Queen Mother, after some consideration, decided to attend the ceremony. There was a demonstration. The controversy did not end there. In October, the Queen made a State visit to Germany, going to parts of former Eastern Germany previously behind the Iron Curtain, including Dresden. Here she encountered protests about the wartime bombing and the Queen Mother's involvement with the Harris memorial. At one point the Queen, accompanied by the German President, Richard von Weizsacker, was booed, and eggs were thrown at her. The rest of the tour passed off without incident; many crowds turned out to cheer her, and she was given a friendly reception by the German media. Prince Philip received warm praise for reading a lesson, in faultless German, at a church service for reconciliation between the two countries.

On Friday 20 November the Queen suffered the personal blow which caused her to describe the year as "annus horribilis". Windsor Castle, her favourite residence in England, caught fire and was extensively damaged. The fire started just before noon. Beginning in the private chapel in the Chester Tower, in the north-east corner of the castle precincts, it spread rapidly into St George's Hall, where part of the ceiling collapsed, and swept on into the State apartments. At the west end of St George's Hall a fire break was created and prevented the flames reaching the State Entrance. But by early evening the fire had also got to Brunswick Tower. It was not until late into the night that the flames were fully under control.

The damage to the castle's fabric was considered to be much more severe than had been caused by the fire at Hampton Court in 1986, but the vast majority of the art treasures were saved, mainly because a large number of them had been removed while renovation work was being undertaken. Ironically, it was this restoration that caused the blaze: sparks from a halogen lamp had ignited curtains in the private chapel. The Duke of York was the only member of the royal family in the castle when the fire began; he informed the Queen immediately and then joined in the rescue work. The Queen was at Buckingham Palace celebrating her forty-fifth wedding anniversary. She rushed to Windsor, and helped oversee the removal of a large number of art works from her private apartments. Although she did not comment directly to reporters, photographs showed that she was, as her son said, "absolutely devastated". Asked by a reporter what her reaction to the fire had been a Buckingham

Palace spokesman replied: "The same reaction as yours if you saw your home burning."

The castle, like all other royal palaces, was not insured; the premiums would have been prohibitive. It was instead covered by government indemnity, which meant that the taxpayers would inevitably pay for the restoration work, through the National Heritage Department. The castle had not been fitted with a sprinkler system, partly because of the risk that it might be activated accidentally and do vast damage to the art work, and partly because of the difficulty of fitting it into the high vaulted ceilings of the castle.

The next day, Peter Brooke, the Secretary of State for the Department of National Heritage, inspected the damage. He was televised speaking to reporters, saying "The heart of the nation went out to the Queen last night. I am sure she will want to see her home restored in a way that we all see fit." He went on to say that the government would pay for the restoration of the castle, the cost of which was being estimated at the time at £60 million. This precipitated more complaints about the Queen not paying income tax. Within hours Labour MPs were asking why the taxpayer should pick up the bill for the damage when the Queen made no contribution to government revenues. The following day the *News of the World* demanded: "Who will flaming well pay?" By Tuesday the majority of the nation's newspapers were demanding that either the Queen should pay to repair the damage or that she should pay tax. The *Daily Mail*, in a front-page editorial, headlined "Why the Queen must listen", asked, "Why should the populace, many of whom have had to make huge sacrifices during a bitter recession, have to pay the total bill for Windsor Castle when the Queen, who pays no taxes, contributes next to nothing?" The *Mirror*, referring to reports that because of economies introduced by the royal family the fire prevention arrangements at the Palace had become inadequate, complained that the "Windsor Wallies" had no judgement. The *Mirror* said that "Hardly a day goes by without the House of Windsor sowing more seeds of its own destruction ... Meanness, greed and blinkered disregard for the feelings of the people are the mark of a dying, not lasting, dynasty." The *Guardian* said that "all the warm words of sadness for the Queen can't hide the growing wash of public cynicism: not yet republicanism, but carping disaffection."

Four days after the fire, while these views were to the fore in the minds of millions of newspaper readers, the Queen made a speech in public which may rank with the Abdication speech of the Duke of Windsor as the most emotional made by a member of the royal family in the twentieth century. The occasion was a lunch at the Guildhall in the City of London to mark her fortieth year as Queen. This historic occasion was attended by 730 people, including the Prime Minister. In a voice made hoarse by a heavy cold and fumes from the smoking remains at the Castle, the Queen spoke of a "tumultuous year" and an "annus horribilis" for the House of Windsor.

The speech started with the usual pleasantries, but soon changed key:

1992 is not a year I shall look back on with undiluted pleasure. In the words of one of my more sympathetic correspondents, it has turned out to be an annus horribilis.

I sometimes wonder how future generations will judge the events of this tumultuous year. I dare say that history will take a slightly more moderate view than some contemporary commentators. Distance is well known to lend enchantment, even to the less attractive views.

After all, it has the inestimable value of hindsight. But it can also lend an extra dimension to judgment, giving it a leavening of moderation and compassion – even of wisdom – that is sometimes lacking in the reactions of those whose task it is in life to offer instant opinions on all things great and small. No section of the community has all the virtues nor does it have all the vices. I am quite sure that most people try to do their jobs as best they can, even if the result is not always entirely successful. He who has never failed to reach perfection has a right to be the harshest critic.

There can be no doubt, of course, that criticism is good for people and institutions that are part of public life. No institution – City, monarchy, whatever – should expect to be free from scrutiny of those who give their loyalty and support, not to mention those who don't.

But we are all part of the same fabric of our national society and that scrutiny, by one part of another, can be just as effective if it is made with a touch of gentleness, good humour and understanding.

This sort of questioning can also act, and so it should do, as an effective agent of change.

The Queen's speech went far beyond any comments she had made previously which might show that she was personally affected by the criticism that she and her family had been subjected to during the preceding months. Even more notable was the direct plea for tolerance throughout British society.

The press on the whole were sympathetic, though some headlines gave an inadequate idea of the message of the speech as a whole. *The Times* headline was: "Sad Queen dubs 1992 her 'annus horribilis'." The *Daily Mail*'s was: "Please be kind to us". The *Sun*'s, crassly, was "One's bum year". Editorial articles were not entirely supportive. The *Daily Mail*'s editorial, headed "Cri de coeur from the Crown", said "We sympathise with the Queen. Of course we do. But these are hard times for most people. Many of them have had a truly horrid year. They have lost their livelihoods. Even been driven from their homes ... The Queen should pay some tax on her income. And fewer members of her family should be a charge to the Civil List ... She should offer to contribute to restoring the fabric of Windsor Castle. ... If we read it right, this intense and complex speech is not only a cri de coeur, but a prologue for change."

The *Daily Express*'s editorial – "Don't shoot the messenger" – addressed itself to what it thought was unjustified criticism in the speech about the conduct of the press: "... the media does no more than mirror the concerns of the public at large. The Queen's advisers are being dangerously misguided if they encourage Her Majesty to think differently. If they were more in tune with what the public wants and expects from the modern monarchy, the Queen would be less likely to have cause again to bemoan an annus horribilis."

The Windsor Castle fire had raised again in a way which could not have been foreseen the issue of whether the Queen should pay tax or not. For those who wished to attack the monarchy, and the royal family, this was a great opportunity. The issue had been brought up at some point or another, logically or illogically, during every major crisis in the 1990s, from the photographs of the Duchess of York on holiday with her American friend, John Bryan, to news of the separation of the Prince and Princess of Wales.

Throughout the early 1990s the longstanding feeling in the

country that the Queen should pay tax had been gaining political momentum. One of the first people to give practical expression to this was a Liberal Democrat MP, Simon Hughes, who introduced a Private Member's Bill into the House of Commons. Although the Bill ultimately failed, it received some attention from the press, and consequently, as 1992 unfolded, it helped ensure that the issue remained in the front of people's minds.

In January the issue was raised in a different form by the publication of *Royal Fortune* by Philip Hall, the result of ten years' research. Hall, a sociology lecturer, gave an account of the financial position of the monarch, traced the history of the issue, and dealt with some of the myths surrounding the wealth of the royal family. According to *The Independent* Mr Hall's view was: "It's the way that royalty have dodged out of tax – the sneakiness – that's what hurts." Extracts from the book were printed in the *Sunday Times*.

Hall traced the evolution of the financial position of the Crown, and described how on the introduction of income tax in 1842, Queen Victoria, under pressure from her Prime Minister, Sir Robert Peel, was persuaded to "volunteer" to pay it, which she did, albeit rather reluctantly. In 1910, George V was able to persuade the then Chancellor, Lloyd George, to exempt the Civil List from taxation, and in 1933 revenues from the Duchy of Lancaster were also exempted. Finally, taxation on the personal investment income of the sovereign ended some time between 1937 and 1952 (the relevant file at the Public Record Office appears to have been destroyed in 1977). So by the time the Queen acceded to the throne in 1952 she did not pay income tax of any kind.

It is at this point that speculating about the Queen's actual income begins. Some sources of income are known about. The Civil List is published. In 1992 it comprised the following:

The Queen	£7,900,000
The Queen Mother	£640,000
Duke of Edinburgh	£360,000
Duke of York	£250,000
Princess Royal	£230,000
Princess Margaret	£220,000
Prince Edward	£100,000

Princess Alice	£90,000
Duke of Gloucester ⎫	
Duke of Kent ⎬	share £630,000*
Princess Alexandra ⎭	

Total: £9,560,000

* Since 1975 has been repaid by the Queen to the Treasury

The Queen also receives a tax-free income of about £3 million from the Duchy of Lancaster. The Prince of Wales and his wife receive a tax-free income from the Duchy of Cornwall. In 1991 the Prince received about £3 million.

The government also pays for:

Palace Maintenance	£25,600,000
Royal Yacht	£9,300,000
Queen's Flight	£6,700,000
Royal Train	£2,000,000
Civil Airfares	£800,000
Overseas Visits	£600,000
Publicity	£400,000
Honours Administration	£200,000
Equerries	£200,000
Yeomen of the Guard	£200,000
Security, estimate*	£30,000,000

Total: £76,000,000

* *Source*: The *Mail on Sunday*, 9 February, 1992

Between 1982 and 1990 the Duchy of Lancaster made a disclosed profit of £8.7 million, which was invested. This raises the question of the income on this investment, which is dealt with below. Mr Hall acknowledged that his estimate of what the monarchy cost, £53.5 million, did not exceed the revenue of the Crown estate, £57 million, which goes to the State. But against that, he said, if the cost of security, estimated at £30 million, and the tax-exemptions are taken into account, expenditure greatly outweighs the return. Moreover, he pointed out, the Queen has other vast wealth such as Windsor Castle, the Crown Jewels, the largest private art collection in the world, and a valuable stamp collection. Admittedly these are unrealisable assets, increasing the Queen's wealth on paper but not affecting her real position in terms of income, all these assets being regarded as "inalienable" since they are part of the national heritage.

The Economist, in a lengthy review of Mr Hall's book, considered several of the issues he had raised, and put forward a number of reasons why it was impractical for the Queen to be taxed. Taxation of the Civil List, said *The Economist*, would give rise to a number of problems. The majority of the List, seventy-five per cent, goes to pay the Palace staff. Any taxation of it would, in effect, be double taxation, and lead to staff cuts or to an increase in the List. *The Economist* stated that "No part of the Civil List provides a salary for the Queen." The Civil List has always provided the easiest part of the rebuttal of the royal tax issue as it can be argued that it would lead to the Exchequer "giving with one hand and taking with the other". The revenue the Queen receives from the Duchy of Lancaster pays for a number of semi-public items but also provides an amount of personal spending. *The Economist* argued that it would be difficult to divide these various parts, though it could be argued that in these respects the Queen is no different from any self-employed person. Finally, the Queen's private income, by definition, is private. *The Economist* conceded that this would be taxable, but covered that with the general arguments against the Queen being taxed.

The Economist dismissed the contention that since revenue is raised in the name of the Crown it would be contradictory to tax the Crown as mere "confused semantics". It also dismissed the argument that the monarch on accession to the throne surrenders the Crown Estates to the State. The argument that this is an implicit tax deal between monarch and State was rejected by *The Economist*, since "for most purposes, the Crown Estates are State-owned".

The Economist's final objection to the Queen being taxed was that it "could become the thin end of an awkward wedge". If the Queen were to become liable for income tax it would be prudent for her advisers to make plans with regard to her tax affairs. But this would be difficult to reconcile with her position, since anything that could be regarded as tax avoidance could cause a sensation in the media and in political circles.

The Economist also set about analysing the size of the Queen's personal wealth, a subject of considerable speculation and dispute.

In 1992, the *Sunday Times* Magazine's annual list of Britain's richest people put the Queen at the top with an estimated fortune of £6.5 billion. This figure was inflated: it included all the inalienable assets, such as Palaces, Crown Jewels and the Royal Collection, which belong to the nation. In 1993, although still at the top, her fortune had been revised down to £5 billion. *The Economist* said that such figures were misleading. The size of the Queen's fortune, it claimed, depends on what is included, and lists of contents are often inaccurate. First it is necessary to distinguish between what belongs to the Queen as a person and what belongs to her as a function of the position she holds. These are the inalienable properties of the monarchy. These fall into two categories: those inalienable by law and those by custom. Those by law include the Crown Jewels and the royal palaces. Those by custom include the Royal Collection. These put together make a sizeable fortune, but do not "belong" to the Queen in the true sense of the word. She holds them while she is alive but is bound to pass them on to her successor – she could not realise their worth even if she wanted to. To include these in the true size of her fortune, therefore, would be misleading.

The Crown Estates and the Duchy of Lancaster can be discounted as they are effectively State owned, it was argued by *The Economist*. That leaves the Queen's real private wealth, which consists of her private investments, her racing stables and her two country houses, Sandringham and Balmoral. The two houses are an interesting case as they are the monarch's personal property: to obtain them her father had to buy them from Edward VIII after the Abdication.

The area of most speculation, *The Economist* said, is that of the Queen's investment portfolio. During the taking of evidence by the Select Committee on the Civil List in 1971, the Lord Chamberlain had said of reports that the value of the portfolio was £50–100 million, "She [The Queen] wishes me to assure the Committee that these suggestions are wildly exaggerated." He did not vouchsafe what the real amount was. In its documentary on the Queen's wealth in 1991 the ITV weekly programme *World in Action* asked a stockbroker to take a portfolio of £30 million in 1971, invest it sensibly in UK shares, and estimate what it would be worth in 1991. The answer was £496 million. *The Economist*, while not disputing the method of calculation, pointed out that the investment could reach such a level only if the capital had remained untouched and the dividends had been re-invested. But this had not been the case: the Queen had not been able to do this: "she has spent the dividends and dug deep into the capital, mainly to help other immediate members of her family. The result is that in real terms the value of her private portfolio seems actually to have shrunk. The best estimate, from those in a position to know, is that her private investments are now worth 'under £50 million'. The conclusion of the article is that the Queen's private income is perhaps "between £1m and £5m a year. If she were to pay income tax, the yield to the Treasury would be about £2m at most."

It was generally accepted that *The Economist* article had been written with the aid of information from the Palace, which had approved it. Times change. In 1971 the monarch had conveyed her message through the Lord Chamberlain; in 1992 she was now doing so through an informed article in a respected magazine. *The Economist* article shed much valuable light on the subject, corrected much misinformation and ended some myths. But discussion of the royal finances, still in a fairly unsophisticated form, went on until the end of the year when the Queen agreed to pay tax.

When the announcement was made some commentators pointed out that the argument that the revenue generated by taxing the Queen would be small did not take into account the sensitivities of the public on the issue. The issue for most people was not that they wanted to extract vast quantities of cash from the Queen but that they felt that in this matter she should be treated like everyone else. The current recession had caused widespread hardship. The question the media asked was: "Why should the Queen and her family not pay tax when the rest of the country is suffering?" With this went resentment of the behaviour of some of the younger royals: "Why should the people pay for these antics?" But for the public, the final straw had been the thought that the nation, not the Queen, would have to pay for the repairs to Windsor Castle. The Queen's "Annus Horribilis" speech was sympathetically received, but overnight the majority of the newspapers returned to the tax issue.

On 25 November, it was announced that Parliament's official watchdog, the National Audit Office, would investigate the cost to the taxpayer of the financing of the five royal palaces. This was considered to be a first step in looking at the finances of the royal family as a whole. The next day John Major announced to Parliament that the Queen had offered to pay income tax on her private fortune and Prince Charles would also pay tax on his income from the Duchy of Cornwall. At the same time it was disclosed that the structure of the Civil List was to be changed; only the Queen, the Duke of Edinburgh, and the Queen Mother would have their expenses paid by the List. The remaining members of the royal Family for whom the List had previously provided – including the Princess Royal; the Duke of York; Prince Edward; Princess Margaret; and Princess Alice, the Duchess of Gloucester – would now receive allowances directly from the Queen.

The Palace said that the Queen viewed the change as "an appropriate step to take in the 1990s". They also emphasised that the Queen had been behind the idea and that it had been first discussed in July, months before the restoration of Windsor Castle had become an issue. In early February 1993 more details were given: the Queen would pay full rate income tax and capital gains tax on her private income, starting with the tax year 1993/94. Although the Queen had agreed to pay tax voluntarily it was said that she and her successors had every intention of continuing to do so indefinitely. The taxable income would not include the Civil List or revenues from the Duchy of Lancaster, which were to be considered for her official duties and working expenses respectively. The arrangements had been worked out between members of the royal household, the Inland Revenue and the Treasury.

Not everyone was satisfied. Some complained that the arrangements had left the sovereign exempt from inheritance tax on what would be handed to his or her successor. The Prime Minister, John Major, dealt with the matter in the House of Commons. This arrangement, he said, existed to prevent the monarchy's assets being "salami-sliced" away.

The details were announced by the Lord Chamberlain, the Earl of Airlie, at a press conference. He referred to estimates of the Queen's private funds, often ranging from one hundred million to billions of pounds, as completely wide of the mark. "Her Majesty has authorised me to say that even the lowest of these estimates is grossly overstated." Commentators settled on an approximate figure of £50–60 million as the value of the Queen's private funds today, a figure with which the royal household's Director of Finance and Property Services, Michael Peat, did not argue when he was interviewed on BBC1 and ITV news the same day. These announcements got a mixed reception from the press. *The Times* editorial, headlined "Pay as you reign", stated that, "The Queen, an astute reader of the political scene, rightly judged that the public mood was changing in respect of her financial affairs. But she has now done enough to satisfy most of her subjects' concerns." The *Mirror*, on the other hand, headlined the front page "H.M. The Tax Dodger", and went on to say: "The Queen is set to become Britain's biggest tax 'dodger' – paying as little as £2 million on her vast fortune." Its editorial called for Buckingham Palace, with the exception of the Queen's private apartments, to be opened to the public. The *Sunday Times* revived complaints about the Queen's immunity from the inheritance tax: a front-page article reported that the Labour Party was considering making the Queen's exemption from inheritance tax a party political issue.

For the Queen her year ended on an unpleasant note. The *Sun* got hold of a copy of the Queen's Christmas Message and published it two days before she was to make it under the headline "Our difficult days, by the Queen – Her Christmas TV message tells of the Royal crisis year." This broke the agreement that the speech is embargoed until Christmas Day, when it is broadcast on radio and television to Britain and the Commonwealth. The *Sun* claimed that the text had been provided by a BBC employee, although an internal BBC inquiry failed to find the alleged culprit. The Palace let it be known that the Queen was disappointed and upset at what had happened. One MP said it was like opening someone else's Christmas present three days before Christmas and telling everyone: a tawdry act. The *Sun* remained unrepentant and on 2 February, solicitors acting for the Queen initiated legal proceedings against the newspaper, claiming damages and costs for breach of copyright. Her lawyers claimed, "Your story gave great offence to Her Majesty." The *Sun* said it would contest the action and in an editorial the next day came out fighting: "We don't consider that we did anything wrong. It was a good old-fashioned journalistic scoop, nothing more. No bugging, no stealing, no skulduggery. Her lawyers say it was copyright. But how could it be, any more than the Budget is Norman Lamont's copyright? Public pronouncements do not belong to anybody. Her Majesty is seeking cash damages. The *Sun* will obviously be contesting the action. We reckon that we already pay enough taxes to keep Her Majesty in the style to which she has become accustomed."

The *Sun* soon changed its tone. An open letter to the Queen published on the front page on 15 February, signed "All at the *Sun*", read: "Dear Ma'am, Last week you proved that you are in touch with ordinary people by agreeing to pay income tax. No small thing. You have responded to public opinion. So the *Sun* is making a gesture of its own. We accept that, unintentionally, we caused you personal offence by publishing your Christmas message two days in advance. We regret that."

The *Sun* then went on to say that, while it believed that what it did was legal, it would donate £200,000 to the Save the Children Fund. The Queen accepted the offer, indicating that half the money should be donated to the Leonard Cheshire Foundation, which was featured in the programme and of which the Queen is patron, and the other half to the Save the Children Fund. The *Sun* also agreed to pay an undisclosed amount in costs. The Palace statement said "The making of the payment by the newspaper must be seen as recognising the basis of the claim."

The year, the fortieth of her reign, had been the worst the Queen had experienced as the monarch. The next chapter describes the worst year of her life as a mother.

12

Annus Horribilis – as mother 1992–3

NONE OF THESE happenings to her as monarch in "Annus Hor-ribilis" caused the Queen so much unhappiness as the marital problems of her children. By far the most serious was the rapid disintegration of the marriage of the Prince and Princess of Wales. That was not just a family affair but had great potential constitutional importance. The various other problems were significant because in one way or another and in varying degree they shocked so many people. The conglomeration of the problems as a whole gave the impression of a family and an institution under siege.

In early 1992 the main offender seemed to be the Duchess of York. In January the tabloids reported that through her Private Secretary, Sir Robert Fellowes, the Queen had advised the Duchess not to go on seeing her friend Steve Wyatt, the Texan millionaire. The *Daily Mail* had printed photographs of the two of them on holiday together with the two young Princesses. On a visit to the United States the Duchess had brought hostile publicity on herself by visiting a night club which banned Jews and blacks. It was widely reported that on the aircraft which brought her back to London she had behaved badly; she had put a paper bag over her head, had thrown bread rolls at her father, and had been very noisy. According to the tabloids she had been reprimanded for other things she had done, including giving permission to the magazine *Hello* to photograph the interior of her home, and her children being bathed and changed. Opinion polls revealed the Duchess to be in a bad light.

On 18 March, it was announced that she and Prince Andrew had decided to separate, and that her public duties would cease forthwith. It was reported that the senior members of the royal family were very angry with her. The Queen's Press Secretary was reported to have given a briefing to two journalists, one of whom, the BBC correspondent, subsequently said: "The knives are out for Fergie at the Palace. I have never known such anger here."

Despite such intimations the separation seemed initially to be much more amicable than the press might have foretold. Within a week of the announcement Andrew and Fergie were together again for their daughter's birthday, where all present seemed to be in good spirits. The Queen was photographed with the Duchess at the Royal Windsor Horse Show, looking happy and relaxed. The Duchess, it had often been asserted, was the Queen's favourite of the younger generation. Meanwhile Prince Andrew was credited generally with being a perfect gentleman during the whole affair. He made practically no public comment, and increased his quota of public engagements, in many cases taking over the commitments arranged for his wife. There were speculations during the early summer that the Duke and Duchess were to be reconciled. But other reports conveyed the idea that the Duchess might withdraw into a form of semi-anonymity similar to that of Captain Mark Phillips. Those who hoped for this were soon to be disappointed.

In April Princess Anne's marriage to Captain Phillips was legally dissolved. Due to sheer hard work and her "hands on" approach with the International Olympic Committee and, most notably, the Save the Children Fund, she had become, if not the most loved the most respected of her generation of the royal family. For a number of years the press had romantically linked her with her former equerry, Commander Tim Laurence, five years younger than herself, the writer of the letters to her which the *Sun* had gained possession of in 1989. Soon after the announcement of the dissolution of the marriage to Captain Phillips, Princess Anne began to appear in public with Commander Laurence. There was very little adverse criticism of their association: it seemed to be taken as inevitable and desirable that she would and should remarry. Throughout the year more and more was heard of Anne's decision that if she got married again the service would take place in Scotland within the Scottish Church so there would be no problem for her mother as Head of the Church of England. There was no mention of an engagement, but after many rumours an announcement was made on 5 December, that the marriage would take place seven days later. The prospect was seen as at least one high point in the year for the Queen, all the more noticeable for coming so soon after she had made her speech at the Guildhall about her "annus horribilis".

It was unfortunate for the Queen and all concerned that statements made about the arrangements for the wedding caused some puzzlement and controversy. First, the press reported, and it was assumed that they did so on the basis of information coming from Buckingham Palace, that the Queen Mother would not attend the ceremony: some reports conveyed that she was not in good enough health to make the journey to Balmoral, others that she was committed to a longstanding prior engagement which could not be put off. The explanation generally accepted by the media and public was that the Queen Mother would not attend the ceremony because she did not approve of divorce and did not want to be party to a remarriage of a divorcee, even if that divorcee was her granddaughter. For the next few days the message of the royal spokesmen was that no formal decision had been made one way or the other. Eventually, it was announced that the Queen Mother would attend the wedding. The truth was that she had been uncertain about travelling so far in inclement weather. Her attendance became almost irrelevant to the media, who were now focusing on the announcement three days earlier that the Prince and Princess of Wales had agreed on a separation.

The marriage ceremony took place as planned. The Princess Royal was able to have her wish: the ceremony was a small family affair; the newspapermen and the television cameras were kept at a distance from the church. Several newspapers went out of their way to contrast it with the pomp and ceremony of the Princess's first marriage in 1973, pointing up how much things had changed for the royal family.

Ever since 1985, when the *Daily Mail* had reproduced Tina Brown's article for *Vanity Fair* on its front page, there had appeared reports that the Prince of Wales's marriage had its difficulties. Little or no hard fact had been adduced, and most people dismissed the reports as speculation by newspapers trying to find another royal story to boost circulation.

Suddenly, on 1 May 1992, the gossip column of the London newspaper, the *Evening Standard*, reported: "As speculation continues about the Duchess of York's marital traumas other members of the Royal Family are bracing themselves for further unwelcome intrusions into their private lives. Andrew Morton's forthcoming biography of the Princess of Wales quietly entitled *Diana: Her Own Story* has reached the proof stage and is currently with the Princess." On 7 June, the *Sunday Times* carried the first extracts from Mr Morton's book under the headline "Cries for Help". The following week the *Sunday Times* ran a front-page story headed "Diana's dilemma as marriage rift confirmed". The *Daily Telegraph* and the *Sunday Telegraph* condemned their competitor for publishing extracts from the book; most of the other newspapers reprinted parts of the excerpts, or ran stories about the stories. The *Sunday Times* increased its circulation, though some of its regular readers cancelled their subscriptions. Yet again the story became the story, and the true state of the marriage became obscured.

Thus even before its publication Andrew Morton's book had created a sensation. No previous book had so altered the public's perception of life in Buckingham Palace. Two aspects of Morton's revelations drew immense attention. First, it gave a detailed account of the longstanding unhappiness of the marriage, putting the blame for this on Charles. He was portrayed as a cold and callous husband, a remote and unfeeling father, selfish, opinionated and arrogant, and a male chauvinist. Secondly, the book claimed that its information came from Diana's family and friends, some of whom were named: Diana's brother, the 9th Earl Spencer; Carolyn Bartholomew, a very close school friend and later flat-mate; and James Gilbey, also a close friend, later to emerge as the man of the "Dianagate" tape.

The fact that many of the Princess's friends had supplied information to Morton, and that her late father had allowed him access to the family photographs, was generally interpreted as evidence that the Princess was involved in the production of the book, or had given it her tacit approval, or had done nothing to discourage the writing of it.

The Princess's motives for allowing her friends and family to co-operate with Andrew Morton remain speculative. Was it yet another "cry for help" similar to those mentioned in the book? Or was it, as a number of the Prince of Wales's friends have asserted, the carefully planned opening of a campaign by the Princess to secure a divorce on her terms and not those of the royal family?

The book opens with a sympathetic picture of Diana growing up in an unsettled environment, child of a broken marriage, her mother leaving home when Diana was six years old, the subsequent ugly divorce case resulting in Earl Spencer retaining custody of the children. Morton describes the additional unhappiness which came with the arrival of the "wicked stepmother", the Earl's second wife, Raine, or "Acid Raine" as Diana and the other children dubbed her. Diana is portrayed growing up as a likeable and quiet, if somewhat emotionally insecure, girl and moves on to describe her early relationship with Prince Charles, that of a very naïve and romantic girl, completely besotted by her Prince Charming, addressing him as "Sir" until the time when they became engaged. She was only just twenty when she married.

On her early life as a Princess we learn of her difficulties in coming to terms with the demands of public life, and with life as a member of the royal family. Apparently Diana first began to feel the new pressures when after the announcement of the engagement she moved from her flat in Coleherne Court to an apartment in Clarence House, the residence of the Queen Mother and Princess Margaret. As for advice or assistance in becoming royal, "Diana was given less training in her new job than the average supermarket checkout operator".

Before the marriage there had been problems and rows between her and the Prince, but soon after they became more serious. Some of these explosions of temper, according to the book, were the result of the Prince keeping up connections with old friends: two days before the wedding Diana almost called it off because of Charles's continuing relationship with Mrs Parker-Bowles. The book stated that Charles's refusal to end that relationship had much to do with the breakdown of the marriage.

The first major surprise in the book was the disclosure that very early in the marriage Diana began to suffer from bulimia nervosa, a disease, common in young women, often called the "gorge-purge syndrome", as a result of which the victim eats ravenously and then makes herself vomit. It can cause grave imbalances in the body's supply of vitamins and minerals, and, in extreme circumstances, can cause death. As the Princess herself has described it, "From early childhood many have felt that they were expected to be perfect but didn't feel that they had the right to express their true feelings to those around them – feelings of guilt, self-revulsion and low personal esteem, creating in them a compulsion to dissolve like a Disprin and disappear."

The Princess's bulimia problem began during her engagement. Its origin could be attributed to the enormous emotional pressure from the media to which she was subjected. It continued well into the marriage. In 1987, according to Morton, the Princess's close friend, Carolyn Bartholomew, issued her with an ultimatum: unless Diana sought medical advice, Carolyn would tell the press about the Princess's condition. This forced the Princess's hand: she went to a specialist.

About a year after the publication of the book, Princess Diana addressed a major London conference, Eating Disorders '93, on the problems faced by bulimia sufferers. She started with, "I have it on good authority . . ." and went on to describe the sufferings of women for whom "the illness they developed became their shameful friend". The speech, much praised, was interpreted as a reflection on her own experience.

The most disturbing disclosure in Morton's book was that early in the marriage the Princess had tried to commit suicide not once but on five occasions. From Morton's descriptions the Princess's "suicide attempts" appear to have been more like "cries for help" than determined attempts to kill herself. According to the book Prince Charles was unmoved by these happenings, and went on his way unperturbed.

Morton also disclosed one sad irony: early in the marriage, when Prince Andrew's marriage to Sarah Ferguson was still smiled on by all, Charles and other members of the royal family wanted Diana to behave more as the new Duchess of York did: "Why can't she be more like Fergie?"

The book went on to describe the deterioration of the marriage. Morton claimed that Diana had considered it over after the birth of Prince Harry in September 1984. He also revealed that for years the Prince and Princess had not shared the royal bed. The final chapter, entitled "I did my best", goes on to state that the Princess had overcome most of her earlier problems and now felt in control of her own life. It also said that she would prefer a divorce but could not have one since she did not want to lose custody of the children. In a final and possibly most interesting revelation Morton disclosed that she believed that not only would she never become Queen but also that Charles would never become King.

The publication of Andrew Morton's book evoked more discussion about the royal family and the monarchy than there had ever been before. The Palace was silent on the contents of the book, except for the comment that the Princess had not co-operated with the author in its production. Andrew Neil, editor of the *Sunday Times*, came under criticism from some of his fellow editors and by many politicians. Lord St John of Fawsley said on radio: "A warning needs to be uttered that our institutions are fragile, and if we do not respect them, and if we do not exercise some self-restraint about them, we shall destroy them and we shall all be the sufferers." The Labour MP, Clare Short, said: "Quite a lot of women suffer from post-natal depression, and none should expect to have that splashed over all the pages of the newspapers. It's outrageous." The Conservative MP, Nicholas Fairbairn, asked whether Andrew Neil wanted "to destroy somebody's else's marriage and the great institutions of the state".

Attention now began to focus on whether, the statement from the Palace notwithstanding, the Princess had in one way or another, contributed to Morton's book. Andrew Neil publicly insisted that it would have been impossible for the Princess not to have known about the book in the course of its preparation, that she had made no attempts to stop her friends and family talking to Mr Morton, and had done nothing to prevent its publication. During the weeks of controversy that followed a well-publicised incident seemed to support Mr Neil's opinion. The Princess made a visit to her friend Carolyn Bartholomew, who, as mentioned, was a major source for Morton. Obviously having somehow acquired notice of the Princess's visit, several photographers were on hand outside the Bartholomew residence to take pictures of the Princess warmly embracing her old friend, the affectionate meeting disposing of any suggestion that Princess Diana disapproved of the part Carolyn Bartholomew had played in helping Andrew Morton to write his book.

In the middle of August the attention of the press switched back to the Duchess of York. The Duchess had rented a villa in the South of France, Le Mas de Pignorol, for a holiday with her two children, accompanied by her friend and "business adviser", John

Bryan, an American. Photographs indicating that she and Bryan enjoyed an intimate relationship, taken outside the villa by an Italian freelance photographer, a Mr Agnelli, using a telescopic lens, had come into the hands of *Paris Match* and the *Mirror*. Prior to the taking of the photographs, Bryan had strenuously denied any romantic involvement with the Duchess. He had previously referred to himself as a friend of both the Duke and Duchess. On 19 August it became known that lawyers employed by Bryan were trying in London and Paris to prevent *Paris Match* and the *Mirror* printing these photographs. Mr Bryan's attempt failed. That evening, the *Mirror* put out advertisements on television claiming that in next morning's edition the photographs of the Duchess with Mr Bryan, in some of which the two little royal grandchildren also appeared, would "not amuse the Palace" and "would amaze the world".

The photographs appeared the next morning. It was obvious at once why such efforts had been made to prevent them being published. The headline above them was: "Fergie's stolen kisses – Truth about Duchess and the Texan millionaire". The front page carried two photographs, one captioned "Poolside embrace: Arms entwined, Fergie and Bryan kiss and cuddle on a sun lounger at their holiday retreat"; the other "Topless in Tropez: Fergie peels off for a session by the pool at St Tropez with her Texan pal". The paper then promises "More sensational Photos – see Pages 2, 3, 4, 5, 6, 12, 13, 20, 21."

As if to emphasise their scoop, the *Mirror* printed a statement of copyright on the page: "MGN LTD has acquired exclusive UK publication rights to these photographs. No unauthorised reproduction permitted."

So far as is known, no other member of the British royal family has figured in a photograph which could be compared to those published in the *Mirror*. Publication caused a storm. The *Mirror* ordered an extra print run of half a million copies. The *Sun*, meanwhile, bought and published similar pictures supplied to them by Mr Agnelli.

Buckingham Palace issued a statement with the backing of the Queen and the Duke of York: "We strongly disapprove of the publication of photographs taken in such circumstances." The *Mirror* and the *Sun* rejected accusations that the privacy of the Duchess had been invaded. The news editor of the *Sun* said: "This is the Duchess of York. This is a woman who milked her role as a member of the Royal family for all it is worth. You live by the sword, you die by the sword."

The appearance of more photographs in the *Mirror* and the *Sun* the following day started two public arguments. The first was about the right of privacy and what should be done to protect it. The second was about what should be done with the Duchess. The first argument, about the right of privacy, was a continuation of an argument which had been going on for a long time, and is going on today. But the second argument, about what should be done about the Duchess, was new. The general feeling seemed to be that although taking the photos had been an invasion of privacy, and was wrong, Mr Agnelli had provided further evidence of how unsuitable the Duchess was to be a member of the royal family, and how important it was that her connection with it should be brought to an end. A *Sunday Express* poll reported that eighty-six per cent wanted her title to be taken from her. The Press Complaints Commission received only forty telephone calls complaining on the Princess's behalf. An editorial in the *Daily Telegraph* entitled "Conduct Unbecoming" might well have summed up the view of the press as a whole:

> The photographer ... behaved wrongly, and so, by extension did the tabloid papers that published these pictures. He and they have no right to invade her privacy. But it is interesting and significant that the actions of the press have aroused so little public indignation. It shows how low is the standing of the Duchess ... For the fact is that the Duchess has been behaving without dignity and sense.

At the beginning of that week the Duchess of York had been with the Queen at Balmoral, accompanied by her two little girls. Within a few days of the photographs appearing in the *Mirror* she and her two daughters left. There was speculation that this would turn out to be the last holiday she would spend with the Queen. Such was not to be the case: the Queen invited the Duchess and her two daughters to spend Christmas with the royal family at Sandringham.

In retrospect the publication of the Duchess of York photographs seems to have terminated a long period in which the newspapers somewhat protected the royal family and opened a new one in which the newspapers would print if they were so inclined everything they knew. A kind of concordat had come to an end.

On the day that most of the press was reporting the "flight" of the Duchess of York from Balmoral, a new, and, again, sensational report appeared in the *Sun*. This was the beginning of the story of the "Dianagate" or "Squidgygate" tape, which purported to be the recording of a telephone conversation between the Princess and a man not then identified. "My life is torture", ran the headline. The five-page article began: "Princess Diana has been named as the woman on a sensational tape telling a mystery man her husband 'makes my life real torture'." The term "Squidgy" was used to identify the tape because the man recorded on the tape so often used "Squidgy" as a term of endearment to the woman he was talking to. On the tape the woman was heard bitterly criticising her family and expressing warm affection for the man she was talking to on the telephone. Voice-test analysis in America had confirmed that the female voice was that of Princess Diana.

The story was exploited immediately by all newspapers. Once an edited transcript of the tapes had been published in the United States the *Sun* printed it in Britain. The *Sun* stated that the conversation had been taped accidentally by a retired bank manager, who enjoyed listening to random radio conversations on his scanner, and had put the tape at the newspaper's disposal. The *Sun* set up a "hot-line" telephone number which people could dial to listen to the tape – more than 40,000 calls were made in one day. The *Sun* explained its reasons for publishing the contents of the tape at this particular moment. The tape, said the *Sun*, had been in their possession for two and a half years. When they had first received it, the *Sun* said, they knew that there were problems with the marriage and that there was concern for the Princess's health. The *Sun* had not wanted to add to her problems, but on learning that a book was soon to be published containing a transcript of this tape, it decided to publish, "to spike damaging rumours about Diana which were circulating in Fleet Street, Westminster and the Court of St James." If the *Sun*'s version of events is to be taken at face value the tape was published for altruistic reasons to help, not harm, the Princess: it was not a response to being "out-scooped" by the *Mirror* the week before with the photographs of the Duchess of York and John Bryan in the South of France.

Diana may have believed that the *Sun* had intended to help her but she could have had no doubt about the damage their helpfulness caused. The tape became the talk of the world. By the end of the week the consensus was that the man at the other end of the telephone was James Gilbey, already well known as one of the main sources for the information to be found in Andrew Morton's book.

As the week went on it became obvious that the press was being sympathetic to the Princess. According to the Sunday tabloid, the *People*, "Opinion polls prove the public has enormous sympathy for the troubled Princess. SO DO WE." Such sentiments were based on the fact that despite initial speculation, there was no evidence that Diana was having an affair with anybody, but that she was a very sad young woman trapped in a loveless and difficult marriage. The "Dianagate" tape confirmed much of what had been reported in the Morton book.

The spokesmen in Buckingham Palace were in a difficult position. Their first statement about the tapes was: "This is an absolute fake, part of a shabby and malicious smear campaign." Within days they made a somewhat different statement: due to "voice quality" what the tape amounted to was "inconclusive".

At the end of that week there was another blow for the Princess: some newspapers reported that photographs in the possession of a national newspaper showed the Princess "hugging Major James Hewitt". Major Hewitt, billed as "handsome bachelor – Gulf War hero", had helped to teach Prince William and Prince Harry to ride. Nothing came of these allegations, but they were grist to the mill for those newspapers who were convinced that the "Queen's men" in Buckingham Palace were out to undermine Princess Diana.

In the *Mail on Sunday* on 30 August the headline was "The Plot – Princess Diana and the bitter Palace campaign to discredit her". The article suggested that there was "an inner circle close to the Royal family" orchestrating a campaign against her. It went so far as to suggest that the Palace sources had approved the publication of the Dianagate tapes. Other papers took a similar line, for example the *Daily Star*: "Dianahate – Revenge plot by Palace to nail Princess". If these tabloids had indeed been trying to be helpful to the Princess they were not in receipt of her gratitude. Their stories caused her great anguish.

According to the postscript to the paperback edition of Morton's book published well after the hardback edition: "At the height of the Dianagate scandal, the Princess seriously considered packing her bags and leaving the Royal Family and public life forever. Several friends who spoke to her have confirmed that she felt 'destroyed' by the coverage."

Whatever view the royal family took of the disclosures that summer, of Diana's role or her indirect responsibility for some of them, and whatever measures were taken in Buckingham Palace to try and reduce the damage they may have thought had been done, there is no doubt that Prince Charles and his friends and his staff had been very upset. They were convinced that Diana had encouraged the production of the Morton book if she had not participated in it. They resented the impression which had been created of Diana the wronged woman, married to a cold and heartless husband. They believed that Diana had manipulated the media in her favour: to take a simple example, on her visit to India with her husband she had allowed herself to be photographed sitting alone against a background of the Taj Mahal.

Friends and admirers of Charles supported him by supplying newspapers with information doing credit to him and less credit to her. These easily understandable responses from both sides could prove to be an undesirable precedent. They did neither party any good, and they were not good for the royal family.

In early November, Charles and Diana went together to South Korea. The visit already has a place in history: it was the last they made before their separation was announced. If conceived as a public relations exercise it was a complete failure: it might even have hastened the sad dénouement which was imminent. Like all royal visits, it had been scheduled well in advance, and had encouraged much speculation. There had been rumours that Diana did not wish to go on the tour, but newspapers referred to Palace sources indicating that the Queen had insisted that the four-day visit to Korea must go ahead as planned.

It was a gruelling assignment. The schedules provided for Diana and Charles, some separate, some shared, were exhausting. Charles attended business forums and seminars, trade fairs promoting British products, and delivered a lecture on environmental problems to Korean businessmen. Diana visited welfare centres and old people's homes. What the Prince and Princess did when they were separate met with nothing but praise, each exuding their natural charm. It was a different story when they appeared together. Problems arose. Photographs showed unfriendly glances being exchanged between them, expressions of disinterest while the other was speaking, and other indications of mutual hostility. Royal spokesmen were quoted as having spoken of this visit in advance as a "togetherness tour". Newspapermen had gossiped that the Queen's spokesmen had encouraged them to report the possibility of a reconciliation. At the end of the tour, Peter Westmacott, Deputy Private Secretary to the Prince, approached James Whitaker, the *Mirror*'s royal correspondent, and told him that the couple were deeply distressed by the amount of intrusion into their privacy. When asked if he was saying the marriage was a happy one, Peter Westmacott was said to have replied, "No, I'm not saying that." This exchange was widely reported in the British press.

Diana returned to Britain: Charles went on to Hong Kong. Newspapers reported that the Prince looked considerably happier than he had in the company of his wife in Korea. Back in Britain the Princess released a highly unusual statement:

> The Princess of Wales would like to single out from the recent waves of misleading reports about the Royal Family, assertions in some newspapers this week specifically against the Queen and the Duke of Edinburgh. The suggestion that they have been anything but sympathetic and supportive is untrue and particularly hurtful.

It was generally accepted that the Princess had made this public statement to counter remarks in the new postscript to the paperback edition of Andrew Morton's book. Although the press noted that the Princess's announcement publicly denied that there were such problems, it was also pointed out that in breaking a long silence on such matters the Princess had not denied the existence of any problem between her and Prince Charles. Was the absence of such a denial an implicit admission that such a problem existed? Why, asked some newspapers, had she denied only the reports about her relations with the Queen and the Duke? She had not denied statements made in Andrew Morton's book in the earlier part of the summer, nor had she denied statements about her having colluded with him or with his sources of information, in spite of the fact, some newspapers said, that Palace spokesmen had hoped that she would do so.

This was the signal for the Sunday newspapers to announce in full voice that the marriage was now no more. "Separate Lives", was the headline in the *Mail on Sunday*. "Diana to go it alone", said the *Sunday Express*. They reported that the marriage was over in everything but name. The *Mail on Sunday* stated that, "Charles and Diana have ruled out divorce, which they recognise would throw the monarchy into further chaos." The *Sunday Express* took the same view but for different reasons: "Diana has decided against divorce in order to stay with her children and guide her eldest son, Prince William, to his destiny as a future king." Both papers stated that arrangements were being made for the Princess to set up a court separate from that of the Prince which would be a potential rival of his.

That Sunday was Remembrance Day, and the royal family gathered at the Cenotaph for the traditional laying of their wreaths. Prince Charles was still in Hong Kong, so there was no possibility of "rift" photographs. The demeanour and expressions of the members of the family were scrutinised with as much zeal as Kremlinologists in earlier years had studied the members of the Politburo lined up for the May Day parade. The following day various pictures appeared in the newspapers, including one of Diana smiling at Anne, who seemed to return a stony stare.

With the Prince still in the Far East, the Princess made a well-publicised and successful visit to Paris, where she was fêted by the President and numerous celebrities. There was widespread comment on her looks and her manner: she had never looked happier and more confident. It was pointed out that she had taken to wearing high heels again, a practice she had long since given up in deference to Charles, who is noticeably shorter. This was thought to be symbolic. On her return to London she made a widely reported speech supporting European Drug Prevention Week. Her theme was that children need to be shown love and affection if they are not to seek substitutes and "cushion themselves behind mood-changing drugs". In a passage in her speech interpreted by some as a direct criticism of the way that the Queen had brought up *her* children, including Prince Charles, she said: "Hugging has no harmful side effects. If we all play our part in making our children feel valued, the result will be tremendous." The contrast in attitudes and the distance between the Prince and Princess could not have been highlighted more clearly.

More revelations from Morton's forthcoming paperback made

front-page headlines. The book claimed that Diana had wanted to have a third baby in an effort to hold the marriage together, but that her idea was rebuffed by Charles.

In the middle of November the *Mirror* let it be known that they were in possession of a tape which revealed an intimate relationship between the Prince and Camilla Parker-Bowles. Over the course of a number of days they released details indicating that the tape was of a compromising nature, and which provided the basis of such stories as "Camilla and Prince planned secret trysts". The reports of such a relationship were dismissed by Camilla's husband, Andrew Parker-Bowles, as "pure fiction". In early December Prince Charles was criticised for making a speech in Paris in which, his critics claimed, he had supported French farmers who had set fire to lorries carrying British lamb, and had praised the French for their opposition to the GATT Treaty. In fact, Charles had simply said that the French had set an inspiring example to their neighbours by defending their rural traditions, but once again the facts of the matter were almost irrelevant: some newspapers presented him again as an eccentric out of touch with the realities of the modern world.

It is difficult to believe that the marriage could have survived any more revelations or speculation. Be that as it may, the stage was now set for the announcement which was issued by the press secretary to the Queen on Wednesday 9 December 1992:

It is announced from Buckingham Palace that, with regret, The Prince and Princess of Wales have decided to separate. Their Royal Highnesses have no plans to divorce and their constitutional positions are unaffected. This decision has been reached amicably, and they will continue to participate fully in the upbringing of their children.

Their Royal Highnesses will continue to carry out full and separate programmes of public engagements and will, from time to time, attend family occasions and national events together. The Queen and The Duke of Edinburgh, although saddened, understand and sympathise with the difficulties that have led to this decision. Her Majesty and His Royal Highness particularly hope that the intrusions into the privacy of the Prince and Princess may now cease. They believe that a degree of privacy and understanding is essential if Their Royal Highnesses are to provide a happy and secure upbringing for their children, while continuing to give a wholehearted commitment to their public duties.

The guidance issued with the announcement tried to deal with the questions which would obviously follow such an unprecedented course of action. It ruled out a divorce, saying that neither party planned or wished for one. It categorically stated that "there have been no third parties involved, on either side, in this decision; they would strongly deprecate any such suggestion."

It then tackled the two main areas of constitutional importance: the succession; and Charles's role as Head of the Church of England. There were no constitutional implications from the decision, it said: Charles would still become King, and "there is no reason why Her Royal Highness should not become Queen." Similarly, the Archbishop of Canterbury had indicated that the separation caused no problem for Charles becoming Head of the Church.

The announcement came as no surprise to the press or public: the revelations throughout the year had shown that there was something radically wrong with the Wales's marriage. The timing of the announcement caused raised eyebrows, coming so soon after the "annus horribilis" speech and only three days before the wedding of the Princess Royal. There were hints that Charles and Diana had decided to make the announcement for the sake of their children, feeling that they would be more harmed than they had been already by continued speculation, especially when they returned to boarding school after the Christmas holiday.

The announcement of the separation was also made public in the House of Commons by the Prime Minister. When in the course of Mr Major's speech he stated that the separation would not prevent Princess Diana from becoming Queen there was an audible gasp. Both sides of the House seemed staggered. After his speech there were the expected expressions of sympathy from the Leader of the Opposition and Leader of the Liberal Democrats, and Sir Edward Heath, in his role as father of the House, described the statement as one of the saddest that a Prime Minister has had to make in modern times.

The reaction of the media was surprisingly mixed. The majority view seemed to be that the right thing had been done: the marriage was now obviously a loveless failure. It was sad for the Prince and the Princess, and for the children. As to who had been to blame, and about what would happen next opinion was divided. The *Mirror* was on Diana's side: "Home Alone – No kids and no husband – back to an empty house". It reported: "The Princess, wearing no make-up, looked pale as she was driven back to Kensington Palace following a day's official engagements. With both sons away at school, she had no family to welcome her." The *Sun* parodied the same film title: "Throne Alone – MPs say that Charles won't be King, Di won't be Queen. It's down to Wills." But it was markedly less sympathetic to Diana than its competitor. Inside the paper under the headline "Victory for Di" the *Sun* said: "1. She wanted the kids – She got them. 2. She wanted the cash – She got it. 3. She wanted her staff – She got them. 4. She wanted a palace – She got it." Further inside the paper, Richard Littlejohn wrote: "What a result for devious Diana," and went on to say that the Prince "could have divorced the little gold-digger and renounced the succession ... he is a weak, dismal, arrogant little man with a third-rate intellect." The *Mail* and the *Express* carried the same headline "End of a Fairytale". They both concentrated on the past with "photo-specials" of the history of the marriage. The "heavies" were factual: they reported the official announcements.

It was soon clear that the Prime Minister's statement that the separation would have no constitutional implications had surprised some politicians and some newspaper editors. Downing Street felt obliged to reiterate the Prime Minister's statement later in the day, adding that before it there had been consultations with the Lord Chancellor, the Attorney-General, the Archbishop of Canterbury and the Secretary to the Cabinet. Some politicians and some newspaper editors remained unconvinced. An editorial in *The Times* agreed with the Prime Minister that "there is today no constitutional crisis. There is barely as yet a constitutional issue. [But] the Position of the Princess of Wales may yet bring greater problems ... Although there are no constitutional reasons why she should not become Queen one day, there may now be several practical difficulties. A reigning Queen who was separated from her husband could not carry out all her public duties, still less act as a unifying symbol." The *Mirror* said: "This latest royal mess is making a mockery of the Monarchy. Unchecked that mockery will destroy the Monarchy itself." The *Independent* predicted that "if the agreement proves to be short-term or insufficiently robust to withstand continuous newspaper investigation of their private lives, then what lies ahead is the prospect of a diminished and broken-backed monarchy."

During the next few days discussion centred on the Princess of Wales, and in particular on the question of whether or not she should become Queen. The consensus between MPs, commentators and the public opinion pollsters was that she should *not*. There seemed to be some inconsistencies in public opinion: most people, apparently, believed that the Prince and not the Princess had been responsible for the break-up of the marriage, but also believed that he should become King without her as his Queen. Underlying this belief, perhaps, was the feeling that sympathy with the Princess was one thing: what was right for the monarchy was another.

There was also much speculation in these few days about whether Charles might wish, or be forced, to renounce his right to the succession. It looked as though the "let's skip a generation" opinion was popular with the press and had substantial support up and down the country. There was a swift reaction from the Palace. By the end of the week a number of front-page stories had appeared such as the one in the *Express* headlines "I will be the King" and stating: "The Prince says he wants to take over from the Queen and serve Britain the best he can." These stories did not end the speculation. The *Sunday Times* editorial that weekend insisted: "We must jump a generation and must look forward to the succession of ... King William V." Other Sunday newspapers reported that the Princess had long since given up all thought or hope of becoming Queen. .

In January 1993 rumours started that a second compromising tape existed, this one recording a conversation on the telephone between Prince Charles and Camilla Parker-Bowles. At first the indications were that no British newspaper would publish its contents, but after a transcript had appeared in Australia, and countless copies of the article had been faxed to Britain, some being sold at street corners, it was published by the *People* and by the *Sunday Mirror*, many other newspapers also reproducing excerpts. The *Sun* at first refrained from publishing anything of it: "Why? To show the country what it will be like if the Government brings in the half-baked Calcutt law to gag the press. If they have their way we'll be able to tell you damn all about major issues like the marital infidelity of the next King and Queen." The *Sun* complained that "millions of people all round the world yesterday read the words of love Prince Charles poured out to Camilla Parker-Bowles – everywhere except in Britain." An article headlined "Smutty schoolboy who would be king" described the contents of the tape as "puerile, inarticulate ramblings ... the kind of love-play you expect from two schoolkids whose sexual experience is limited to a quick fumble behind the bike sheds or in the back row of the Odeon" confirming "what we all suspected about the heir to the throne: he is an emotionally immature twit." The article noted that some people "see the fact that the tapes emerged in an Australian magazine in which the owner of the *Sun* has a stake as further evidence of a republican plot to bring down the monarchy."

It was clear from the transcript published that the relationship between the man and woman concerned was sexually and otherwise of a very intimate kind. It was soon accepted that the tape had indeed recorded a conversation between Prince Charles and Mrs Camilla Parker-Bowles. The tape was widely interpreted as confirming that it was Charles's relations with other women which had brought about the breakdown of his marriage.

At the same time, Princess Diana came under severe criticism. The previous year, Lord McGregor, Chairman of the Press Complaints Commission, had examined widespread rumours that some of the reports which had appeared in the newspapers about the state of the royal marriage had done so as a result of direct or indirect assistance from the Princess. In the course of his inquiries Lord McGregor had talked with the Queen's Private Secretary, Sir Robert Fellowes, who assured him that rumours linking the Princess and her friends with the press were "baseless". McGregor concluded that these assurances had been given to Sir Robert by the Princess herself. McGregor consequently denounced some of the stories which had appeared in the newspapers as intrusion on the part of the Press into the lives of the Prince and Princess: some newspapers, he said, "had dabbled their fingers in the stuff of other people's souls". But in the process of making further inquiries McGregor had talks with several newspaper editors, and as a result of these talks he came to a different conclusion. "I was told that the Prince and Princess had been involved in making statements about their marriage. I did not at the time [receive] nor have I subsequently received any evidence of any involvement by the Prince leaking to the press anything of that nature. I made inquiries to the editors of newspapers and was satisfied that the intrusions were contrived by the Princess herself. I feel I was used." The Private Secretary to the Queen must also have felt "used".

The reputation of the Princess was badly damaged by Lord McGregor's disclosures. Many newspapers and several politicians condemned her for the deceit. Only the ongoing story about what was now being called the "Camillagate" tape saved her from further criticism. As it was, the question of whether both the Prince's staff and the Princess's staff had played "dirty tricks", and who suffered more in consequence, was featured in the newspapers for several weeks to come.

In early March 1993 the Princess made her first official foreign tour since the announcement of the separation the previous December. With Baroness Chalker, Minister of State for Overseas Aid, she spent five days in Nepal, visiting relief agencies and charity operations. Just before she left, an Australian television programme broadcast hitherto-unreleased excerpts from the "Dianagate" recordings, these extracts being more compromising than those released the previous year. Their contents were reported in the British press. There was some speculation in various newspapers that the release of these extracts was part of a "dirty tricks" campaign against the Princess at a time when her much advertised visit to Nepal might further enhance her popular reputation. Newspaper commentators remarked that compared with usual royal tours this one was apparently being downgraded: one newspaper reported that those in charge of protocol in Nepal had been told not to play the national anthem during the Princess's trip: the *Daily Telegraph* reported: "Nepal rolls out a second-class carpet for the Princess of Wales." There was much discussion.

Reportage, comment, speculation and gossip throughout the summer of 1993 raised many questions about the future of the Prince and Princess of Wales, of their relationship, of their two sons and about the future of the monarchy. But after the holidays newspaper coverage seemed less intense; and tension surrounding the royal family appeared to lessen. The lull may have reflected a widespread and growing opinion that the royal family had been subjected to too much suffering, more than was fair, and that they should now be left alone. Some people said publicly that the editors of the tabloids felt guilty about the quantity and quality of the coverage they had given to the Prince and Princess of Wales, and now wanted to make some amends.

Such hopes were not to be realised. On 7 November the *Sunday Mirror* printed close-up colour photographs of Princess Diana taken of her lying on her back on an exercise machine, wearing a leotard, her legs in a cycling position. These photographs, for which the camera had to be fixed in a well-planned position, had been taken in the private gymnasium which she visited regularly. The manager of the gymnasium had contrived to have the camera fitted, the photographs taken, and had offered them to several newspapers, finally selling them to the *Mirror* for, it was reported, £100,000. The publication of the photographs made it clear that Princess Diana would continue to be pursued by the tabloid press. The editor who had published the photographs claimed that they could "only enhance her image and popularity with the British people". He claimed also that the photographs had been of use to the Princess since the fact that it had been possible to take them showed that measures for her security were inadequate. The following day some newspapers denounced publication, as did Buckingham Palace as a gross invasion of privacy; "outrage at 'peeping tom' pictures of the Princess of Wales", predicted *The Times*, "will give extra ammunition to those who would put limitations on the freedom of the press." The issue of privacy and the press flared up again.

Two weeks later the *Financial Times* reported in some detail complaints by the Prince of Wales that his visits abroad to improve British trade relations were not being given the support they deserved by the government: "The Prince of Wales is frustrated at what he sees as lack of support from some powerful government departments for royal visits abroad which could help secure business for Britain." Similar stories appeared in other newspapers. The following day *The Times* reported: "Major backs Prince's business envoy role", and stated that "Downing Street officials said Mr Major was keen for the Prince to play an active part in helping to win business abroad."

The Prince of Wales might also have said that his business trips did not get sufficient support from the media. The day after the world had boggled at the gymnasium photographs of Princess Diana, Charles was in Saudi Arabia in the interests of British trade: *The Times* gave the visit a few inches on an inside page. Many people may have thought that so long as Diana was available to the press Charles would not be news. There was much speculation that nobody was more aware of this than the Prince.

What thoughts passed through Princess Diana's mind when she saw the photographs in the *Sunday Mirror*, and pondered their implications, we do not know. But four weeks later, on 3 December at a charity lunch in London, she astonished nearly every one of the 500 guests present by announcing that "my plans for the future ... have changed ... At the end of this year, when I have completed my diary of official engagements, I will be reducing the extent of the public life I have led so far." The Princess explained that when she started her public life twelve years previously she had understood that the attention of the media "would inevitably focus on both our private and public lives ... But I was not aware of how overwhelming that attention would become; nor the extent to which it would affect both my public duties and my personal life, in a manner that has been hard to bear." From now on her first priority would be her children. The Princess hoped that "you can find it in your hearts to give me the time and space that has been lacking in recent years". Having explained why she was taking this step the Princess said: "I would also like to add that this decision has been reached with the full understanding of the Queen and the Duke of Edinburgh, who have always shown me kindness and support." She made no reference to the Prince of Wales. She read what was obviously a carefully prepared statement in emotional tones.

The following morning the front-page headline in the *Daily Telegraph* was: "Princess Retreats from the Glare of Public Life"; in *The Times*, "Princess of Wales leaves Public Arena". Lord Rees-Mogg, the leading columnist of *The Times*, blamed the tabloids – "I would not like this morning to have the conscience of the editor of the *Daily Mirror* ..." But the *Daily Mail* headline was "Charles Drove Her To It", basing this contention on information from an anonymous "close confidante" that the Prince had "pushed her out".

The announcement that the Princess thereby cancelled her agreement to make dozens of appearances for charities disturbed many charity organisers who had been counting on her to bring in funds for future programmes they were already committed to. They sympathised with her in her predicament, but at the same time some of them felt let down. Newspaper comment was sympathetic but not uncritical. While the leader in *The Times*, headed "A mature decision that deserves respect", was entirely supportive, the *Daily Telegraph*'s, headed "Retreat into Privacy," though also sympathetic, expressed regret that "she should have chosen to unleash a new royal melodrama by making so prominent a declaration when she might simply have allowed her list of future engagements to tell the story for itself."

A few days later, on 8 December, *The Times* published an article by the Archdeacon of York in which he raised the question of Prince Charles's moral fitness to accede to the throne. Charles had broken his marriage vows, said the Archdeacon: could he then be trusted to keep the vows he would have to make at the Coronation? Several newspapers reported that many high-placed clerics thought that the Archdeacon had done well to raise the question, and that they would prefer that Charles did not become King, largely because of his association with Mrs Camilla Parker-Bowles.

On the page in *The Times* opposite that which carried the Archdeacon's article appeared a leader entitled "Fit To Rule" with the subtitle "A king need not be a model husband". The leader listed the many proofs which Charles had given of his dedication to his vocation, examined the nature of kingship and challenged "the equivalence of coronation and marriage vows ..." The leader advocated, not for the first time, the repeal of "the archaic law", the Royal Marriages Act, "which limits considerably the monarch's freedom to marry, divorce or remarry". The last sentence of the leader summed up the view of *The Times*: "The misfortunes of the Prince's private life have been a regrettable chapter in the history of the monarchy: but they are an unjust, unreliable and uncon-stitutional test of his fitness to rule."

The posing of the question started discussion about whether Charles, if a party to divorce, should be allowed to come to the throne anyway. This in turn raised the question of whether the time had come for the disestablishment of the Anglican Church and to sever the connection between Church and State established in the reign of Henry VIII. There was further speculation that Charles might choose to give up his right to the throne in favour of his son, Prince William. Friends of Charles, notably Churchill's grandson, Nicholas Soames, assured the nation publicly that Charles had no intention of not becoming King: when the time came Charles would consider it his *duty* to succeed his mother, and nothing would prevent him from carrying out that duty. On 15 December the Archbishop of York wrote an article for *The Times* headlined by the newspaper "An adulterer can be king, the Archbishop of York says".

Dr Habgood began his article by saying: "One of the curious features of the present controversy about the Prince of Wales is that it erupted out of nothing." He mentioned that the Archdeacon was "well known for his readiness to speak to the media," and dismissed the controversy about the Prince's fitness to succeed to the throne and supreme governorship as "a classic example of media-created news". He pointed out that *The Times* had already "disposed of the fallacious argument that someone who broke their marriage vows might treat lightly any other vows ...", adding, in a point which may have most impressed his readers, that:

> The other aspect of this strange hypothetical controversy centres on the question of whether a monarch with moral flaws would be fit to rule. Put like that the answer is obvious. Sovereigns are not required to be saints.
>
> Nevertheless, is the Supreme Governor of the Church of England required to be at least as morally sober as an archbishop? If supreme governorship were the same as spiritual leadership the answer might have to be yes. But this would represent a serious misunderstanding. A monarch's personal involvement in the Church is welcome. The role of the Supreme Governor, however, is not personal but institutional.

Dr Habgood then went on to define and explain what many people for a long time may have misunderstood, the nature and meaning of the relationship between the monarchy and the Church, and to draw an important conclusion:

> The monarch is the visible representative of the unity and identity of the nation, and it is the Church's commitment to the nation, and responsibility for its spiritual welfare, which is symbolised by supreme governorship. It would be theoretically possible to hold to the symbol even if in personal terms the monarch only fulfilled the minimum requirement of belonging to the Protestant succession.

Various polls threw some light on public opinion at this time. On the question of who had emerged with greater credit following the separation fifty-four were for Diana and fourteen for Charles. Asked whether the separation had altered their respect for the monarchy sixty-eight replied that it had not, twenty-nine that it had. Only nineteen thought that the monarchy should be abolished; seventy-seven believed it should be retained. On the subject of divorce, fifty-five were for, thirty were against. In the event of divorce, sixty-six thought Charles should become King, and twenty-nine not. Charles should be allowed to re-marry, said seventy; twenty-five said he should not. If he re-married Charles should be allowed to become King, said fifty-seven; thirty-five said he should not. When the Queen dies, said twenty-nine, William should become King; fifty-eight said the next King should be Charles. A few days later, an *Observer*/ICM poll showed that two-thirds of those questioned preferred to retain the monarch as Head of State, only one-fifth opting for an elected President and one-tenth for the Prime Minister. Nearly one-third hoped the crown would "bypass" Prince Charles and go to his son. There seemed strong feeling about the financing of the royal family: seventy-three of those people questioned wanted to end the £7.9 million a year Civil List and associated payments of nearly £1 million to the Duke of Edinburgh and the Queen Mother. Only twenty-one of them believed the taxpayer should continue to foot the bill. Two-thirds of those interviewed blamed the press for the royal family's problems.

In her Christmas Day message the Queen struck an optimistic note. Dealing wih international affairs she said: "This year has seen significant progress made towards solving some of the world's most difficult problems – the Middle East, for instance, the democratic future of South Africa, and, most recently, Northern Ireland." Speaking as the Queen of Northern Ireland she appealed for a settlement there: "May 1994 bring to those who live there ... the reward they deserve – peace." In general she made a plea for optimism, which combined with realism could lead to making the world a better place:

> If we can look on the bright side, so much the better, but that does not mean we should shield ourselves from the truth, even if it is unwelcome ... the more we know, the more we feel responsible, then the more we want to help.

Epilogue

THE THEME OF THIS BOOK is that after more than forty stressful years on the throne the Queen has proved herself to be a woman of unique charisma and professional skill who deserves the admiration and affection on both counts which the great majority of the people of this country obviously have for her; and that this feeling towards her personally is the greatest asset in the possession of the monarchy. It is mainly the product of the Queen's own personality and manifest sense of duty. But it is in great measure the result of her relationship with her consort. The Duke of Edinburgh has been a powerful husband to her. He has not been the easiest man to live with: he is as short-tempered, brusque and self-willed with his wife as he has been with everybody else. But he has loved her, revered her and supported her – sometimes imparting valuable advice – from the earliest days of their marriage. In her few moments of doubt and decision he has spoken out boldly, clearly and consistently. She knows he looks up to her as woman as well as Queen, and this has given her the ultimate strength which has made her in times of stress and danger as firm and steady as a rock, and given her a reputation which nobody and nothing can take away.

This is not to deny that critical questions have been asked about the Queen, and even more about the future of the monarchy. The two, the Queen and the monarchy, are separate matters, though intimately connected: if regard for the Queen were to diminish the monarch would suffer, and if the monarchy came to be looked on as useless or an encumbrance the Queen would not be seen in the same light as she is today.

As a result of the breakdown of the marriages of three of her children, many people have wondered if the Queen were at any rate in part to blame. Could she not have foreseen the vulnerability of these marriages, and have advised her children in advance that they should not enter into them? Could she not have warned, ordered or prevented? Has the Queen been a good parent to her children?

The Queen had a happy childhood, though even for a royal child it was unusually sequestered, partly because of the personality of her father, and the circumstances of the war. To a great extent she sheltered behind her self-confident, extrovert and attractive younger sister. Elizabeth grew up a shy and inexperienced young woman. She was not demonstrative; on the contrary she was withdrawn. All her adult love, as though waiting to pour out, has gone to Prince Philip, and focused on him. Whatever she meant to him he meant everything to her. In some marriages the woman's love is lavished on the children, and the relationship with the husband is secondary; in other marriages it is the other way about. The Queen's marriage belongs to the second category. By nature she would not have been a dominant parent, telling her children what and what not to do. She could not have been the heavy Victorian who wagged her finger at her children as Queen Victoria did at her son and heir when he was nearly sixty, and as George V did at the future George VI. And even if she had it in her she would not have done it. Though her childhood and early youth was happy as she grew older she came to realise that being royal had cut her off from many good things in life and had imposed many burdens on her. To be born royal was to be born handicapped, and she did not wish to add to her children's problems by being censorious to them. She wanted them to have as much freedom to be themselves as possible. What discipline there was she left to her adored husband. By nature the Duke tended to criticise rather than cultivate, and to bark at wrongdoing rather than discuss at length the right way to behave. The royal parents were closer to their children than thousands of parents have been, but they were not as close as is taken to be the norm nowadays. By the standards of their day, they have been good parents.

There were other factors. The Queen travelled an immense amount and was absent for long periods in the years when her two younger children were small. When she was at home, conscientious about her duties to a fault, she was working at her state papers, giving audiences or talking to her secretaries, when other parents would be with their children. Doing so, as she had seen with her father, came to her much more naturally than entering the inner lives of her children, and doing what came naturally may have been an excuse for not doing what did not come so easily. Unflinching and courageous in her duties, but eschewing conflict and confrontation in her private life the Queen's attitude to her children was permissive. In their youth and early adulthood whenever they wanted to come and talk to her she would respond immediately – break off what she was doing and make time for them at once. But they did not do this as often as many children. They had become used to living, emotionally, at a distance. In their recent years of troubles the Queen has deeply involved herself in the problems of her children, and has been closer to them than she has ever been before. But the past, and its effects, cannot be changed.

The personality of the Prince of Wales as it shows itself today is that of a man whose life was shaped to some extent by a lonely childhood. He was a shy child, and his parents, though devoted to him, were not demonstrative in their affection. The Queen, herself shy, did not cope with his shyness. His father, extrovert, hearty, unsentimental, unsoftened by family life in his own childhood, believing that children should develop self-reliance, left him to make his own way. The Queen was too shy to talk much to her son, except about undemanding family matters and about public affairs; she did not talk to him much about either, since she is not very communicative by nature. Nor did the Duke talk much to the Prince, Prince Philip is communicative, and he is a thinking man, but he believed, possibly because of his own childhood experience, that children learned more from example than precept. The result was that Charles grew up in a degree of solitude, with a sense of not being wanted and of not being understood. He went to a school which did not suit him, and for ideas and information about the world outside he turned to people outside the immediate family because they gave him what his parents did not.

Critics say that the Queen has not only been out of touch with her family but out of touch with the world outside the Palace. Anybody who has extensive professional or personal dealings with the Queen knows that she is very well informed. She sees it as part of her duty to know as much as possible about what is going on, and her duty is her life. Influenced by the example of her father, she works her way conscientiously through the dispatch boxes, the contents of which provide a great deal of information on a wide range of subjects. The Queen is not an intellectual, would not rate a very high IQ and has had limited formal education. But she is perceptive, shrewd and curious. She likes to know, and she has an accurate memory. She makes very good use of what she picks up in talk on tours and visits. Her "long cool stare" continues to provide her with a wide variety of knowledge, including knowledge of people. For more than forty years she has been in the habit of asking questions of a range of people from prime ministers to postmen. And she is briefed by her Private Secretary, not only on the political, diplomatic and general matters she has to know about in order to deal with government at home and governments in the Commonwealth, but with every other piece of information which in his judgement she ought to know.

The Private Secretary has more access to the monarch than any other person outside the royal family. And consequently no one has as much influence on the monarchy as he has. George V said that his Private Secretary, Lord Stamfordham, had taught him how "to be a king". According to Sir John Wheeler-Bennett, official biographer of the Queen's father,

> The Private Secretary is the eyes and ears of his Sovereign. [He] plays a leading role, perhaps *the* leading role, in the maintenance of friendly relations between the Sovereign and the Ministers of the Crown. ... He must owe loyalty to none but the sovereign, whose complete confidence he must enjoy. Never must he be a Civil Servant in forced allegiance to the Government of the day. ... He must know all that is going on and must be ready to advise upon all. ... With the emergence of the New Commonwealth the Private Secretary has become the sole link between the Sovereign and her Governors-General overseas and between Her Majesty and her Prime Ministers, not only in Westminster but also in Ottawa, Canberra, Wellington, Cape Town, Colombo and Accra.

... Such is the task and the trust of one of the least known but most responsible officers of the Crown, for in his hands, more perhaps than in those of any other individual in the Commonwealth, lies the continued well-being of the Monarchy.

The Private Secretary and his assistants know that if they do not tell the Queen something which she ought to know the chances are that she will learn it sooner or later from one or another of her other sources of information, of which there are many: Prime Minister, ministers, members of her family, friends, newspapers, television. If that happens they will be taken to task. But their motive in maximising the amount of information they give her is not fear of being found wanting, but of being required to do *their* duty. This is not to please but to inform. Their job is to be the Queen's men. Part of their service is to protect her and the monarchy, but they know they will not protect either and may damage both if they withhold information or opinions which sound judgement indicates that she should have, even if what they tell her is unpalatable. The Queen's men take a high view of their responsibilities. One of the most famous and successful of her former Private Secretaries, a gifted man who could have had his choice of careers, has said: "To be in the service of the Queen is the best thing a man can do."

The Private Secretary, therefore, currently Sir Robert Fellowes, keeps in close touch, confidentially, frequently by necessity secretly, with many sources of information. The Deputy Private Secretary, Sir Kenneth Scott, and the Assistant Private Secretary, Robin Janvrin, both former members of the Diplomatic Service, collect information about international and Commonwealth affairs. The Press Secretary, Charles Anson, who gives out information about the Queen and the royal family, can also bring in information from his wide range of contacts in the media. The Private Secretary is in touch with many people well placed to supply him with information from many walks of life. On politics he has the information coming from his special relationship with the Secretary to the Cabinet and with the Prime Minister's private secretaries, a two-way flow of information which forms the basis of the Prime Minister's weekly Audience with the Queen: the Queen gets to know in advance what the Prime Minister feels he should tell her, and the Prime Minister gets warning of what the Queen would like to know. All that is known about the Audiences is that there is no one present at them other than the Queen and the Prime Minister. Each Prime Minister will have his or her own approach to what he will choose to raise with the Queen. Personal matters are not taboo – nor are they with the Private Secretary.

The contention, therefore, that the Queen is not sufficiently informed about what is going on by those who work in close relationship with her, would require some proof. If anybody thought it fit to criticise any action or inaction on the part of the Queen it would be hard to blame lack of information from her secretaries.

Uniquely important as the Private Secretary is in constitutional, political and family business, he is not the senior member of the Queen's Household, that position being held by the Lord Chamberlain, the key figure in management and finance. The Lord Chamberlain is responsible directly to the Queen for overseeing the conduct of the business of the Household and for co-ordinating those matters which have implications for the Household as a whole, including appointments to it. He chairs meetings of the six Heads of Departments, of which the Private Secretary's Office is one. The post is held by the 13th Earl of Airlie, a Scot, sometimes spoken of as a handsome aristocratic courtier. This he is, but David Airlie is also an extremely successful businessman, going into the City in 1961, currently Chairman of the General Accident Fire and Life Assurance Corporation, having over the years acquired seats on a number of other boards. A wise and reforming character, he was involved in the arrangements for the Queen to pay tax, the changes in the Civil List, the opening of the Palace to the Public, and the financing of the restoration to Windsor Castle.

It has been mooted that it would be to the advantage of the Queen and the royal family, and to the working of the monarchy, if the Queen were provided with a small council of elders who could give her information and advice about matters of interest or concern to her. Those who see merit in setting up this council must belong to that school of thought which assumes that the Queen is not given enough, or good enough, information by her secretaries, and is, therefore, cut off from the kind of information and advice which she ought to have. There are many arguments against setting up such a council.

One is that really valuable information, especially if it is unpalatable, is more or less easy to exchange between two people, or even three, but is less likely to emerge when several people are in hearing; and if the elders gave information to her separately they might be inhibited by wondering what she was being told by their colleagues, or, speaking boldly, contradict each other.

A second is that the opinions of such well-qualified elders are already available to the Queen via her Private Secretary, who is in a position to sift and cross-check what he is told.

A third is the question of who would choose its members, and on what basis? It would be difficult to identify a suitable person or body qualified to advise on the membership of such a council, and even more difficult to persuade such a person or body to take on the responsibility.

The overriding argument against the proposal is that in any case the Queen would not agree to it: she wants her information and advice to come from persons who are close to her professionally because their advice and information will be the best information, and the best information does not come from a Committee.

During the discussion precipitated by the events of 1992 and 1993 some newspapers put forward the view that the role of the Private Secretary to the Queen was now out of date and inadequate to provide the sovereign of a multinational Commonwealth with the services currently required. Various suggestions for change were put forward, varying from the selection of the Private Secretary by the Prime Minister, not by the Queen, to the replacement of the Private Secretary's office by a small secretariat modelled on Civil Service lines which would serve the Queen much as the Cabinet Office, headed by Britain's top Civil Servant, currently serves the Prime Minister and his government.

One view is that such a department, and its head, would have more authority with the Queen and over members of her family since it would speak for the government. Another view is that it would convey information and advice of a more professional character than the Queen is given at the present time. It would speak more frankly to the Queen than do her present secretaries. It could not be dismissed because it gave advice which the Queen, or the Duke, or the Prince of Wales, did not like to hear. Thoughts like these are expressed not only by people without much knowledge of how the royal secretariat works, but by some who do. However a majority of the latter are against the proposal, and for one key reason. In the words of an official, located outside Buckingham

Palace, who can be regarded as an expert on the situation which the proposal is meant to deal with: "The problems which have become public in the last two years have not been due to faults in the secretariat in Buckingham Palace, but to the personal behaviour of some members of the royal family. No change in the structure or personnel of the Household which could be envisaged would have prevented those problems from arising." His view is at least in part supported by remarks coming from some of the younger members of the royal family; in particular from protests from the Duchess of York that officials at the Palace tried to bully her into doing what she did not want to do.

The assurance that it has been the personalities of some members of the royal family and not the structure and personnel of the Household which have caused the problems we are familiar with is in itself an argument for being cautious about change. But there are others. The present arrangements have served the Queen and her predecessors well. If the Queen does not wish to alter the persons and arrangements which are there to serve her personally it would be difficult to change them for her. If there is to be a Queen, she must be allowed to run her secretariat her own way. There has always been a close personal relationship between the monarch and the Private Secretary. Today, the Queen knows she can count on her principal secretaries. The introduction of a kind of Civil Service secretariat would put an end to such a relationship, and supply the Queen with nothing which is not available to her already. Civil servants are there to serve the government of the day. Any "government" secretariat appointed to the Queen if it did not actually become partisan could be seen to do so, no matter how wise the advice it supplied, one political party or another would criticise it as "party-orientated.". The entry would be entirely on the debit side, and the loss would affect not only the monarchy in Britain but the monarchy in its relationship with the countries of the Commonwealth.

This is not to say that the working of the Household is not in any need of change. It changes all the time. Change, if it were not planned, would in any case be forced on it. Some uncomfortable lessons have been learned. One is that of timing. For example, some members of the Household regret that the announcement that the Queen would pay income tax was not made sooner: as a result it seemed to some to have been forced on the Queen as a result of public resentment at the idea that the taxpayer would have to pay for the damage done by the fire at Windsor Castle.

Other changes are being considered. The combination of a larger number of members of the royal family with far more attention being paid to them by the media than ever before has led to an increase in the number of satellite secretariats, who have planned their principals' activities and engagements independently without consultation with each other. There is a strong case for fewer members of the royal family appearing with the Queen and the Duke of Edinburgh in public – for instance on the balcony of Buckingham Palace – and for the activities and publicity for the members of the "reduced" royal family to be put into the hands of a single office which would co-ordinate what their principals were doing and deal with the publicity for their activities.

Much has been heard about the desirability of "reducing" the numbers of the royal family who are exposed to – or who may seek – the public gaze. It is true that if the royal family did not get the appropriate amount of publicity its future might be in jeopardy, and in the past several members of the family have said so publicly. To justify its existence the royal family must do things, and it must be seen to do things, good things. And for this it must rely on the media, just as parts of the media rely for their existence on the royal family. But beyond a point, the members of the royal family do not want publicity, and there are some members of the family who do not want it at all. The "rationing" of appearances of the royal family, if anybody were faced with the task, presents some problems. If in order to reduce the number of members of the family appearing in the public eye an official suggested, for example, that Princess Alexandra should no longer make "royal" appearances there would at once be vociferous opposition from many people who greatly admire the Princess. Different members, and sections, of the public have different predilections about the royal family. There is a request for this one to open a new institution, for that one to open an exhibition, for another to open a hospital. It is impossible to refuse all these requests.

Nevertheless there seems little doubt in the minds of those who should know that the number of members of the royal family seen in public performing public functions will be significantly reduced. The process has begun, and has been commented on by the press. Nothing will hasten it more than the fact that some members of the royal family in this generation do not have a sense of vocation for, a sense of duty about, their traditional responsibilities, and prefer private life, however quiet, to publicity as members of the royal family.

The absence of brown, black or yellow faces at Buckingham Palace or in Kensington Palace, some critics say, indicates that the Queen is racist. The facts, however, speak for themselves. For many days in the year when on tour in the Commonwealth the Queen is surrounded by brown, black or yellow faces, and in many countries there is not a white face among her companions, advisers, secretaries and staff. When she is in London, she is visited and entertained as Head of the Commonwealth by people of many different races, whether from Commonwealth countries or from others, and she reciprocates. Though many people are employed at Buckingham Palace the number of significant posts is very small, and for these specific qualifications are required. Anybody who wanted, for instance, to become the Queen's Press Secretary, and had the qualifications, would be considered for the job whatever the colour of his skin. On the other hand, to give that job to somebody for the sake of having a coloured face in the Palace, and to pass over a white man who had qualifications more appropriate to the job, would be to practise race discrimination in reverse, and risk a reduction in efficiency.

As for the Ladies-in-Waiting, their main qualification is that they know their responsibilities, and, indeed, have known, for a long time, without having to be trained or indoctrinated. These are not complex. These women do not require academic excellence, technical knowledge, or high political or diplomatic experience, but they require character and commonsense, the ability to get on with a great variety of people from a quick start, and most important they require knowledge of the duties of the Queen and how she likes to perform them. The combination of qualifications required is most likely to be found in women who have known the Queen and the Court from an early age, and have to a degree, grown up with her and it. Hence the number of Ladies-in-Waiting who, it is complained, come from a social background comparable to the Queen's. Their duties would not appeal to many women, even if they were highly paid for carrying them out. Their principal duty is to accompany the Queen on public engagements. In the Palace they join the Queen when she wants, or needs, company, and are present with her when she gives a small lunch or dinner for guests drawn from a variety of walks of life. They deal with a great many of the three hundred or so letters from all over the world which arrive at the Palace daily, especially those from children.

If there is to be a Queen there will have to be women to be Ladies-in-Waiting and it is difficult to imagine how the existing incumbents could and would be replaced, at anything like the level of cost that is now incurred. They are chosen by the Queen for personal qualities: she would take care not to select a woman conspicuously political in a party sense. The practice of appointing Ladies-in-Waiting, including the Ladies of the Bedchamber, with political allegiance was brought to an end, after some controversy, in the reign of Queen Victoria. All who work for the Queen in the Royal Household accept their positions on condition they maintain a political posture which is completely non-partisan.

There are many people who in spite of some criticisms think highly of the Queen as a person and as a professional, but think the institution with which she is associated is in need of overhaul and reform. Many people want Britain to continue to be a constitutional monarchy but, they say, would like it to be demystified, relieved of its pomp and circumstance, simplified, the royal family to live in a more down-to-earth style, and cost the taxpayer far less than it does today. In short, they would like the monarchy to continue, but for the royal family to behave much more like the Scandinavian monarchs behave and be treated much more as they are treated. Scandinavian monarchs, such reformers say, are not crowned; they do not ascend the throne or get married trailing clouds of religious glory, and they do not nourish nostalgia for a departed imperial past.

Let us recall one of Bagehot's most quoted observations about the monarchy: "There are arguments for not having a Court, and there are arguments for having a splendid Court; but there are no arguments for having a mean Court." Those who depend on Britain's tourist trade would agree with him. Once the novelty of seeing Prince Philip bicycling behind the railings of Buckingham Palace had worn off, the adaptation of the monarchy to a Scandinavian model, if it were practicable, would probably mean an end to the tourists who come from overseas to see the Changing of the Guard, to watch the Trooping the Colour, and to walk through the main rooms of the Palace. It would vastly reduce the television coverage of the royal family overseas which rightly or wrongly projects an image of Britain which is good for her influence in the world in general and in particular is good for trade.

Even if there is widespread agreement that changes should be made to the monarchy in Britain to make it much more like the Scandinavian monarchies it is doubtful if these changes would be practical. It is frequently said that the Queen should divest herself of some of her residences. The question would immediately arise: what should be done with them? She pays for Balmoral and Sandringham out of her own pocket; they are very expensive to maintain, and the combined income from both falls short of expenses. If the government bought these houses, the acquisitions would cost the taxpayer a great deal of money, and to maintain and exploit the acquisitions would cost even more. If Bagehot's advice were to be ignored, and monarchy were to be down-graded, and the Queen were allowed only a much reduced income from the Civil List, and she felt obliged to dispose of these residences, the question of to whom they might be sold would pose problems.

Discussion about the relation of the British monarchy in its present form to class, privilege and unhealthy deference has evoked many ideas and opinions, but has not uncovered an impressive number of facts. Most people agree that there was far more class, privilege and deference in Britain fifty years ago than there is today, but disagree about how much of it remains. The United States does not have a monarchy and most Americans do not want one, but it would be hard to prove that American society, whatever claims are made for it by its admirers at home and abroad, is essentially an egalitarian country. In the Soviet Union after the revolution of 1917 there was no monarchy, but after the slaughter of that year which was necessary to establish the people's democracy, and the even greater exterminations of the kulaks in the 1920s which were necessary to preserve it, a considerable degree of privilege continued to be enjoyed by a wide section of the Russian people.

Class, privilege, and deference of various kinds, motivated for different reasons can be found in many countries where there has been no monarchy for a very long time – in France, for example. Many people, some of whom may deplore the existence of the monarchy, feel that deference, albeit in degree and kind, is not undesirable: when there was more deference in Britain there were better manners and less crime. Fewer children got into the hands of the police.

Protests against the existence of the monarchy in this country are made by thoughtful people who have a right within the law to bring about the changes they would like to see. But the opinions are based on feelings; they are subjective; they are not always based on facts. The people who express them are logically in a position far less strong than are the monarchists, who can point to the benefits of a monarchy, which can be identified, described and listed. If the monarchy continues to adapt to the need for change, as it nearly always has, and never so much as in the last five decades, these benefits will increase. Unfortunately for the monarchy, many monarchists simply make assertions about its merits and fail to support it with argument based on fact. They support their cause in terms as subjective as do their opponents, and make claims about the amount of popular support for the monarchy which cannot be factually verified.

Many people say that the monarchy as it is today feeds nostalgia and strengthens the shackles which bind Britain to the past. Thoughtful Britons, certainly, very conscious of what their liberties and way of life owe to what has gone before, are grateful for it, and may look with affection on the monarch not so much as creator of the benefits as symbol of them. Their view makes far more sense than that of those contemporaries who press the view that they would have been better off if the monarchy had not existed; they are not in a position to prove it. The monarchists cannot prove or disprove either, but they have the advantage of being able to refer to the fact that Britain with its constitutional monarchy has much to be thankful for, and that a comparison with the condition of other countries substantiates this.

One hears that the kind of monarchy which exists in Britain today encourages escapism, and escapism is something the people of Britain cannot afford to indulge in, is a drug that is capable of destroying them. This is a theoretical argument, and if it were generally accepted, and led to a major change in the nature of the monarchy, its advocates might refute it. Escapism is to be found in many if not all societies. If the existence of monarchy as it is today encourages escapism, a change in the character of the monarchy would be less likely to reduce escapism than to divert the demand for escape into other channels, a demand which the United States has for many years satisfied with the output of its film industry. If the monarchy were to be abolished, we might find that a baby had gone out with the bath water. The myth, fiction and unreality of the monarchy, which has diminished, is diminishing and ought to be diminished, but which continues to adhere to the monarchy, is attached to something which is real. Out of Hollywood comes nothing but illusion, illusion created by and for the box office. To exchange a characteristically British escapism for an American one, and to do so influenced by opinions based on so-called facts which on inspection turn out to be unverifiable assertions, does not seem to be a prudent course of action.

This takes us from criticisms of the Queen and of the working of the monarchy to the radical question of whether, however much the Queen may be admired, there should be a monarchy at all, why Britain should not be a republic. There has for centuries been a school of thought in Britain which has advocated the abolition of the ·monarchy and the establishment of a republic. It is sometimes forgotten that for eleven years, from 1649, when Charles I was beheaded, to 1660, when his son was invited back from exile to become king as Charles II, England *was* a republic. Monarchists have pointed out ever since that the experiment of a republic in Britain was tried, failed, and once is enough. Republicans point out that the principles on which the American republic was founded in 1776 were imported from Britain and put into effect by political leaders, many of them of English descent, familiar with British political institutions. The creation of a republic in France after the revolution of 1789, they say, also owed much to the familiarity of leading French politicians and philosophers with British political institutions. Republicanism in Britain, as British republicans point out, is not a foreign importation but is home grown. There have been earlier periods in British history when the demand for a republic has been stronger than it seems to be today, but what has happened to the royal family, if it has not increased opinion in favour of a republic, cannot but have created publicity for the alternative.

The arguments put forward for the establishment of a republic are to a great extent composed of the arguments put forward for the abolition of the monarchy: monarchy is not good for a democracy, so let us get rid of the monarchy, and replace it with a republic, which is. Just as many monarchists assert that monarchy has many undesirable attributes and effects but do not, or cannot, prove that these are intrinsic to it, many republicans claim virtues for a republican form of government which they cannot prove to be intrinsic to it. So far the argument can only be conducted on the basis of principles and preferences: very little of it can be conducted on a basis of fact. Many of the arguments against monarchy are introduced by republicans explicitly or implicitly with the phrase "it stands to reason", and go on to say that the mystique, religiosity, choice by heredity and the pomp and circumstance which surround and prop up the British monarchy cannot be accepted by a reasonable human being.

This again is a matter of opinion. It is a matter of fact that many reasonable men and women *have* accepted the idea of monarchy, some of them with devotion to the point of death, and that many reasonable men and women continue to do so. It is not possible for a reasonable and objective republican to maintain that most people in Britain would prefer to live in a republic, or that they would be better off in a republic – he cannot know. Opinion polls may not be totally reliable guides to what people think but they are more reliable than assertions made by a single individual generalising from his own limited experience. And polls in Britain indicate that eighty per cent of the British people are content to live in a monarchy and do not want a republic.

The republican who bases his argument for the replacement of the monarchy on the view that a republic is a more democratic form of government has a particularly difficult problem to overcome. This was brought out very clearly at a conference on "The Monarchy, the Constitution and the People" organised by *The Times* in association with Charter 88 in May 1993. Mr Christopher Hitchens, an out-standingly thoughtful, eloquent and persuasive republican, said at one point in his speech: "If you're on the left as I am you have to trust the common people," but in his honesty he felt compelled to add that when he talked to the common people about the monarchy they produced pro-monarchist responses – which he thought were "programmed", but which could not be ignored – so that, he said, "It was terrible for me as someone on the left to find myself despising my fellow democrats." It looks, therefore, as if honest men like Mr Hitchens who want to remain good democrats – which means respecting the views of their fellow democrats – may have to give up hopes of bringing a British republic into being for a considerable time to come. Another interesting example of the difficulty of advocating republicanism on rational grounds was provided by the novelist, Sue Townsend, who in a warm and moving speech, applauded by some monarchists for its skill as well as the republicans for its content, said that whereas in Britain, a monarchy, she felt restricted, when she was in a republic she felt free. Only Mrs Townsend can know how she feels, but perhaps she would not feel so free as she implied in some of the South American republics, or indeed in some parts of the greatest of all republics, the United States of America.

Practical measures required to substitute a republic for the monarchy would automatically raise some important problems. It would in the first place be a very expensive process. Second, it would be disruptive in the sense that much time and money would be expended in making and consolidating the change. To mount a Presidential-type election, it has been calculated, would cost a country the size of Britain at least £45 million every five years. Third, it would create controversy of various kinds: would, for instance, the British republic follow the French model, the American model, or some other model, or be devised as it were from scratch? Even for a new country it is difficult to devise a constitution on the basis of an abstraction; it would be even more difficult to do so for an old country.

Would the Prime Minister become the Head of State, a politician with allegiance to one party, who might disappear from power every time there was a general election, perhaps within six months of taking up his office; a politician who while he was in office was already overworked in the process of running the government and the country? Or would the Head of State be a politician who, after a career in politics, or possibly on account of achieving national distinction outside politics, become President for a legally set period after being elected to the office by, for example, a national plebiscite, or by some process of selection agreed by the political parties?

How would agreement on whether there is to be a republic, and what kind of a republic, be reached? And when it had been agreed that a republic of some kind would replace the monarchy, and there had been agreement about the process by which the monarchy would be abolished and the means by which the republic would be established, and what kind of a republic it would be, what would come about as a result?

In all things there must be change, and in nearly all things there *will* be change, but there are always, too, the risks of change. The French Revolution began in 1789 as a movement against the absolutism of the French monarchy which was subjecting the French people to a burden it could no longer tolerate. The object of the men who led it in its early stages was to replace that absolute monarchy with a constitutional monarchy similar to what the French saw operating satisfactorily in Britain. The attempt to do so failed, and four years later a republic was established. There followed a reign of terror, the guillotine, civil war, bloody disorder, brought to an end by the dictatorship of Napoleon, who subsequently made himself Emperor. In less than forty years after Louis XVI had been sent to the guillotine France had become a monarchy again.

Replacing the monarchy with a republic is one thing; constitutional reform which would affect the working of the monarchy is another. Many monarchists would agree with many republicans that there is a good case for changes which would affect the existing powers of the Crown, notably that of the use of the prerogative. Most of the use of the prerogative is made not by the Queen or her representatives, but by the government of the day. It relates to such various functions as the command of the armed forces, the appointments of bishops, the administration of justice, the proclamation of a state of emergency, the declaration of war and peace, and the making of treaties. It is frequently complained that in the name of the Queen the government of the day can do things for which it has no warrant from Parliament and that this in effect puts the Prime Minister of the day above the law, and that when he uses these powers he is protected from investigation or control by Parliament on the grounds that Parliament is not free to discuss any matter in which the monarch is involved, let alone criticise or seek to control the role of the Crown in such a matter. Many eminent and wise people have supported the voicing of this complaint and have urged reforms which would give Parliament more control over the Executive. This would require legislation.

This problem has little, if anything, to do with the monarchy. If citation of the prerogative powers of the monarch enables the government of the day to do things which the House of Commons thinks the government should not be entitled to do the remedy is in the House of Commons's own hands. If the House of Commons succeeds in depriving the government of the use of the monarch's prerogative powers they will take nothing away from the monarchy. On the contrary, the House of Commons would do the monarchy a favour: they would make it clear that the monarchy does not have, and has not had for decades, and does not wish to have, a power of a quite undemocratic nature.

If change is required it is up to Parliament to recognise it, and to effect it. If Parliament wishes to circumscribe or abolish the prerogative it can do any time it wishes by introducing the appropriate legislation. There might be a long and heated debate – governments, whichever party is in power, do not take easily to the introduction of measures to limit their freedom of action – and in the event Parliament might fail to get the control of the prerogative which it set out to achieve. But if Parliament were determined to obtain it nothing the Queen could do would stop it. To return to Bagehot again: "She must sign her own death-warrant if the two Houses unanimously send it up to her."

If legislation to deprive the government of the use of the prerogative were enacted some of those who pleaded for it might have regrets. The use of the prerogative enables the government to get measures through on a wide range of matters which do not merit parliamentary debate and legislation, and on many of which there is already agreement, and therefore save a great deal of time and expense. In the United States the President as head of the Executive wastes a great deal of his, the House of Representatives' and the country's time and money by having to submit legislation to Congress on a myriad of matters which in Britain can be dealt with by the prerogative.

Though there are many good monarchists who believe the prerogative puts power in the hands of the government of the day which it should not have and that this power should be taken away it is not that part of the prerogative which comes in for criticism from the reformers so much as two other powers: first, the power to grant a dissolution to a Prime Minister who wants to hold a general election; second, the power to appoint the next Prime Minister after the result of the election is determined.

As we have seen earlier the use of the second power can raise problems, and if proportional representation were to be introduced the existence of that power could raise more. For the time being the importance of it has been much reduced by the fact that the monarch no longer has to seek information about which member of the party which has won the election can command a majority in the House of Commons; the identity of that member will have been determined in advance by the result of the annual intra-party election. The Queen could not possibly choose anybody but him, or her, to form a government.

The key question that has to be asked nowadays about the use of this particular part of the prerogative is this: if it is not to be used by the Queen who then should use it? It would have to be used by somebody. Many people believe that, if necessary, it should be used by the Speaker of the House of Commons. There are, of course, pros and cons. The Speaker, whose main responsibility is to preside over and regulate debates in the House of Commons, takes an oath to respect and preserve the liberties of the House of Commons, and to behave impartially towards Government and Opposition. The Speaker gets to know a great deal about the state of opinion within the parliamentary parties, and the Speaker, aided and advised by the Clerks of the House of Commons, is an expert in precedents and possibilities. The Speaker is selected for his, or her, ability to chair debates and preserve order in a sometimes unruly House, but also for the wisdom and common sense which he can bring to bear on any matters which affect the House of Commons. He, or she, must be respected for integrity and impartiality. In the event of, say, a hung Parliament, which would require an act of judgement as to whom should be invited to try to form a government, there would be much to be said for referring matters now dealt with by the monarch to the Speaker.

On the other hand, the Speaker's responsibility is to the House of Commons, not to Parliament as a whole. The Speaker is a member of a political party, and would not be sitting in the Speaker's Chair if it were otherwise. The Speaker does not have a responsibility to the nation; the Queen, on the other hand, *does*. There is no reason to suppose that the Speaker would be any better than the monarch in the event of a hung election or any doubt arising as to who should be the next Prime Minister. Once the Prime Minister of the day has given in his resignation he has no power to recommend a successor, though he may offer advice if asked for it. The monarch is free to consult with anyone. It may make many people, including monarchists, feel better if this particular power of the prerogative were taken from the Queen and allotted to the Speaker, or to an alternative, but nobody can make a case, and prove it, that such a change would result in better judgements being made than those which have been made in the past.

It is important for the people to feel that in the choice of a new Prime Minister in these special circumstances the "right" procedure has been adopted and the "right" decision arrived at. There might, indeed, be greater trust in the Queen's decision than that of a politician, who, however respected, might lose his seat at the next election.

The desire to take away the prerogatives of the Queen which remain to her personally is partly the result of a feeling on the part of some of the critics that the monarch not only ought not to have, in Bagehot's words, the right "to be consulted, the right to encourage, the right to warn," is not equipped to use it, and almost certainly does not use it. The right is a sham, and Prime Ministers and monarch pay lip service to it because it suits them to. There are not many people who have sufficient knowledge of the occasions when the Queen may have used this right to confirm whether it is real or indeed a sham, and they are sworn to silence about such occasions – notably Prime Ministers after they have had their weekly Audience of the Queen. As one Private Secretary to a Prime Minister said, "They may come back from the Palace smiling like a Cheshire cat but they don't tell you a damned thing."

The silence to which the Queen's officials and her Prime Ministers, and she herself, observe, therefore prevent her and the political role of the monarch from being assessed at their true worth. However, the silence is, up to a point, occasionally broken.

In his memoirs, published in 1987, the former Prime Minister, Lord Callaghan, recounted "an incident which gives substance to the text-book principle that the function of a constitutional monarch is to warn, advise and encourage her Ministers." The incident occurred not when he was Prime Minister but when he was Foreign Secretary in 1974–6. Information reached Callaghan that at last the Prime Minister of Southern Rhodesia, Ian Smith, had decided that he might have to concede majority rule to the black Africans, and that if a compromise with their leader, Joshua Nkomo, could be backed by the United Kingdom, Smith would be prepared to accept it even if it meant splitting his own party. Callaghan, who by now had become very sceptical about the chances of Smith accepting a compromise, was sufficiently open-minded to ask Lord Greenhill, until recently Head of the Foreign Office, to undertake a secret mission personally to find out if Smith was indeed at last ready to compromise. When he got back to London, Lord Greenhill confirmed that Smith had expressed his readiness for a compromise. The Foreign Office, however, continued to advise Callaghan that "they had no confidence that a settlement could be reached at this stage." Lord Callaghan's account of what ensued is as follows:

> Although I was bound to agree that the official assessment was probably correct, it seemed to me that sufficient had emerged from [Lord Greenhill's] visit to warrant following up. It was at this juncture, while I was considering what to do next, that by chance I had an opportunity of talking with the Queen. ...

The occasion was a performance of Rossini's opera, *La Centerentola* at Covent Garden, which the Queen attended with the wife of the President of Italy, who was visiting London at that time, the Italian Ambassador entertaining them to supper at the Embassy afterwards. Callaghan – who had been placed next to the Queen – went on to say:

> During supper I described to her Lord Greenhill's visit to Rhodesia and the aftermath, and discussed the alternative courses of following the matter up, or of letting it simmer for the time being, adding that I had not decided which would be the better ...
>
> The next afternoon a letter was handed to me from Sir Martin Charteris, the Queen's Private Secretary. He said that the Queen had told him how much she enjoyed our conversation about Rhodesia. She had reflected on our talk, and "She recognises that any initiative you take may prove ineffective, but none the less believes it would be worthwhile to make the effort. ...
>
> Inevitably the Queen's opinion was enough to tip the scales, for she is an authority on the Commonwealth and I respect her opinion: I decided to go ahead.

Callaghan immediately sent a message to Smith promising that if he was willing to make a public commitment to majority rule the United Kingdom would broker a compromise between him and the African leaders. Unfortunately, talks between Smith and Nkomo broke down, and he was unable to proceed with his initiative. But that did not prevent him from concluding:

> I have always thought since that the Queen's initiative on Rhodesia was a perfect illustration of how and when the Monarch could effectively intervene to advise and encourage her Ministers from her own wide experience and with complete constitutional propriety.

As well as change that is perceived to be needed and is intelligently put into effect there is the change that is suggested by circumstance. The greater number and variety of religions now practised in Britain, for example, will put great pressure behind the argument that a monarch who claims to rule and serve the British people as a whole can no longer be seen to favour only one of the many existing congregations. Can the monarch claim to be a truly national monarch if he or she rules out the possibility of marrying one of Britain's three million Roman Catholics or one of Britain's two million Jews, or, more to the point, a foreigner who belongs to either of these two religious groups? At the moment the monarch is prevented by law from doing so. But the law can be changed, and there is no reason why it could not be changed to permit the monarch to end the exclusive connection of the Crown with one religion or another or to marry somebody whose religion was different from his or her own.

As well as change being made in response to circumstances there is change which is imposed by them. If Britain moves much further into the European Community, accepts more of its rules and regulations, becomes bound by its courts, whatever is said to the contrary British sovereignty of the monarch is bound to be diminished. At the moment the ultimate authority in Britain is a law which has passed through the House of Lords and the House of Commons and has been approved by the monarch. As things are now progressing – the process may of course be arrested or reversed – a law enacted in Britain by the British Parliament in Westminster may be overridden by a law enacted by the European Parliament in Strasbourg. It will then be impossible to speak of the British Parliament as being sovereign in the full sense of what the word meant in the past. There is talk of Britain surrendering "some" sovereignty. This does not make sense: sovereignty is absolute. It should be noted however, that the role of the monarch would not for practical purposes be reduced. In the view of the expert on the subject, Vernon Bogdanor: "Many fears have been expressed as to the position of the monarchy which are misplaced. Since more than ninety per cent of the sovereign's prerogative powers are now in the hands of the government, integration into the EC is unlikely to affect the position of the monarchy." But the claims currently made for the monarch's role and powers will have to be amended if they are not to be inconsistent with Britain's responsibilities to and within the European Community, and descriptions of these powers unamended, for instance in the Coronation service, would have to be changed if they were not to seem fanciful to the point of being ridiculous.

Some people take what might be considered a gloomier view of what would be the British monarch's position in the EC. It is generally assumed that the European union is moving as the American union did to the creation of a "federal" state with a "federal" government. If so the status of the British monarch would have to change. The Head of State for the American people is the President of the United States. It is to him that the citizens of the states of California or New York swear allegiance, not to the governors of their states. As a member of a "federal" Europe the British citizen would recognise a European President as the Head of State. The effective status of the Queen would become analogous to that, say, of the governor of California. The British Army, Royal Navy and Royal Air Force would owe their loyalty not to the Queen but to the President of the "federal" government of Europe. They could still be called "Royal" but they would cease to be so in the sense that they are now.

Unless a European "federal" government enacted legislation to abolish the monarchy in any or all of the member countries the monarchy in Britain, if the British people wished, could carry on its activities much as it does now. There could be a state opening of Parliament, a Trooping of Colour, garden parties at Buckingham Palace and banquets for visiting heads of state at Windsor. The Queen could attend Royal Ascot, the Chelsea Flower show, and open Parliament, and perform many other public duties. In short the monarchy could carry out its public programmes very much as before.

It is difficult to see, however, how the monarch of a United

Kingdom within a "federal" Europe, or in a Europe in which national sovereignty was substantially reduced, could remain the sovereign of a member of a Commonwealth country which was not a member of the European union and did not wish to be. For the Queen to remain the Head of State in Australia, for example, would mean that the Australian people would ultimately acknowledge the authority of the European organisation which their Head of State acknowledged, a European organisation to which they do not owe or wish to owe allegiance. It is inconceivable that the Australians in any circumstances would accept such a situation, and even if they were willing to tolerate such a relationship in theory it would be impossible to give it any practical effect. Such a relationship would be intolerable also to the government of Europe. That government could not allow one of its member countries to have constitutional responsibilities to and for a state which did not accept the overriding authority of a European "federal" government.

Given the state of the United Kingdom's relations with Europe, it looks like being a long time before such problems become real and pressing. There is far more likelihood of, for example, Australia severing the relationship with the British monarchy because the Australians want to become an independent republic than of the Australian government having to end the relationship with the British monarchy because it owed ultimate allegiance to a European government in Brussels. Several of its members being monarchies there is far more likelihood of the still immature European government bending its principles and practices to accommodate monarchies than there is of them trying to impose on them unpalatable and unnecessary restrictions, regulations or change. It would be reasonable to predict that by the time the position of the British monarchy in the European Community might theoretically raise the question of sovereignty the role of the British monarchy will have become so modified that the issue will have become, and will generally be seen to have become, of no importance except perhaps to purists, pedants and political fundamentalists.

The future of the monarchy will be determined by many factors, some personal, some political, some of an international character. But just as it has been influenced by the conduct and reputation of certain individuals in the past so it will be considerably influenced by the image of a few individuals in the public mind in the present and immediate future. The Prince of Wales is the heir to the throne; the Princess of Wales is the mother of the Prince's heir. When two ordinary individuals separate or divorce though there are many problems which they have to face they do not have to face the non-personal constitutional problems in terms of which Charles and Diana have to live. They cannot have a truly private life.

The Prince will be in such a glare of limelight as no potential heir to the throne has been in before: unless he can present the image of a monarchy which accepts change, symbolises change and leads change, and the image of a person whom the people feel, however vaguely, is "good" he may find that he as a person and the monarchy as an institution are losing support. No heir to the throne has shown as much potential for establishing that image. If he has the determination, the application, the will, these with his other qualities should enable him to succeed. Opinion polls, even in the worst days of the last few storm-tossed years, indicate that four people in five in Britain want the monarchy to continue and have no wish to see it replaced by any other system of government. Only a minority would prefer to see his son rather than him as the next king.

The Prince may be much helped by the attitude of the British people towards the European Community. It would be difficult to substantiate the view that the British people have ever been enthusiastic about joining the EC or about remaining in it: the majority of them have "gone along" with the idea of going into Europe and once in have "gone along" with the idea of staying in. The debates, confusions, setbacks and controversies of the 1990s have increased not diminished their misgivings about being a member of the Community. The divisions of opinion in Parliament about whether to sign or not to sign the Maastricht Treaty have disturbed many people. The decision taken very late to enter the ERM, and then the decision taken very early to get out of it, has bewildered many people. The devaluation of sterling as a result of initiatives taken by some of Britain's partners in the EC have hit many British people in their pockets. The people of Britain are not in a mood to give up any more than they have given up already to comply with the rules of the European Community. They are in a mood to support and cherish not what makes them feel part of Europe but what reminds them that they are British. Whether it is rational that

Acknowledgements

IN THE COURSE of preparing this book I have had conversations with a number of people who know, or have known the Queen personally, some who have served her, and with civil servants who have had dealings with the Royal Household. Some would have been happy about information being attributed to them, others not; in consequence I have not listed any names.

My thanks are due to the authors of those books and writings about the Queen, the monarchy and the period who are cited in the text, but in particular to the following: Sarah Bradford: *George VI*; Robert Lacey: *Majesty*; Elizabeth Longford: *Elizabeth R*; John Parker: *The Queen*; Kenneth Rose: *King George V*; Peter Townsend: *Time and Chance*; John Wheeler-Bennett: *King George VI*; Philip Ziegler: *King Edward VIII* and *Mountbatten*. Quotations from *The Little Princesses* by Marion Crawford are reproduced by kind permission of Gerald Duckworth and Co. Ltd. The Queen's Press Secretary and his staff at Buckingham Palace have been most helpful in supplying factual information.

I am indebted to Mark Malcomson for research, to Keith Pye for computer advice, to Carol Johnson, my copy-editor, to Catherine Lightfoot for pictures and, above all, for advice and encouragement to my publisher, Ion Trewin.

it should do so or not, the monarchy symbolises simply and colourfully the sovereignty they are fearful of seeing diminished. Of even more value to Prince Charles is the reputation of the reigning monarch. Even the most confident of republicans, and the most pessimistic of monarchists, may be heard to say of the monarchy from time to time: "Well, it will last for as long as the Queen is alive. After that ..." It is an irrational view, but irrational views, if they are held by enough people with enough tenacity, can be more influential than the most powerful of rational arguments. The institutional mystique of the monarchy is dissolving but the Queen may have created her own personal mystique. So long as she is there the monarchy seems secure. And by the time she goes her son may well have given it another, most promising, lease of life.

Index

NOTE: Ranks and titles are generally the highest mentioned in the text

Index

Victoria, Queen: reign, 2–3, 103, 253;
  Elizabeth likened to, 49, 69, 87;
  marriage, 86; and Melbourne, 134;
  popularity in old age, 205;
  payment of income tax, 265; and
  children's upbringing, 299; and
  Ladies of Bedchamber, 308

Wales: nationalism in, 188, 211, 214
Walesa, Lech, 255
"walkabouts", 194–5, 211
Ward, Stephen, 167–8
Washington Daily News, 196
Washington, D.C., 195–6
Waterhouse, Colonel Sir Ronald, 19
Waverley, John Anderson, 1st Viscount,
  145
Weizsacker, Richard von, 261
Wellington, New Zealand, 194
Wenner-Gren, Axel Leonard, 43, 66
Westmacott, Peter, 285
Wheeler-Bennett, Sir John: on George
  VI's interest in constitution, 13–
  14, 106; on George V's
  indifference to George VI, 19–20;
  on George VI's view of children's
  upbringing, 30; and George VI's
  unpreparedness for throne, 36; on
  appointment of Bevin as Foreign
  Secretary, 73; on Queen's
  engagement to Philip, 84;
  completes life of George VI, 149;
  on Private Secretary, 301
Whitaker, James, 285
White Lodge, Richmond Park, 27
Whitlam, Gough, 201, 209–10, 258
William III (of Orange): King, 101
William IV, King, 103
William, Prince, 283, 286, 290, 295,
  297
Wilson, Harold (*later* Baron):
  premiership, 173; relations with
  Queen, 173–5, 177; and honours
  list, 175; and Rhodesia question,
  177–8; and Harewood divorce,
  182; 1970 election defeat, 192; and
  Civil List, 196; 1974 government,
  203; resigns, 207
Windsor: as royal family name, 111
Windsor Castle: as wartime home, 62;
  fire and reconstruction, 261–2,
  264, 269–70, 306

Windsor, Edward, Duke of (*earlier*
  King Edward VIII; David):
  abdication, 3, 37–8, 94; on father's
  temper, 6; upbringing and
  relations with father, 8, 10; George
  VI feels overshadowed by, 12–13;
  in Great War, 13; at Oxford, 14;
  and social unrest, 16–17, 45; and
  Freda Dudley Ward, 24; visits
  Queen and Princess Margaret as
  children, 32, 41; behaviour as king,
  34–5; involvement with Mrs
  Simpson, 34–6, 41, 44, 94; on
  international affairs, 35, 45;
  relations with George VI, 39–40,
  43, 67–8, 90–1, 94–5; "offending
  letter" to George VI, 40, 95;
  associations with Germans, 43–4;
  and USA, 45, 90–1; Churchill
  supports, 58, 60; wartime
  activities and intrigues, 58, 63–7,
  90–1, 148–9, 176–7; as Governor
  of Bahamas, 63; not invited to
  Queen's wedding, 87; attends
  George VI's funeral, 95; and
  mother's death, 114; and
  modernising of monarchy, 119;
  and Wheeler-Bennett's life of
  George VI, 149–50; 1965 London
  visit, 175–6; health decline, 175–
  6; Queen's improved relations
  with, 183; invited to White House
  by Nixon, 195; death and burial,
  198; Queen visits in France, 198;
  Queen buys property from, 268;
  A King's Story (memoirs), 94–5,
  176
Windsor, Wallis, Duchess of (*formerly*
  Mrs E. Simpson): marriage to
  Edward, 3; involvement with
  Duke, 34–5, 41, 44; and husband's
  "offending letter" to George VI,
  40; refused title of Royal
  Highness, 40, 63, 67, 94; relations
  with Queen Elizabeth, 42–3, 63,
  66, 183; US view of, 46; in
  London, 183; at Nixon's White
  House, 195; at Duke's funeral,
  198; reclusiveness and death,
  198
"winter of discontent" (1978–9), 214
Wolfgarten Castle, Germany, 177

340